D1027995

The Teacher's Classroom Companion

A HANDBOOK FOR PRIMARY TEACHERS

School

The Teacher's Classroom Companion

A HANDBOOK FOR PRIMARY TEACHERS

Mary Coons

Teachers' Handbooks
San Rafael, California

Teachers' Handbooks, San Rafael, CA

© 1993 by Mary H. Coons
Reprinted 1997, 1998

All rights reserved. Published 1993

First Edition
Printed in the United States of America

Illustrations by Morgan Appel at age 6; illustration on page 18 by Ellen Tilden

Cover design by Janet Bollow

All of the names mentioned in this book are fictitious.
Many quotes throughout this book in boldface italics are from Edwards, Tryon D. D., *The New Dictionary of Thoughts*, printed in the United States of America: Standard Book Company, 1966.

ISBN 0-9634938-0-9

Library of Congress catalog card number 92-085215

How to order more books

Contact Teachers' Handbooks, P.O. Box 2778, San Rafael, CA 94912; telephone (415) 461-0871.

DISCLAIMER

The ideas and opinions stated in this book are based on the author's own personal experience. No representations are made as to any specific experience necessarily arising from use of this work.

The author and Teachers' Handbooks shall have neither liability nor responsibility to any person or entity for any loss or damage caused, or alleged to be caused, directly or indirectly, by the information in this book. Although the author has exhaustively researched all sources to ensure the accuracy and completeness of the information contained in this book, neither she nor the publisher assumes any responsibility for errors, inaccuracies, omissions, or any other inconsistency herein. Any mistakes, either typographical or in content, which may inadvertently occur in this book, as well as any slights against people or organizations, are wholly unintentional.

Dedication

For my mother, Bernadetta Holland, who became a nurse in 1904 in
spite of raised eyebrows at that time and encouraged me to further
my education as she had. She was excited to think that her daughter
might be a published author before she died two years ago at age
ninety-seven. I am also ever grateful to my husband, Fred, who
stuck with me through all the years of labor with this baby,
The Teacher's Classroom Companion.

Acknowledgments

My thanks for the helpful advice, encouragement, and editing I received from Rosaleen Bertolino, Lynne Hacklin Coons, Dorothy Lobrano Guth, Bharti Kansara, and Jean Kidd. For their interest, advice, and encouragement I would also like to thank Mary Crosby, Ph.D., Carol Carr-Colglazier, Sherrin Bennett, Jeanne Gibbs, Carole L. Swain, Ph.D., and Patricia Mitchell, Ph.D.

Foreword

Spending time in Mary Coons's classroom while I supervised my student teachers was a wonderful experience for me. Mary's classroom was a laboratory for student teachers where they found opportunities to practice the approaches they were studying in their credential program. My students learned so much while student teaching with Mary Coons.

Now, for those who have not been able to learn directly from Mary Coons in her classroom, there is *The Teacher's Classroom Companion*. In this book, Mary presents a synthesis of her ideas for the creative classroom.

The Teacher's Classroom Companion contains a wealth of information that will assist the beginning teacher. This book encourages the new teacher to develop an accepting and safe environment in which children may learn. The emphasis throughout the book is on developing a trusting and respectful relationship with students, which mirrors the relationship that the author had with the children in her own classroom.

In addition to the affective domain, the author provides the new teacher with practical advice on such things as the organization of the classroom, effective ways to teach the language arts, checking papers, and parent conferences (to mention only a few). In each of these areas Mary takes the reader logically from philosophy through the day-to-day implementation of her ideas in the classroom.

I am happy that *The Teacher's Classroom Companion* is now a reality. Those who have not had the opportunity to student teach at Mary Coons's side may still learn from this creative and gifted teacher.

Mary Crosby, Ph.D.
Professor, Dominican College Education Department

▼ ▼ ▼

A child miseducated
is a child lost.
—John F. Kennedy

I have perused many books in an effort to select the most appropriate texts for my methods courses at the University of San Francisco, and I have been amazed at the number of authors who have very little practical experience in the elementary classroom. It is refreshing to read a theoretically sound book with so many actual portraits of real primary classrooms that is written by an experienced teacher.

Mary Coons's *The Teacher's Classroom Companion: A Handbook for Primary Teachers* not only provides companionship for primary teachers, but also offers a great resource for all elementary teachers. Any college professor who is in the business of training prospective elementary teachers will welcome this handbook to their library as well.

Coons assuages the fear of an entering neophyte to the teaching profession by providing many examples of strategies that have been tried and have worked in the classroom. She offers a handbook that an experienced teacher can refer to for new ideas and for validation of his or her own work. Once you read the book, I guarantee it will become your companion, something you will keep in your reach for the rest of your teaching career.

This invaluable handbook focuses on the practical and useful techniques of stimulating the students to meet their full potential. It gives you a broad range of effective techniques and materials. It is filled with hundreds of proven learning activities, teaching strategies, games, sample schedules, lesson plans, classroom management strategies, testing strategies, and much more.

I salute Mary Coons for a job well done. *The Teacher's Classroom Companion* is an absolutely superb book packed with useful information that represents the "how to" in teacher education. This information is desperately needed and will help teachers improve their effectiveness in the classroom. I will use the book in my undergraduate and graduate courses.

Patricia Mitchell, Ph.D.
Coordinator, Elementary Education Program
University of San Francisco

▼ ▼ ▼

Mary Coons never retired, she just extended her class. In *The Teacher's Classroom Companion* she has preserved her years of wisdom and experience and is offering it up for a generation of new primary grade teachers and their students.

The early grade emphasis is important in its focus on providing the strong foundation of confidence in and love of learning needed by children to succeed in school and later life.

Now new teachers and those returning from a hiatus from teaching will have a ready resource to accompany them through all the phases of planning and delivering effective instruction.

The durability of Mary Coons's work is obvious. The book is rich in ideas that are grounded in years of reflection and solid practice. She recognizes that a teacher is always developing and that her ideas are best incorporated into one's repertoire over several years of teaching.

The teacher education and school communities are fortunate to have this work to offer its newly credentialed teachers. The book is timely as many colleges and universities are working in partnership with districts and schools to provide new teacher support for a teacher's first several years. *The Teacher's Classroom Companion* is a perfect bridge between the pre-service and induction phases of the teaching profession.

As a teacher educator, I welcome Mary Coons's work and think that there is no better contribution to our future success with young children than a teacher guide so thorough and thoughtful in its presentation.

Carole L. Swain, Ph.D.
Director, Elementary Education
Saint Mary's College

Preface

In the course of teaching the primary grades, when do you finally feel comfortable with your teaching methods? Never! The best teachers are always looking for ways to improve—new methods, new tools, new subjects. But you can reach a point where you are relaxed and confident and *The Teacher's Classroom Companion* is designed to help you along.

This book is directed toward teachers of children in kindergarten, first, second, and third grades. It offers you the fruit of my experience, both my philosophy and practical knowledge, of twenty-three years of teaching the primary grades. *The Teacher's Classroom Companion* is intended to be a guide, like a good friend, not to be followed verbatim, but referred to, to help spark your own creative ideas and methods.

Have you ever experienced that sinking feeling the day before school opens? Perhaps you've forgotten something and, oh my, there's the rest of the school year too? I have! And I have searched for practical reference books that would help me plan for the school year and solve day-to-day problems. After fifteen years of describing my methods to student teachers, I finally decided, with their urging, to write a book myself.

When I graduated from college in 1946, I taught kindergarten and first grade following the techniques I had learned in college. I grouped the children by ability into low, middle, and high levels. Everyone in the class read from the same basal reader series, the only difference was that the different levels read from different sections. Within a group, I gathered children in a semicircle to read aloud, having the children start at one end of the semicircle, each reading one or two sentences, until the last had a turn. The remainder of the class were in their separate desks in rows, silently doing busy work. The only sounds heard were that of the struggling reader and me correcting the reader's mistakes.

In 1953, I took a fifteen-year sabbatical from teaching to raise my three sons. During this time my two younger sons were having difficulty learning to read, one son, Paul, more severely than the other. We discovered through testing that although Paul had a high I.Q., he also had a minimal learning disfunction called dyslexia. Because he understood only parts of what people said, his spoken and written language were impaired.

For Paul, being forced to read out loud was so frightening and humiliating that he once responded by crawling under his desk. He remembers that he would often practice the sentence he was to read over and over, trying to memorize it, so nervous that he did not follow the words when others read. He remembers being ridiculed by his classmates and the shame of being segregated into the low ability group.

My experiences trying to get help for Paul awakened me to the idea that all children learn differently and that each child has his own special needs.

I became aware of different approaches to learning while serving as a superintendent of a church school in 1967. Workshops I attended about church curriculum taught me there are individual differences in learning. When I returned to teaching, I searched for classes and books to learn other ways to teach reading to beginners. The way I had taught previously now seemed an impediment to learning because the role of the teacher was authoritative and the child's own input was negligible.

I enrolled in a workshop given by Dr. Mary Reiss Collins. Mary was well aware of the latest methods in education and she was a teacher's teacher. She was just what I was looking for and I found myself taking her workshops summer after summer, always learning something new.

I began to experiment with different methods and attitudes. My new teaching style was based on the premise that learning is a twofold process in which the child must play an active role. I now saw the teacher's role as that of a triggering mechanism to stimulate the child's own imagination, curiousity, and creativity. By trial and error and years of research and instruction, I developed my own method in which I became a partner in the learning process, more of a facilitator than an instructor.

My methodology developed into a practical system that children could understand. In this system, the child is respected for his integrity and viewed as a responsible person who can change his behavior. I created concrete ways to express these ideas through actions, often using different techniques with each child. Because these techniques respected rather than violated individual personalities, each child gained a strong sense of self-worth. In order to use this method, a teacher must be a person who can prize, trust, accept, respect, and care for the learner. And before you can understand and be empathic to children, you must know yourself.

It was difficult for me to give up the traditional power of the teacher over the child but the results after five years showed me that it was well worth it. Children who had been considered problems in other classrooms were blossoming in mine. Slow learners often had sudden breakthroughs, which delighted them as much as they delighted me.

My experience from 1968 to 1984 was in teaching the primary grades, usually a combination of first and second, or of kindergarten, first, and second grades. During this time, I spent fifteen years being a master teacher to student teachers. These young people were not only eager to see what made my classroom different from others, they also provided me with their fresh ideas. I am indebted not only to them, but also to my real teachers, the students in my classes. They let me know how they learned and when they didn't learn. If a lesson failed, I found myself scrambling for books, taking classes, and quizzing my students and my fellow teachers.

To sum up, my philosophy evolved from one in which the teacher is a "superior" person into one in which education is essentially a partnership. Although I do not believe in a completely "open" classroom (all children need limits) I do believe real communication between teacher and child involves active listening on the part of the teacher, taking cues from the child's own interests and needs, and helping the child to expand his own world of imagination and creativity.

To change your teaching methods requires courage and faith in yourself, but remember that the rewards are great—the fulfillment of seeing the children eager to learn, of hearing from their parents that their children are truly enjoying your class and are excited about coming to school each day.

Writing this book has been a labor of love. I hope that both new and experienced teachers can find in it some fresh insights into the wonderful profession of teaching.

Contents

Teacher Be Successful in Your Classroom 256 · What to Do with Completed Papers 257 · Evolving from Groups into Independent Learning 258

List of Figures

List of Boxes

What's in This Book and Where to Find It

What does it take to create a pleasant and creative classroom where children are eager to learn? Each chapter in this book is designed to answer different aspects of this question. This book is intended to be a good companion to you throughout the school year, to be used before school starts as a planning tool, and to be referred to as day-to-day problems arise.

Chapter 1 discusses children's needs—how they learn, and how to create a positive climate in the classroom, one which allows for individual differences and encourages creativity. But a positive attitude alone won't work without a well organized program and this can't happen without hard work and months of advance planning. Chapter 2 details what you should do *before* school starts, including how to set your goals, plan the physical layout of your classroom, and obtain and organize your learning materials. This chapter introduces you to the teaching method I developed after years of trial and error. It shows you how to arrange your classroom to facilitate learning in heterogenous groups while providing for private time alone with the teacher. It discusses how to obtain essential materials and tools and where to put them. By the end of Chapter 2 you should be all ready for the first day of school!

Chapter 3 walks you step by step through this first day. Based on a typical first day schedule and lesson plan, it shows what you can do from the first minute the children arrive to dismissal time, and how to ensure that this day is a pleasant and reassuring one for the children and yourself. (If you're interested in seeing samples of class schedules throughout the school year, refer to Appendix A.) This chapter also explains my system of group rotation from learning area to learning area and how to introduce it to the children.

Chapter 4 offers you further ideas on how to remain well organized throughout the school year and includes a section on some of a teacher's most valuable aides—the school's support staff.

Developing a positive, trusting, respectful relationship with each child in your classroom is the best way to encourage eagerness to learn. This is the focus of Chapter 5, which offers a range of techniques to help you get to know your children. Discipline problems are discussed with a systematic plan, using different methods for each child in a nonpunitive, positive manner. Solutions to problem behavior are discussed in detail, as well as ways to become an active listener and how to hold creative and productive class discussions.

Many teachers dread tests, yet I found them to be a valuable tool that I could use to help determine each child's abilities. Chapter 6 shows you how to test children in a gentle, nonthreatening manner and use these results to plan a program for each child individually. This chapter also demonstrates how to group children into skill groups and how to teach these skill groups.

I don't believe any one method is the best way to teach reading and so Chapter 7 offers a variety. This chapter offers summaries of the most influential and common theories and methods of teaching reading, along with my experiences in trying to implement them and their advantages and disadvantages. Chapter 8 is also all about reading. This chapter explains how to use regular individual reading conferences with each child to inspire them to enjoy reading and to assist them in developing skills. It shows you how to help a child select reading materials appropriate to her interests and reading skill level and how to use reading conferences to learn about the child's emotional and educational needs. It also explains alternate ways to inspire children to read, with suggestions particularly useful for slower learners and for children from other cultures.

Writing is an integral part of reading and can awaken in a child a bridge of knowledge as he discovers that what he speaks and writes is also what he reads. Chapter 9 presents a variety of writing projects and tools for beginners, from personal journals to class collaborations, that can make learning to write exciting and fun for your children. This chapter also offers some valuable topic ideas to help spark your children's creativity.

Other topics can be designed to accommodate the individual child—some ways to do this is the subject of Chapter 10. Separate sections explain how to individualize math and spelling. This chapter also explains how to teach subjects thematically, by integrating a variety of subjects around a given theme.

Chapter 11 shows you how to work with some very important partners—your children's parents. In this chapter, you'll learn about conducting a parent/teacher conference, ways to include parents in the educational process, and ways to work with parents when a child is having learning or behavior difficulties.

Think of Chapter 12 as a treasure chest, a place to browse when you need inspiration. In it you'll find ideas for special days and special events along with additional ideas for implementing classroom management.

Those teachers interested specifically in the third grade will find Appendix B useful. Based on the method I developed to teach the other primary grades, this appendix offers suggestions on how third graders should be treated differently, with techniques that focus on their growing independence and their taking increased responsibility for their own learning.

Throughout the book, I provide real life examples of children experiencing learning and behavior difficulties and how I worked with them to solve these problems. To protect my young partners, the names used in the stories are not their real names. You'll also notice that I alternate between using "he" and "she" when describing children—since they come in two sexes, it seems only fair.

Best wishes!

▼▼▼▼▼▼▼▼▼▼▼▼▼▼▼▼▼▼▼▼▼▼▼▼▼▼▼▼

Chapter

1

They Can Because They Think They Can
Creating the Climate for Success

*The secret of education lies
in respecting the pupil.*

—Ralph Waldo Emerson

can read!! The significance of these three little words cannot be overestimated. Teacher and child joyfully share in the excitement of an invaluable achievement.

How do most children arrive at this thrilling moment? My philosophy is on a poster taped to my classroom door, "They Can Because They Think They Can."

Respect the child for being a responsible person who can change her behavior, and you will be rewarded by seeing the child blossom academically and socially.

A CHILD'S NEEDS

Children have many needs that must be fulfilled if learning is to be successful.

Positive Atmosphere

Children feel more relaxed and able to learn in a positive atmosphere. You the teacher create this atmosphere in two ways: by designing a cheerful, functional classroom that is suited to your program and that minimizes frustration, and by keeping a positive attitude towards the class as a whole, each child, and yourself.

Role Models

Children are always on the lookout for behavior models. If a child observes a teacher, adult, or another child who is interested in and likes what she is doing, he will learn from this example to discover and feel positive about his own interests. If a child observes you the teacher being kind to others, then he will learn what kindness is. But the reverse is also true. If the teacher shakes Jim the next time he misbehaves, Jim may conclude that hurting is sometimes okay.

Children become confused and lose respect for a teacher who expects a certain behavior but does not do as she has asked them to do.

Don't try to be perfect, though; smiling all the time is not fair to yourself. Be an example by being a real human being. No person can be at the same emotional level daily; if you're feeling sad about something or you're having a tough day, let them know why you are feeling differently. Children usually feel relieved to hear how you feel. They no longer need to wonder if they did something wrong.

Social Interaction

The teacher must provide opportunities for children to interact socially. When one child is able to talk to another, she can experience other ways of viewing things and come to realize that others do not necessarily share her opinions. When children challenge each other's views, arguments and conflicts are inevitable. They are forced to defend their ideas and justify their opinions. Through this process children begin to internalize and clarify their own thoughts. When Bill expresses his ideas, he formalizes these ideas in his own mind and he gets feedback from other children, which may cause him to modify his original concepts. Many adults use this same technique when they talk with their friends about important issues.

Social Skills

The social skills elementary school children need to learn are to call others by name, let others talk, look at the person they are talking to, remain calm, respond to ideas, share feelings, disagree diplomatically, say "thank you," ask questions, repeat what has been said, talk about work, check others' understanding of work, and give ideas. A child participating in the cooperative learning process should be able to get the group back to work, follow directions, keep track of time, and stay in his seat.

Support for Self-Esteem

The kind of treatment children receive from people in their immediate personal lives is far more important in determining their feeling of self-worth than any outward conditions of status or wealth. In order to feel good about himself a child needs to be accepted and be provided with clear guidelines within which he can explore. A child needs to hear about his successes and receive encouragement to persist. Giving a child clear, positive, sincere messages about his efforts, and not his personality, enhances his self-esteem.

There are three ways you can help a child develop a positive image of himself.

Acceptance. Accept a child for his strengths and weaknesses. Acceptance is expressed through interest in the child and concern for his welfare, involvement in his activities, and support in times of need. Show appreciation of a child for what he is and can do; do not try to change him. When the child experiences the acceptance of a teacher, then the child will want to learn and grow personally.

For example: John is having difficulty understanding how to add two columns in a math computation. The teacher becomes angry and exclaims in a loud voice, "John, you are thick headed, I have explained this to you many times!" John will not be able to learn as fast as when the teacher says softly, "These problems are difficult, let's see if this explanation will help."

Limits. Set limits on specific actions, present them firmly, and enforce them consistently. These limits need to be realistic, reasonable, and open for examination and discussion. If the number of limits is restricted, enforcement of them is less burdensome and stressful. Without limits a child has no way of knowing what is acceptable and will not be able to learn the boundaries of permissible behavior.

Respect. All children, like all people, should be treated respectfully. Put-downs or degrading comments by peers or adults are damaging to a child's self-esteem. You can provide an environment where a child can build his own self-esteem by:

- Giving the child decisions to make and the necessary information to make them
- Giving more responsibility to the child
- Allowing the child to take risks
- Capitalizing on the child's strengths

Treat the child with the same respect and trust you would give to a friend or peer. Avoid talking to her as an inferior. For example, a child expressing her opinion might say, "I think Mr. Lane would be a good president." The teacher's response of, "That's a silly idea," makes the child feel degraded, but "Why do you think so?" gives her a sense of worth.

The child's work also needs to be respected as important. If an in-class assignment is to be discarded, do this discreetly after school. If a child happens to see her work in the wastepaper basket, she will be crestfallen. This is the paper she put so much effort into.

Flattery and the complete expressiveness children are offered in an open classroom may result in a lack of direction and uncertainty, which leads to low self-esteem. Self-esteem is enhanced by limits and can be built by positive attention.

Establishing Limits

A teacher's adage says, "Don't smile until November."

New teachers want very much for their students to like them; they want to be a friend to their class. Somewhere we get the notion when we first start teaching that in order to have the children like us we must acquiesce to their wishes, but if we do this we risk coming across as weak. When I first started teaching, I thought that I needn't speak out against an inappropriate action. "Who am I to scold this child?" I thought. But this only shoved the problem under the carpet; it didn't go away. When I changed my thinking and began to say, "I do not like that," or, "That's not appropriate for the classroom, Timmy," a resolution to the problem came faster.

Children want and need limits in order to feel secure. It is of the utmost importance to begin the school year letting the children know in a kind, loving manner that you are in charge. Don't worry, friendships will develop, and being firm and directive will add to the children's trust of you.

Fair and consistent limits are essential. The clearer you are about your limits, the more smoothly your class will run.

Individual Needs

When a teacher adjusts her instruction to the abilities and needs of the individual child, that child becomes keenly interested in school. She develops self-esteem because she can find success at her own level and looks forward to coming to school. The reward for you is seeing that moment when you have found the child's mode of learning and she finally understands with a "Now I see it!"

You also need to let the children know, if they question you, that you may establish different requirements for individuals. A boy attending a special education class for an hour each day need not be required to do everything that the rest of the class must do.

A Child Must Be Listened To

Children need to be listened to. Children learn best when being listened to; creativity depends on communications. Active listening is a process of giving feedback to ensure understanding. Active listening helps children to express their ideas and feelings, to make choices and decisions, and to feel that their ideas are important. This process is explained more fully in Chapter 5.

Emotional Needs

Being sensitive to a child's feelings and getting to know what a child might be experiencing is vital. Occasionally a child will come to school upset because a beloved dog died the night before, there was a fight at home during breakfast, or his parents are getting a divorce. Children don't usually offer this information. Be alert to behavioral changes—a friendly child becomes withdrawn, a quiet child throws a tantrum. Academics are not the highest priority on these days. We all need certain times to mourn, reflect, and dream. Giving the child someone to talk to is important. Instead of a regularly scheduled reading conference, take time to talk and listen. A half hour spent with a school counselor can also relieve the child's mind. Creating a place in the classroom, a quiet, hidden area, and/or time in the program structure to allow for the emotional needs of your children is a good idea.

Acceptance of Mistakes

Everybody makes mistakes. Mistakes are our best teachers. Children learn best when they feel they are allowed to make mistakes. Children who are tense for fear they will make a mistake are not able to think and learn for themselves. A feeling of trust, an understanding, accepting atmosphere, and a healthy sense of humor must be built up between the teacher and each child in the class in order to create an atmosphere in which it is easy to learn.

Recognize or admit when you make mistakes. Let your children see you as a human being. Help them learn that mistakes are inevitable by cheerfully admitting your own.

One of my students noticed that I'd spelled a word incorrectly on the blackboard. I found the mistake and asked how the children thought it should be spelled. We soon looked in the dictionary for the answer and this mistake became a lesson.

HOW CHILDREN LEARN

Many different factors affect how a child learns, including his individual emotional and intellectual levels, and the experiences and environment to which he has been exposed. An only child will have different socialization needs than a child from a large family; a boy who comes from a family interested in literature will learn reading at a different pace and in a different style than a boy whose family only watches T.V. and has few books; a girl who comes from another country may be living in two different cultures. Yet for all their differences, there are things all children have in common.

By Saying and Doing

Of course a child needs to learn some facts while in the early grades; kindergarten is more than just playing with sand and paint. However, a typical child does not learn facts if the teacher merely transmits them. Children must discover things for themselves in order to truly learn them.

**Studies have shown that children —
and adults, too — retain only:**

0–20%	of what they hear,
20–50%	of what they see and hear,
70%	of what they say, and
70–90%	of what they say and do.

The fundamental concept around which the kindergarten to second grades should be designed is that children *learn by doing and saying*. They should certainly hear your instructions, but if they are to internalize what they are learning, you need to show them while you tell them, have them repeat what you said, have them do things for themselves, and discuss what they are doing. How many times as an adult have you heard instructions on how to sew a dress or put together a bicycle, but found yourself unable to really understand the task until you saw it being done, and did it yourself?

By Progressing at Their Own Level and Pace

No matter what grade level he is teaching, a teacher has the responsibility to learn the level of each child's educational ability and make appropriate allowances. A child cannot jump ahead of his own level of understanding. Some children are "late bloomers" and take a longer time to develop, while others dash ahead. Some children seem to have a spurt of intense learning and then take a month to sit back and reflect on what they have learned. When children are allowed to progress at their own pace through the normal sequence of development, they regulate their own learning and come to a more genuine understanding of the subject matter. If a teacher attempts to teach too quickly, this may prevent the child from finding out for herself. For example, while Bob is having difficulty learning the alphabet, Sue has mastered not only the alphabet but also the beginning and ending sounds of words. Having Bob and Sue learn the same thing at the same time would either expose Bob to a lesson too difficult for him, or would leave Sue frustrated and unchallenged.

Even when given enrichment and support, children will only learn to read when they are ready. In the beginning the teacher should focus on these preliminary steps, getting them ready to read.

My own experience bears this out. Tammy had been my student the previous year, and I was aware that she was not doing as well as she had been. Her tests showed she had slipped below grade level in her subjects. I sought outside help when, as a second grader, she dropped to first grade levels in reading and in math.

After extensive testing of this student, a group of specialists found that there was nothing wrong neurologically. Tammy was quite intelligent. She just felt she would never read. The committee assured her mother and me that she was perfectly capable of learning, and that we should simply encourage her to keep trying. We began to reassure Tammy that of course she would learn to read.

That was all Tammy needed to hear. She read many books afterwards and reached grade level in all of her reading and math tests. Apparently she had gotten herself stuck in comparing herself to other students in the class. She needed to discover for herself that learning is an individual, personal process.

By Being Creative

A child's imagination is often astounding to an adult. His natural tendency to make connections and draw conclusions is quite remarkable and must be nurtured. Some traditional methods of education have worked hard to force the creativity out of a child so the facts can get in. Yet children are natural learners, and if the curriculum is interesting to them, they will help you to find ways to teach them. Sometimes they will surprise you; you won't know how they learned something. Let go and cater to their creativity; they won't let you down.

By Using Different Learning Modalities

Every person learns differently. Some children pick something up the first time they hear it. Others may not grasp a concept until they've had the chance to see it in print, or to write it themselves. These people all use different learning modalities.

There are four basic ways in which people learn:

- *Auditory:* with their ears
- *Visual:* with their eyes
- *Kinesthetic:* with their muscles and skin
- *Photographic:* with all their senses

Everyone gains information by all of these means, yet some people tend to favor one aspect over another, or rely more heavily on one combination — such as writing down (kinesthetic) what they hear (auditory). A majority of people learn visually, so visual aids are a must. It is best to teach to all of the first three modalities when introducing a lesson with emphasis on the visual.

You can use learning modalities in your teaching by finding out how individual students learn and letting them know what their strongest modes are. They can learn to use this information for themselves, and you can encourage them to strengthen modalities that may be weak. (See the end of the chapter for reference to learning modalities.)

CREATING A SUCCESSFUL CLASS

Create a Pleasant Environment

If the classroom has a cheerful, comfortable atmosphere, then learning will be more enjoyable. Besides, you will be spending a major portion of your time in your classroom; make it a pleasant space. There is no reason to have a sterile classroom. All you need is a little elbow grease, paint, contact paper, a few pieces of furniture (from the local thrift shop or donated by parents), and a good imagination. (Ideas are given in Chapter 2 on arranging a pleasant learning environment.)

Create a Stimulating Program

A flexible, changing program stimulates both student and teacher. When a teacher is bored, her attitude will have a direct effect on the class. I found that the years I risked trying something new were the years that I enjoyed the most and that really stimulated both me and my class. Enroll in college or adult education classes to keep your mind alert and provide new ideas. Keep your eyes and ears open for a changing variety of social studies, math, science, and reading materials. Use ideas from current literature and from other teachers. If they don't succeed, simply withdraw them from the program and try something else.

Take Them Out of the Classroom

Field trips are an important part of the teaching/learning process. Children relish opportunities for stimulating firsthand adventures. Afterwards, a teacher can effectively use these experiences in many different ways. Small group projects are possible since all the children have a common experience to which they can refer. Field trips keep children excited about school. My students were all smiles the day of each field trip and convinced me that all my efforts to take them off campus were worthwhile.

Avoid Direct Competition

You need to keep competition in the right place: the playground. You can divide into teams to play games, but in the classroom, the class should be one big team.

An underachieving or late-blooming child is discouraged and humiliated when his achievements are compared graphically with the class, such as when cards are placed on the bulletin board to show the number of books each child has read, the results of tests, or the recipients of 100% or A+ papers.

Grading on a bell curve in the kindergarten, first, and second grades discourages young children. When all the children are doing well, they should not be pressured into feeling that they are competing with one another. Instead they should be graded according to their own progress.

It is also frustrating to the underachiever or late bloomer to receive low grades consistently. A child may be working and trying as hard as he can to complete the assigned work, but become discouraged and give up trying if graded by some objective standard and not according to his own levels of achievement. A child is motivated to learn by his own individual feeling of accomplishment.

Children have rhythms to their learning; sometimes they will spurt ahead for a while, sometimes they will hang back and focus on other things. This is no cause for alarm. Even adults have peaks and pits in their experiences. Learn to make allowances for your students' spurts and slow spots.

Develop Close Relationships in the Classroom

Children learn best in small groups where they can interact easily with each other and with an adult. In this situation, they also have more of a chance to express their views, ask questions, and talk about events. Within a group, they can help each other. I learned how to arrange my classroom so that these relationships could be developed as part of the learning day, not as a distraction to it, by replacing the single desks in rows with groupings of double desks and tables. Close relationships develop more naturally this way than in traditional seatings. (Chapter 2 discusses classroom layout in detail.)

Provide Positive Feedback

New subjects and ideas are more easily absorbed by children in a positive atmosphere. Immediate and frequent acknowledgement of each child is essential. Children should know that their teacher has utter confidence that they will learn to read eventually, whenever they are ready, that their success is inevitable. A teacher needs to be constantly on the lookout for positive behaviors to encourage. One year I had a student, Hope, who constantly interrupted others. Initially I would point out to her each time she interrupted, and she got negative attention for performing the unwanted behavior, so that the behavior continued. But when I noticed times she listened well and gave her positive recognition for the good behavior, Hope soon decided she wanted to learn to listen. If you look for good behavior, you will find it, and in doing so, will encourage more good behavior.

Don't Expect to Be Perfect

Teachers, especially new teachers, have very high expectations of themselves. Will I fit in to this school? Will my ideas be ridiculed? Let me reassure you — you can't fail. It's okay to make mistakes, don't expect to have every lesson perfect. You won't have the time to spend on lessons that you did as a student teacher, so you have to take more risks. If a lesson is a flop or is a success, the children will let you know. Teaching is a learning process itself; the more you teach, the more you will understand what is needed by your students, and be able to provide it for them.

Deal Positively with Negativity

Negativity promotes depression, impatience, dissatisfaction, and loss of energy. It is easy to feel pessimistic after a negative encounter with a critical parent or principal, and then to let the children follow their tendencies towards negative responses. An example of a vicious negative cycle is recounted in a book, *The Terrible, Horrible, No Good, Very Bad Day*, which begins with the husband forgetting to kiss his wife goodbye. She ends up yelling at her son, who in turn kicks the dog.

Learn to catch yourself when negative thoughts or remarks enter your life; sit back, take a deep breath, close your eyes, and see yourself relaxed and non-defensive. Keep a file of positive remarks or notes you have received from parents, children, supervisors, and principals and read them when you need a boost. Negativity will make teaching a chore. If, on the other hand, you approach teaching with the attitude that you are making the world a better place, that you can make a difference, you will create a wonderful class and feel more energy and increased well-being.

Understand and Accept Yourself

Understanding and accepting yourself is an important requirement for a teacher. As a teacher, you can only accept each child if you have a healthy love of yourself. Only then can you relate to children as fellow human beings with ideas and beliefs and paths of their own. By accepting yourself and being nonjudgmental, you will be able to accept children of various races and socioeconomic backgrounds. Through your example and teaching, a child having difficulty being accepted by her peers will benefit.

Probably the most essential ingredient in a successful teaching career is your own attitude. In a letter to the parents of my students I wrote:

> My concept of each child will reflect on how that child feels about himself or herself. If I like, want, accept, and feel they are worthy, then they will feel liked, wanted, accepted, and worthy.

Creating a positive learning environment, however, takes more than just confidence and praise. A well-organized, physically attractive classroom is also essential. In Chapter 2 I take you step by step through the process of "setting up shop."

BIBLIOGRAPHY

Coombs, Arthur. 1962. *Perceiving, Behaving, Becoming.* Educational Leadership: Alexandria, Virginia. (Gives examples of how our perception of a child affects the way he behaves.)

Gordon, Thomas. 1974. *Teacher Effectiveness Training*. Peter H. Wyden: New York. (This book contains suggestions about teacher-student relationships, students with problems, verbal communication, and active listening.)

Ginsburg, Herbert and Sylvia Opper. 1969. *Piaget's Theory of Intellectual Development*. Prentice-Hall: Englewood Cliffs, New Jersey. (The simplest explanation of Piaget's theory.)

Johnson, David W. and Roger T. Johnson. 1987. *Learning Together and Alone*. Prentice-Hall: Englewood Cliffs, New Jersey. (This book contains theories about cooperative learning.)

Kovalik, Susan. 1986. *Teachers Make the Difference*. Susan Koralik and Associates: Village of Oak Creek, Arizona. (This book contains Wynn Baxter's test for learning modalities.)

Postman, Neil and Charles Weingartner. 1987. *Teaching As a Subversive Activity*. Delacorte: New York.

▼▼▼▼▼▼▼▼▼▼▼▼▼▼▼▼▼▼▼▼▼▼▼▼

Chapter

2

Setting Up Shop

Opening Day Minus Two Weeks — And Counting

*Have a time and place for everything,
and do everything in its time and place,
and you will not only accomplish more, but have far
more leisure than those who are always hurrying, as if
vainly attempting to overtake time that had been lost.*

—Tryon Edwards
American theologian (1809–1894)

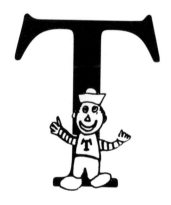

There is nothing magic about a successful first day at school, nor can it be attributed to luck. Many hours of thoughtful planning are required. In addition to setting daily and year-end goals, a teacher must be thoroughly familiar with the required course of study. Finally, the classroom must be arranged to enhance the academic program.

All teachers of the primary grades are required to follow a prescribed curriculum, but each is responsible for his own teaching methods. You can follow the teacher's manual page by page, or you can be creative with your class and construct more participatory and interesting ways of teaching and learning. In this chapter I describe my process for building the structure within which I learned to teach most creatively. This structure has allowed me to tailor lessons to individual students, thus giving them greater responsibility for their own learning.

THE NEW TEACHER

If you are new to the district or school, you must become familiar with the school plant and the people you will be associated with. It is important to:

- visit your school as soon as possible
- prepare questions you need to ask the principal and schedule a meeting as soon as possible
- prepare any questions you have for the school secretary
- check with the custodian as to his availability to help move your furniture
- find a fellow-teacher as a buddy, exchange phone numbers
- write questions you have for the school nurse after reviewing the children's health records
- ask the librarian for books to supplement your class library and ask her about supplementary equipment, games, and literature from the media center

CONSIDER YOUR CLASS LEVEL(S)

Once you find out what grade levels you have been assigned, it is necessary to read the course of study for your district to learn what subjects are required for those grades.

After teaching homogeneous classes of kindergartners, first, second, and third graders for six or seven years, I asked for a combination of first and second grade children in my class. If the kindergarten classes were over the enrollment limit, a few mature, high-achieving kindergartners were placed in my room. This can be a typical arrangement; you might find one overflow class like this in every school, since the number of students enrolled does not always divide neatly into the number of classrooms in a school, and a mixed class eases overcrowding. I found this to be an ideal situation, and my structure of individualized learning suited the combination class perfectly. The children helped and learned from each other. They learned at their own pace, followed their own interests, and found their own inner motivation for learning.

The various ages soon were blended in heterogeneous groupings, first graders doing second grade tasks and a few second graders performing at the first grade level. I never played up the grade differences, and began instead to learn how to match the learning pace of each child, no matter which level he was at. Working in heterogeneous groups at different ungraded levels, the children were not overtly aware of who was in what grade. There was often a surprised exclamation when the nurse or office announced the need for the kindergartners: "Is he a kindergartner?" The traditional boundaries of grade levels came to seem quite artificial after my success in creating heterogeneous groups.

It was tricky sometimes, as I would have children in my classes ranging from pre-primer to fifth-grade reading levels. Yet the class as a group never seemed to mind, and individual students would move along at the correct level for themselves, feeling neither bored nor intimidated. Students became more able learners in this situation, and most continued their good habits in grades to come.

Most teachers, however, breathe a sigh of relief that they are not given this assignment. Granted, it's easier to teach one grade at a time if you use the system of just teaching that grade level and not at individual levels. A teacher can take a child at her individual academic level in a straight second grade, yet, if you acknowledge individual levels of learning, the child may need to have tasks available from various levels from first to third or fourth grade.

Some states, North Carolina among them, have taught via a non-graded school system for many years now. Yet in states where this is not common, I would recommend that beginning teachers not take mixed-grade classes for the first few years. It takes an understanding of the different grade level materials and can be too much to take on all at once, especially without the support of the entire school system. Wait until you are secure about using individual learning methods and comfortable in your school, before you ask for a multi-grade level class.

SET YOUR GOALS

It is impossible to say, "This summer I'm going to switch gears and not even think about teaching." On the contrary, thoughts creep to mind, such as, "Next year I can really do..." or "It would be nice to try...," or "I wonder if the teachers' store has that book I needed last year...," or "How can I make math or reading or writing more interesting?" Thinking about school leads to action; let your creativity flow! If you are facing burnout, seek help for turning things around. There are many teachers out there who want to share their knowledge with you.

Taking a summer course at the local college or university and reading the latest book on the subject never fails to inspire new ideas and solve old problems. Once you get your credentials, your continuing education can be fun. Most popular education courses and workshops are exciting and stimulating, especially if you can find one to suit your particular needs. New ideas from these courses can readily be incorporated into teaching methods. For example, I use this list of goals I received from a class I attended one summer, as I consider my class each year.

Goals to Work Toward
- Increasing Self-Esteem in the Classroom
- Having Children Help Each Other
- Developing Independence by June
- Helping Children Think for Themselves
- Getting the Children Involved in Their Work
- Face-to-Face Communication, Making Choices
- The Importance of First-Hand Experiences
- Meeting Children's Individual Needs
- Providing Positive Learning Experiences
- Self-Initiated Learning Opportunities
- Building Close Relationships Among Children
  —and Between Adults and Children
- Problem Solving in the Classroom *

* Source: Mary Reiss Collins, Ph.D., Instructor, California State University at Sonoma, 1973.

ORGANIZE YOUR MATERIALS

By taking time to organize your materials before school starts, you will have extra time when you are overwhelmed with reports, meetings, conferences, and preparing for special class activities. When reviewing the state-adopted text and teacher's guides for different grades, look for overlapping areas, especially in the subjects that the whole class will be studying as a unit. These include social studies, music, science, art, and health. Take notes as you read these books, and list what will be covered. Then plan a simple theme for the first month.

Whether teaching a single grade or mixed grades, organizing all the materials that pertain to the same subject is worthwhile. For example, if the subject of kindness is taught in social studies, you can reproduce worksheets on kindness, list and gather books to read to the children about kindness, order films pertaining to kindness, make a notation of the page in the social studies book on kindness, and list ideas for study activities, such as writing a letter to someone who is ill or elderly. All of this material can be placed in a box or file marked "kindness." It will be ready to go when it is time to study the unit.

FIND NEW MATERIALS

Search for new and different materials. With your goals in mind and a list in hand of the specific areas to be taught in social studies, health, reading, science, math, and English and an inventory of the books and duplicating materials already available to you, investigate the teachers' store and the instructional media center at the district office. You can buy duplicating materials in books at the teachers' store, or they may come with the teacher's manuals for textbooks. They provide added practice of the skills that have to be covered. After a few years of teaching the same grade or grades, assembling only the challenging, creative, and interesting materials will become automatic.

It is important to note each year whether there is a concept that the majority of the children found difficult to learn. Be aware of new sources—games, stories, puzzles, and worksheets—which teach this concept. Always keep your goals in mind. Will the materials make the children think? Are you finding a variety of ways to present the same idea? Are you gathering a supply of materials at different levels of challenge to meet the individual needs of each child? Are you getting problem-solving material? Above all, are you sure you are providing more than busy work? Children should always be required to do more than just fill in the blanks.

ENVISIONING YOUR CLASSROOM

Most classrooms come with desks in standard rows, with a big teacher's desk in the front and the blackboard behind it. But you don't have to run your class by the

Reprinted with permission from Ellen Tilden

divide-and-conquer method of teaching; you can create a more dynamic space for a more creative class. I traded in the rows of individual desks for a number of double desks, U-shaped, and circular desks (see Figure 2.1), which were arranged in areas around the room.

Visualize

Two weeks before the opening day of school, begin preparing the space in which your class will spend its days. Measure the classroom, the desks, bookcases, cabinets, and all other large pieces of furniture and cut out scale models (see Figure 2.2).

Draw a scale diagram of the room, and decide where the furniture should be placed using the model.

Figure 2.1 The circular desk

Figure 2.2 THE SCALE MODEL

Measure each large piece of furniture and rug and, using graph paper, reproduce each piece. Save these for next year. The pieces need to be cut out individually.

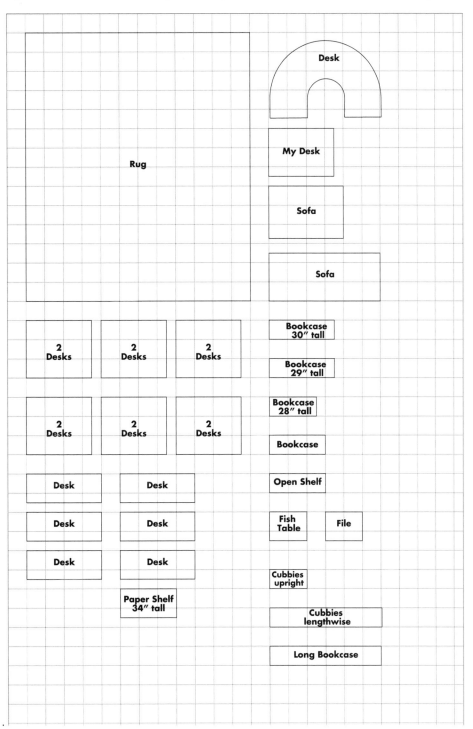

See Figure 2.3 showing a room diagram. Keep your goals in mind as you set up the room. For example, because children need to talk to each other, face-to-face and side-by-side seating is best. Circular desks or four double desks in a U-shape meet this need perfectly. A circular seating arrangement increases the ease and speed with which a child can be helped. The daily contact with an adult or peer helper should be face-to-face.

When you discover how well young children learn in small groups, you will never return to individual desks. Children need to communicate and to learn other children's points of view. When they are at desks, in rows, they have little chance to interact with other children. Not having neat rows of desks, however, does not mean that a classroom needs to be noisy or that the children have license to run around the room. On the contrary, they can talk, softly, and will learn to move around in an appropriate fashion so as not to disturb others.

Divide Your Class Into Heterogeneous Groups

I have found that the best way to manage a class is to divide it into heterogeneous groups of seven or eight children each, and assign each group a color. The colors my classes used were yellow, orange, and green, and this kept organization of materials simple. The class was organized into learning areas, and for the first two hours of the day, the groups rotated from one to another, until each group had spent time in each area, and the day's tasks were completed. This system is structured so that it can be extremely flexible, and each child can learn at her own rate while at each area, working on individual tasks. It works equally well with single-grade and mixed-grade groupings.

In the beginning of the year, choose groups arbitrarily and alphabetically. Later on, when the children get to know each other, a small sociometric study can help you to regroup them heterogeneously to the children's preferences and interests. (See Chapter 12 for this procedure.)

Design Your Program

Consider the program you'll adopt. In my years of experience, a program focusing on language arts early in the day is best. The children's concentration on reading, writing, and language arts skills is best when they are fresh and rested.

Later, after recess, the children tend to be restless. This is when programs of active participation, such as math, math manipulatives, science, health, or art are favorites.

In our school we have two morning periods, separated by a twenty-minute recess. In the first period, the language arts time, the three groups rotate among

Figure 2.3 **ROOM DIAGRAM**

Using graph paper, measure your classroom and fixed built-ins. Now you have a model for your scale classroom. Make several copies for next year.

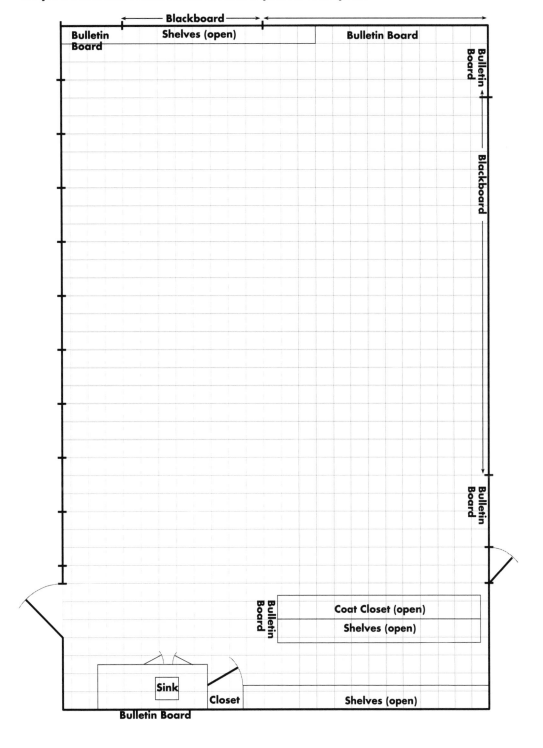

reading at the Reading/Meeting Area, listening at the Listening Area, and writing at the Writing Area. (See Figure 2.4.) An extra set of tables becomes the Language Arts Task Area, for the children who have completed their work at the Writing Area. Shelves nearby contain individual tasks children can choose from to work quietly. During the second period the rug area is not used (math manipulatives on the rug can become unmanageable without close supervision), and all three sets of tables (areas 2, 3, and 4 in the Language Arts Diagram) are put into use. I have found it good to start with math manipulatives, math papers, and puzzles, working your way into social studies, science, and health later when the class is functioning as a unit.

A word of warning: too many groups can be confusing for the younger children. They can't remember where to go. You must not introduce too many different subjects at first during the second period. Your goal should be to help make the children comfortable and relaxed with the program, the routine, the teacher, aides, and — if you're lucky enough to have one — a student teacher.

Try to keep everything simple, especially in the first few weeks of class. You must establish a rhythm before introducing the melody. If children find everything in the classroom too complicated they will become upset and spend their time worrying about the program instead of concentrating on their schoolwork. Do not feel guilty about omitting certain subjects at first. It will pay off in the end when a learning environment is established. When the children are comfortable with the routine, then you can concentrate on learning in all of the subject areas.

ARRANGING THE CLASSROOM

Placement of the Furniture

Take your scale drawing of the classroom and the scale models of the furniture and determine where to put the Reading Area, the Writing Area, and the Listening Area. Choose a quiet area for reading, away from the busy door or the sink, but near a blackboard, since the Reading Area can also be used for meetings. The Writing Area can go near the sink and door. The Listening Area needs another quiet area. Slide the scale drawings of the furniture around on the scale drawing of the classroom with all of this in mind.

Take another look at the floor plan to determine if each area is arranged so as not to disturb the quiet areas. This is important. When children are in the quiet area, they should be respected for wanting to concentrate on their books. (See Figure 2.5.)

Figure 2.4 LANGUAGE ARTS ROOM DIAGRAM

The four areas are not used at the same time. During Language Arts 1, 2, and 3 are used with a few children at 4 for individual tasks. Later in the school year, 2 is used for listening twice a week and 4 is used three times a week. Two, 3, and 4 are used during the second period for math, science, and art.

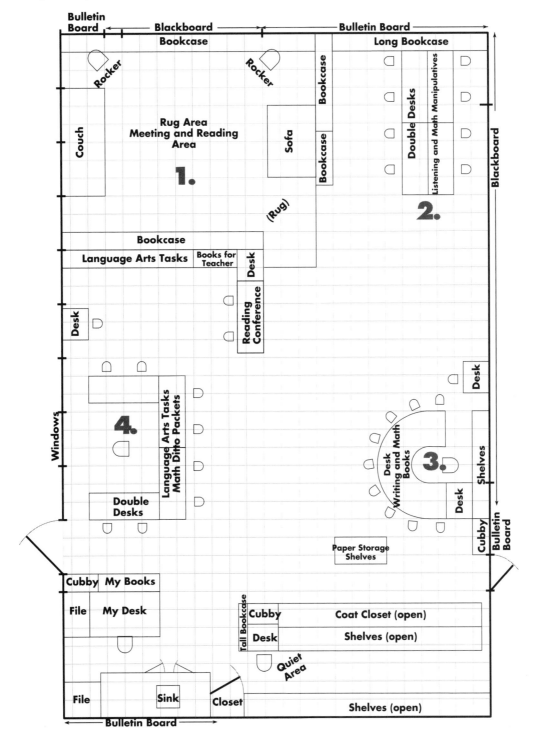

Figure 2.5 QUIET AREAS

The Meeting/Reading Area is in a quiet section of the room, away from the entry door.
The personal quiet desk or castle is near the coat closet, shelves, and cubby.

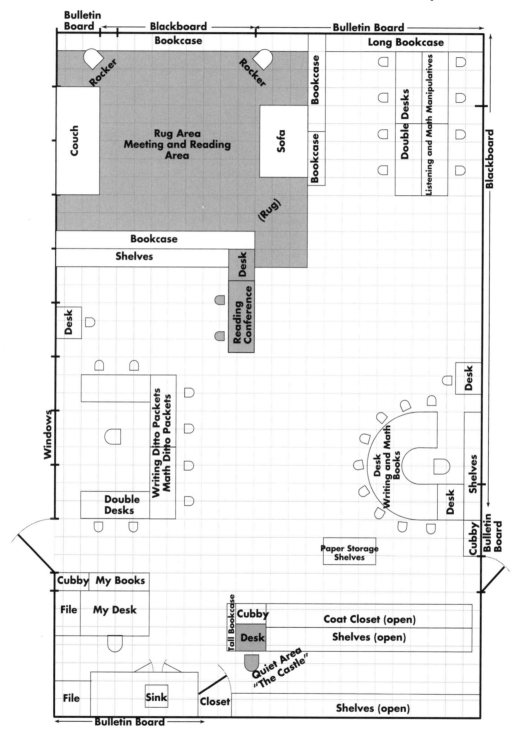

The Rug

Designate a 9'x12' to 12'x14' area near a blackboard, in a well-lit place, for the rug or, if you have wall-to-wall carpeting, for some open rug space. The rug doubles as both the Reading Area and the meeting place for attendance and class discussions.

An Isolated Quiet Area: The "Castle"

Try to create a quiet, screened-off area for children who need to be alone. Perhaps there was an upset at home before school, or perhaps this child is easily distracted by others. My children dubbed this area the "castle," and it was requested many times by children aware of their need for isolation. A child's work must be complete, however, when that time period is over for the class. The castle should be equipped with paper, pencils, and crayons.

Circular Desk Pattern

Arrange the cluster of desks in a circular pattern so the groups can rotate from one learning area to the next smoothly since they never sit in one desk for more than twenty minutes at a time. The U-shaped desks have a chair for an aide, who is available for assistance to the children.

Teacher's Desk

In my classrooms, the mystique of the teacher's desk did not exist. Children were never called to it for discipline or to be made examples of, and there was no ruler in the drawer. I also never found tacks or whoopie cushions in my seat. The teacher's desk should be tucked away in a corner, since you will sit in it only after school to write lesson plans, or to consult private files. Keep a bookcase near your desk for teacher's reference books, and books that can be lent to parents. You will still have a special place in the room, a chair or rocker of your own in the Reading Area.

Reading Conference Desks

Never hold reading conferences at the teacher's desk. Have reading conferences at a table where you can see all the children. During reading conferences, you need to be aware of what is going on in the classroom at all times. Notice the placement of the reading conference tables in Figure 2.5. They were positioned for maximum privacy and so the teacher can see the rest of the classroom easily.

Individual Desks

The next step is to check the list of children assigned to your classroom. If you are not assigned the maximum number of children, you would do well to expect additional children the first day of school. (Try to accept their presence gracefully. I've had principals complain of facing pained expressions from teachers when bringing extra children in to classes.)

If you end up with more than twenty-four children, eight children can be seated around a U-shaped desk. One or two extra desks can be placed near each area to seat the overflow or to put children who need to work by themselves but near enough to the teacher or aide so they can interact with an adult and seek help when they need it. Individual desks are helpful for children who have difficulty concentrating or those who need to be encouraged to keep their hands to themselves. The not-too-far-away isolation enables the rest of the children in the classroom to do their work in a less distracting atmosphere.

Cubbies

Since the children in my classroom didn't have their own desks until third grade, we had cubbies made for our school, one-foot open cubicles or "cubbyholes" the children could call their own. These boxes were built in stacks of eight, which could be arranged vertically or horizontally, and were used by each child for storing papers, books, and individual supplies. Lunches had their own shelf in the coat closet, since they tend to leak. Cubbies can be arranged like furniture for easy access and aesthetics.

Open Low-Storage Shelves

Open shelves near each learning area allow children to choose activities or supplies, saving steps for the teacher and enabling the children to become more independent and make choices of their own.

Traffic Pattern

After deciding where everything should be placed, take a moment to trace through your classroom diagram with a pencil to establish a traffic pattern. (See Figure 2.6.)

Starting at the classroom door, think about where the children will go to hang up their coats, put their lunches away, walk to their cubbies, get to the meeting area, or move from one learning area to another. If the pattern is not an easy, flowing one, now is the time to change the arrangement. When you are satisfied with the arrange-

Figure 2.6 **TRAFFIC PATTERN**

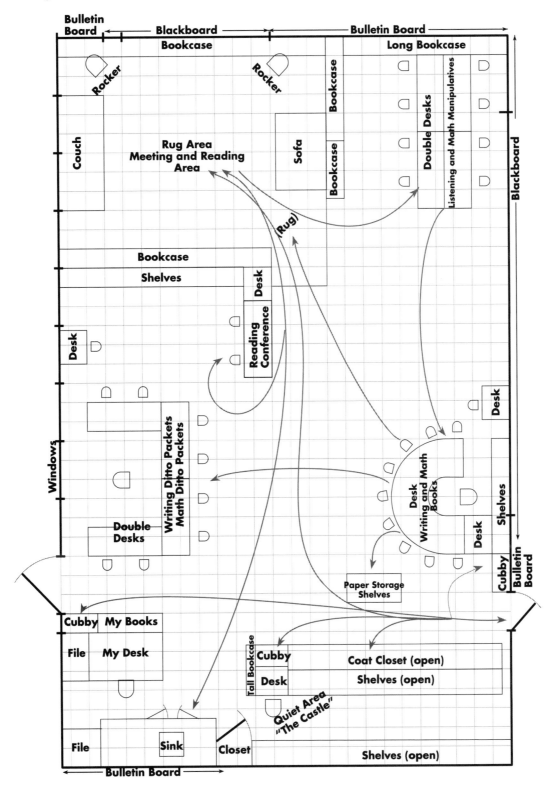

ment of the furniture on your scale model, it is time to move your actual furniture into place. The earlier you start, the less busy the custodian will be and the happier to help you arrange your room. Two weeks before classes start is your best bet.

Walking Through the Areas

When the arrangement of furniture in the classroom is complete, walk through the areas and around the room to be certain that the children can move about without bumping into things or each other. Stand in each learning area and decide how the children will go to the bookcase or their cubby to get their materials and then return to the area. Is there enough room? Are the necessary materials in the nearest location? Is the cabinet too near a group of tables where children who are working might be disturbed?

ORGANIZING MATERIALS FOR THE CLASSROOM

Organizing the materials for the classroom is your next step. It is best to completely stock the materials in one area at a time. Getting everything out of the storage cupboards can become very confusing, and the room becomes impossibly cluttered. Start with the Reading/Meeting Area on the rug. If the room has been used during the summer, you may find that it will be necessary to unpack all of the books that have been stored in boxes. (See Figure 2.7.)

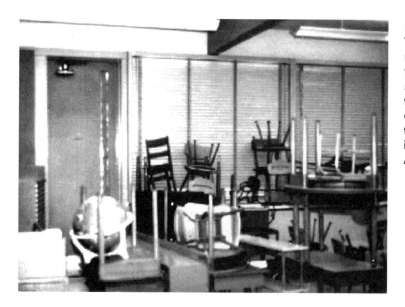

Figure 2.7
This is the way the room looks when you come back to start school. After the floor plan is chosen, start with the rug down first in the Reading Area.

Preparing the Reading Area

The Reading Area is used by the entire class for meetings, but only small groups of seven to nine children are there during the reading area time.

Place three colored containers to coincide with the three groups on a shelf under the blackboard. Yellow, orange, and green (if these are the colors you choose for your groups) boxes or posting tubs available in an office supply catalog or office supply outlet are easily identified and accessible. The children can put the book they are reading in the appropriately colored container for their color group at the end of the reading period and easily find it the next day. Make a sign for this area with a picture of children reading and "This is the Reading Area" written above the picture. After a month the children will no longer need this as a reminder.

Steps to Prepare the Reading Area

- Study your floor plan.
- Move all of the furniture and boxes from the 12'x14' space to be used for the Meeting/Reading Area.
- Lay the 12'x14' rug down.
- Move the bookcases to their designated areas.
- Move the couch, sofa, rockers, and chairs onto the carpet.
- Finally, place the supplies, containers, and books in appropriate locations.

Make the Reading Area as attractive as possible. Reading should be a pleasurable experience. You can include freshly painted bookcases, rockers, comfortable sofas, lamps, chairs, and, of course, books, lots of books. Make sure you keep a special rocker or chair for the teacher.

The carpet and/or sofas can be donated by a parent or bought at a local thrift shop. You can find child-sized bookcases in the school district storeroom. The custodian is always helpful, knows where all the extra furniture is, and will deliver it to your room!

So that they can see each other during discussions, it is best to have the children sit in a circle. The rug space should be large enough for everyone. Keep the following items in a bookcase by your chair:

- books to read to the children

◆ books with ideas of things to do if you have five minutes of extra unplanned time (like Sponges, the Peabody Kit, and Finger Plays; these are described in Chapter 12)

◆ a roll or pad of large (36"x 48") unruled paper (newsprint) and two large magnetic clips in case you wish to clip the paper and magnets to the blackboard to write ideas during a discussion

◆ the finished-paper basket to show them on the first day (you may choose to keep it elsewhere)

◆ the attendance folder, class lists, pencils, pens, chalk, and felt pens

Books and More Books

Since the purpose is to have them read, the children should be surrounded by books. Always be on the lookout for books to put in your class library. Check the instructional media center for old basal readers and supplementary texts that are no longer used in the curriculum. Check books out of the school and public libraries, and buy used books. Scholastic Book Services has two excellent services for the elementary grades: the See-Saw Book Club for kindergarten and first grade, and the Lucky Book Club for second and third grades. You'll get promotional materials in your mail from which you and your students can order books. This exercise in consumerism really involves the children. When the class orders a certain number of books, often the teacher and/or class can choose a bonus book or game.

Reject no book that might be suitable for the children. The objective is to get books and hundreds of them. The books can range from pre-primer to fifth-grade reading levels. Start with at least 100 to begin a class, work up to 500 if you can.

Color Coding and Organizing Your Paperbacks

Color-code the paperbacks for the reading area by reading level or difficulty. This takes some time but is very important. I'd begin by sorting the books on the shelves from easy to hard, from books with many pictures and few words to books with many words and few pictures, then go through and mark the bindings with magic markers. In my system, red ink on the spine indicates short books with very few words that take a short time to read. Paperbacks with purple on the back or spine take a little longer to read. Those with orange ink are longer still and take about two days to read, and the ones with brown ink have chapters and take a week or longer to read.

The color-coding system must be carefully explained to the children. You can then arrange the books in different ways, by author or by subject, making it easy for the children to find Dr. Seuss books or horse books or science books. (Sometimes you'll have a student or two who will be fanatics about the library and will spend hours on a special project or clean-up days arranging the books.) By using this system the children who are reading can determine which book they want to read or look at.

Hardbacks

In a separate bookcase place dictionaries and only six to eight copies of each state basal reader and textbook used in your district throughout the years. This gives a wide assortment of books for the children who have a variety of interests. Later on, in the second half of the year, books and journals that are written by the children can be added to the class library.

After a few years of teaching, you will recognize titles that have not been chosen by the children for the last two or three years. Trade or sell the paperbacks for new titles and put the never-used old basal readers away in the storeroom or return them to the instructional media center.

Preparing the Listening Area

When the Reading Area is complete, the next area to organize is the Listening Area. After you have arranged your desks and chairs according to your floor plan, this area should include a record player, a tape recorder, and an earphone jack with nine or ten headsets. The record player should be within easy reach next to the seat occupied by the resource and record chairperson. This person, who is a new child each week, is in charge of turning the record player or tape recorder on and off and adjusting the volume. Find a record or tape that is about ten minutes long, and play the record to time it. An efficient way to do this is to put the time the record started on the blackboard and go about preparing the rest of the room. When the record is finished put the time above the starting time and subtract. Write the length of time on the jacket or record. If it is not the right length, play another while preparing the next area. When a record of the right length is selected (allowing for both movement to and from the area, as well as clean-up afterwards), place the books and a plugged-in earphone in front of each chair and the record in the record player. The same procedure can be used for tapes. Do an equipment check to determine that everything works and is plugged in.

This is one less task you will have to think about on the first day of school. Making these preparations means extra time will be available when needed for attention to the class. Store additional records and books in marked envelopes on a shelf nearby. Make a sign for the Listening Area that says "This is the Listening Area," and put a picture of earphones below the title.

Preparing the Writing Area

Let's move to the Writing Area. Once your U-shaped desk, chairs, paper storage shelves, and bookcases are in place you are ready to add the supplies. You can place sharpened pencils on the table in juice containers made attractive with contact paper and erasers in small baskets. If your aide is to be based in this area, he can arrange things to suit his own needs.

Paper Storage

Store different shapes and sizes of lined and unlined paper in an open cabinet near the Writing Area. This easily accessible storage saves many trips for the teacher to the main classroom supply closet. You can simply send a child to the nearby shelf for the needed paper.

Keep open posting tubs with 9"x12" alphabetical file cards near the U-shaped table. A folder with each child's name is filed alphabetically in the tub. These folders can contain papers for the aide to use for each child when it is noted that extra help is needed in certain areas, such as manuscript writing. Another posting tub could contain colored folders corresponding to the color groups. These folders will be used to place the papers the children in each group need to complete or correct, before they are given a new task. You could keep a similar file of unfinished and to-be-graded math papers here, and use this area during the second period for a math area. Organize these files with a class list in front of the first file to designate the level and pages each child has completed of open-ended work page packets. When each packet is completed, the aide checks through for completion. (This is explained in detail in Chapter 10.) For the first day of school, prepare lined paper with the first names of the children written on the first line as an exercise for them to copy. This is good practice for kindergarten, first, and second grades.

Dictionaries and Thesauri

Put various levels and types of dictionaries, from picture dictionaries to a college edition for the teacher, on shelves near the Writing Area. Elementary-level thesauri can be stored with the dictionaries. After instructing them on the best use of each book, encourage the children to use them.

Individual Chalkboards

If you can obtain some, keep pieces of old blackboards on the open shelves near the Writing Area. Cut into 12"x14" slates, and make them available for children who wish to write their story in chalk before copying it onto paper. They read what they have written on the slates to an aide and correct any errors simply by erasing the part to be corrected on the chalkboard and then they are ready to write it on their paper. Not all children enjoy doing this, but the chalkboards are helpful to those who wish to use them.

Individual Tasks Area

Near the third set of desks that are not manned by an aide during the language arts period, I place quiet individual tasks on open shelves. Children who have completed their writing assignment before the others in their group can be sent to this area to choose an individual task.

Ideas for Independent Tasks

- ◆ Putting pictures into sequence.
- ◆ Putting cut up comics into proper sequence.
- ◆ Putting the alphabet in the proper order.
- ◆ Matching pictures with the letter sound they begin with.
- ◆ Unscrambling sentences (made by cutting simple sentences into words or phrases).
- ◆ Putting together pictures of words that rhyme or sound alike, or compound words.
- ◆ Using shufflebooks (large cards with phrases or words and pictures) to form a sentence or story.
- ◆ Playing with sequential picture cards, rhyming cards, and association cards.

These are just a few of the individual tasks that can be found in school supply catalogs such as Educational Insights, Media Material, or a teachers' store.

Organizing Ideas

By arranging the classroom one area at a time, you will experience less anxiety. As ideas occur to you, resist the urge to skip around the room to implement them. Rather, write the idea on a piece of paper and place the paper on the desk in the corresponding area, put the paper on the blackboard held with a magnet, or simply write notes on the blackboard. The idea can be completed when that particular area is being set up, or after all of the areas are complete. You can start a second list of ideas or projects to be completed throughout the year and store it in your plan book.

Extra Supplies

On a low bookcase or in a cabinet near the Writing Area, place extra supplies of crayons in baskets, felt pens and pencils in holders, scissors, rulers, and boxes of erasers. This bookcase should be easily accessible. It will be used by the monitor from each group to provide the needed supplies.

The Bulletin Boards

Bulletin boards can be used for many things. For example:

- A calendar (The calendar helper can mark off the dates each day.)

- A seasons and weather chart

- A helper's chart showing children's jobs for the week (see below)

- To show manuscript writing examples

- To display bright, cheery messages such as "Welcome Back!" (You can change this written message according to the season or current event.)

- To show a featured book, news items, current events, and student of the week

The Blackboard

The next step is to put the *daily schedule* on the blackboard in the Meeting/Reading Area. Be complete. (See Figure 2.8.) The children become very aware of the schedule each day and enjoy calling attention to things that need to be corrected or updated. I also put *pictures of the areas* on the board and under each picture a list of the children who will be in each area, attaching these to the blackboard with magnetic clips. (See Figure 2.9.)

The blackboard near the Writing Area should announce the day and date:

> **Today is Tuesday, September 9, 1992**

Each day, the children can refer to it when they date their papers.

Figure 2.8 FIRST DAY SCHEDULE:

8:55	Name Tags, Attendance, Fire Drill
9:30	Tour the school
10:00	Back on the rug, Bathroom procedures, Color groups
10:15	Snacks
10:20–10:40	Recess
10:45–10:50	Storytime
10:50–11:10	First Area rotation
11:10–11:15	Back to the rug
11:15–11:35	Second Area rotation
11:35–11:40	Back to the rug
11:40–11:55	Third Area rotation
11:55–12:00	Back to the rug, Dismissal
12:00–12:45	Lunch
12:45–1:00	Storytime
1:00–1:20	Game
1:20–1:30	Discussion
1:30–1:45	Art
1:45–2:00	Discussion, Dismissal

Figure 2.9 ROTATION DIAGRAM

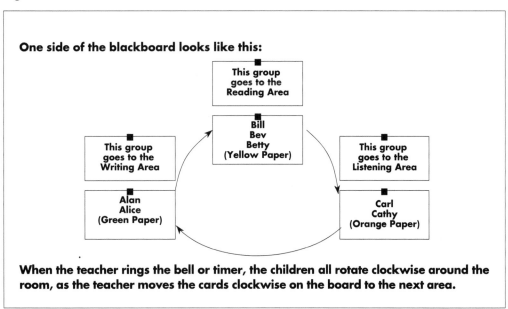

One side of the blackboard looks like this:

This group goes to the Reading Area

Bill Bev Betty (Yellow Paper)

This group goes to the Writing Area

This group goes to the Listening Area

Alan Alice (Green Paper)

Carl Cathy (Orange Paper)

When the teacher rings the bell or timer, the children all rotate clockwise around the room, as the teacher moves the cards clockwise on the board to the next area.

On the blackboard near the door I put the bathroom sign out for the children who I allowed to leave the class two at a time, one boy and one girl. They printed their name by one of the numbers to go out of the room to the bathroom, and erased it when they returned. This is so I knew where they were at all times.

OUT
1. _____
2. _____

YOUR TURN TO HELP	
LEADER	NAN
FEED FISH	ALICE
ROCKER	ANN
ATTENDANCE	BOB
SOFA	
TAKE DOWN CHAIRS	
PENCILS	
COUCH	
LUNCH TABLES	
SOFA	
PAPER	
MESSENGER	
COUCH	
FLOORS	
CLOSET	
COUCH	
LUNCH TABLE	
COUCH	
HOT LUNCHES	
YARD CLEAN UP	
COUNT P.E. EQUIPMENT	
LIGHTS	
CALENDAR	
SIT NEXT TO MRS. COONS	
BLACKBOARD ERASERS	

The Helper's Chart

A helper's chart is essential. It is best to have a job for everyone. It makes the children feel needed and lets them participate in the functioning of their classroom. It also frees the teacher to attend to other tasks. This eliminates a one- to two-week wait before each name appears on the chart. The name of each child is printed on a 3"x5" card and placed alphabetically in library pockets that are stapled to the cardboard backing of the chart. After school each Friday rotate the name cards down to the next pocket. Any lost card can be easily replaced into the correct alphabetical order. The children look forward to their next job.

Display of Children's Work

Keep one bulletin board for the children's work on the unit being studied, such as skeleton bones during a health unit. Use the bulletin board near your art area for the children's art work. I used the area near the sink for art (area 4) and displayed the children's art work on the bulletin board above the sink. Layouts for bulletin boards can be purchased at a teachers' store if your talents are in other areas.

The Storage Closet

Put extra supplies and files of books, papers, pictures, and storybooks in the storage closet.

At this point the room should be arranged and all materials ready for the first day of school. If you've planned it right, the opening day of school is still two or three days away. Congratulations!

Helpers or Aides

An occasional day on your own is okay, but I found that I needed at least one helper in my classroom at all times to make this program run effectively, and used up to three for big events. Your assistant can be a hired aide, a cross-grade tutor (usually a sixth grader), a student teacher, friend, or a parent. A hired aide is the very best, as they are paid, dependable, and qualified. You're lucky if you have one and should treat him as a co-teacher. The next best helper is a reliable sixth grader, who comes in for an hour at a time. Talk to a sixth grade teacher concerning volunteers from her class. A teacher's instincts are usually to send the top students, but being a tutor can be a valuable experience for children with discipline or motivation problems. The opportunity to help others builds self-confidence, and the responsibility of teaching younger children basic skills often helps to internalize subjects that have been difficult before. The biggest treat for me was when my previous students came back to help in my classes. It was a good experience for them, too, because they knew the system, and could see how far they'd come.

Student teachers are marvelous. You learn so much from them. They are inquisitive, helpful, and come in with fresh ideas. They are there because they love children and are interested in learning as much as they can. They assume responsibilities similar to yours, teaching a unit, for example, on their own, and eventually a week of full-time teaching responsibility.

In a pinch, an experienced friend or parent can help out. It can be interesting and fun to have a parent in your classroom, but there are things to watch out for. A parent has a vested interest in the classroom, can be extremely critical of the teacher and the class, can show too much interest in comparing their child to other children, and can take one classroom incident and spread it around outside the classroom, out of context. New teachers can be especially vulnerable to criticism, so be attentive to problems, and take them in stride. But most parents are absolutely wonderful, and their support is worth seeking. The school is a community that involves teachers, children, and parents and any support you can build outside the classroom is welcome and needed. As far as a parent's help in the classroom goes, the key thing is that they are patient and helpful with the children, and respect the students and how you run your class.

Before class starts, get to know your aide or student teacher. Involve them in your planning, and inform them of the program, the curriculum, and the rules. Discuss your philosophy with your helpers. Be certain they know your goals, for example, to stress positive behaviors and to guide each child toward independence. You will let them know each day what special tasks are needed from them, so get in the habit of making them a list. Communication is important; an aide is your first mate.

DETAILS

Procedures

Among the many things to think about are your own standards and procedures that you want to enforce throughout the school year, to keep things running smoothly. Ask yourself what your preferences, standards, and limits are in the following areas:

- Upkeep of desks and storage areas
- Care of school materials and property
- Traffic patterns within the classroom
- Drinking fountain and bathroom procedures
- Pencil sharpening procedures
- Lining up
- Entering the classroom
- Emergency drills
- Obtaining help
- Cues to get attention
  (Do you want them to raise their hand or to put out a card? Make it clear, in your rules and in your behavior, that you will pay no attention to their shouting, "Teacher! Teacher!")
- Procedures for obtaining help
  (For example, a student can identify whether the teacher is busy, attempt the task himself, consult examples in the text, signal for help, and if all else fails, go on to the next problem or assignment.)
- Rainy day routines

- Free time (when work is completed)
- Seatwork behavior
- Students use pencil or pen
- Participation in group activities
- Turning in assignments
- Writing procedures: paper headings, cursive vs. manuscript, indentation, skipped lines, etc.
- Homework
- Makeup work
- Out of seat behavior
- Attendance/tardiness
- Responsibility for bringing materials to class
- Personal property brought to school
- Behavior during interruptions
- Talking out
- Put-down language toward others
- Noise level in classroom
- Disruptive outbursts, arguments
- Inattention or lack of interest
- Lying, cheating
- Swearing
- Power struggles with other students or teacher
- Language/culture barriers
- Lack of support from parents

Class Lists

Now it's time to make your class list. Alphabetical by first name, the first class list determines which children belong in each color group. The first seven or eight children on the list might be yellow, the second seven orange, etc. Each adult in the classroom has a copy and uses it to help a child find his or her correct group. (See Figure 2.10.)

A class list can be used to check off many things—who you have called on so far for news, reading conferences, and so on. This is discussed in detail in Chapter 4.

Make at least twenty copies of the class list without the color added. The children's names are listed in alphabetical order by first name because the children usually can more easily pronounce and read each other's first name. Children can take home a list so parents will know who is in the class.

Figure 2.10

		Called on to talk	Returned notes	Read journal to the class
CLASS LIST Week of 11/15				
Orange	Adam Smith			
Orange	Alden Brown			
Orange	Alice Palmer			
Orange	Alison Greco			
Orange	Alan Scott			
Orange	Alma Hubert			
Orange	Andre Baker			
Green	Arthur Glaser			
Green	Ava Wallace			
Green	Barbara Abbott			
Green	Barry Zimmer			
Green	Bert Deyton			
Green	Bertha Rapp			
Green	Blair Perlow			
Yellow	Carl Brooker			
Yellow	Cynthia Vincent			
Yellow	Dale Wilson			
Yellow	Doris Evans			
Yellow	Donald Hobbs			
Yellow	Edna Robb			
Yellow	Elmo McCory			

Study the class list. If you have some children returning for the second year, you are familiar with their skill levels, and these can be recorded on the class list. Of course, you will have to assess new children on an individual basis.

Finishing Touches

Look around the room now that everything is in its place, and places that could use livening up will become apparent. Would a plant help brighten the corner of the Reading Area? How about a hanging light above a plant? Could that bulletin board use a little more color? Is there time to paint the back of the desk that was left unpainted last year? What about contact paper on the outside of that old bookcase? These decisions are more easily made when talked over with someone. Comparing notes with another teacher can be beneficial. Another pair of eyes can make an improvement in some area that you have overlooked.

Last minute tasks include putting away recently arrived supplies and enlisting the help of your student teacher or aide to print name labels to be affixed in alphabetical order in the cubbies, above the coat closet hooks, and lunch shelves or racks. Make name tags for the children marked with the color of the group the child is in. Make alphabet books of lined paper with a letter of the alphabet in both capital and lowercase written on each page for each child. Make journals of unlined paper with a colored paper jacket. Print each child's first name on separate pieces of ruled paper for the first day of school.

Next to Your Chair

Put notes of what you want to say or introduce near or on your chair in the Meeting Area. Have the attendance, class list, three or four storybooks, examples of the writing paper task for writing their names, a dot-to-dot paper to complete, crayons, pencils in holders, and erasers in holders next to your chair. Other examples will be needed when you introduce the journals, alphabet books, and papers. The crayons, pencils, and erasers are used to illustrate the proper procedures for sharing and putting away materials. The finished-paper basket is used to illustrate where their finished papers are placed. Colored folders to match the colors of the three groups are used to show the children where their unfinished papers go.

Look around the room for anything you might have missed, and when every detail is attended to, the books and files and crayons sit ready for children, stand yourself in the middle of the room and enjoy the feeling of readiness. Turn out the light as you leave, and go home feeling well prepared and eager to meet your class.

SUMMARY OF STEPS FOR PREPARING THE CLASSROOM

- Decide on the type of program you are comfortable with.
- Consider how you will utilize the room.
- Measure your classroom and furniture, make scale models.
- Make a floor plan. Arrange the scale models on the floor plan.
- Develop the easiest classroom arrangement for you.
- Decide how many areas you will need.
  - What the areas will be used for.
  - The best placement of these areas within the room.
  - What is needed to be placed near each area.
- Arrange the furniture in your classroom like the floor model.
- Put out the materials for each area one at a time.
- Make notes on the blackboard or at your desk when ideas come into your head.
- Open the boxes of the new supplies and orders after all of the   areas areas are set up.
- Label cubbies and coat hooks and organize files and worksheets.
- Prepare the bulletin board.
- Have the materials and papers ready for the first day.
- Put the schedule on the blackboard.
- A welcome letter about your goals and first weeks plan is ready for the parents.
- Send a note to each child's home, welcoming them.
- You have a supply of apples and graham crackers ready for snack time.

STEPS FOR PREPARING YOURSELF

- Read books to expand your knowledge of personal growth and children's behavior and development.
- Read the teacher's manuals and books about teaching methods.
- Read the school district's course of study.
- Take courses (not just units to upgrade you on the salary scale) about something new you wish to try in the classroom.
- Study the subjects or curriculum you will use.

- Develop ideas for integrating several subjects such as English and social studies (have students write a get well note to help a person feel good about themselves).
- Organize your materials, books, visual aids, dittos, by subject.
- Each year look for ways you can better organize and save time for the next year.
- Develop your philosophy of teaching.
- Make a list of your goals for the school year.
- Develop your strengths.

USEFUL IDEAS

Think about your classroom procedures before the school year starts. This table lists some common decisions teachers must make about procedures and possible solutions to each. (Printed and revised with permission from the Marin Teachers' Learning Cooperative.)

Decisions	Possible Solutions
1. How can you ensure a clean classroom and neat, orderly cubbies?	1. Set aside time after each work period to be certain the areas are tidy and materials are in their places. Have the children help clean the room each Friday, and have desk and cubby inspection.
2. What rules should you have for placement and use of desk chairs?	2. Demonstrate to the children how they are to use and place their chairs and how to sit correctly.
3. How many children should be at each area at a time?	3. Some areas may be appropriate for several children at a time, while others, such as the computer, may only be suitable for one or two.
4. What standards of behavior do you expect at each area?	4. Allow quiet talking at the writing, math, science, and health areas; no talking in the Reading Area.
5. What are your requirements for each area?	5. Children in some areas are required to turn in completed work, while the requirement for the Reading Area is simply to read a book.

6. **What are the children's responsibilities for care and placement of property?**

6. Demonstrate the correct way to handle and replace all materials, and where they go on the shelves. If an area is not neat when a group has moved on, they must return to tidy it up.

7. **What are the rules for the children's contact with your desk, and what private areas do they have?**

7. Explain to the class that they are not to touch anything on your desk, and that you will not touch their desk or cubby.

8. **How many children at a time at the sink, to the bathroom, at the pencil sharpener?**

8. Set up a sign-up to allow two at a time to go to the bathroom. Have a monitor each week to sharpen all pencils before school starts. Allow only two at a time at the sink or fountain.

9. **When can the bathroom, sink, and fountain be used?**

9. They can be used at any time except when you are teaching a lesson or when there is a meeting on the rug.

10. **What method will you use to line the children up?**

10. Some methods are: weekly line leaders, separate lines for boys and girls, quietest person or table first, a person who pushes must go back to his seat.

11. **How will they go to and come from the playground?**

11. Set a rule that if anyone breaks out of line they must go back and start over. Set a place where the children are to meet you on the playground to return to class.

12. **How will you line them up outside?**

12. Before a game is over, announce how much longer they have to play and where they are to meet you when they are done. A signal such as a whistle or a raised hand means time to line up.

13. **What are the safety rules for the playground equipment?**

13. Review the school rules then establish your own for balls, bats, etc. Such rules may be: no one is to stand near the batter or kicker, or the goalie must stand in a certain area.

14. **What are your rules about table manners?**

14. Review how to eat and talk quietly. Some schools have special awards for the best behaved individual or table in the lunchroom.

15. **How will students voice their opinions and answer questions?**

15. Students must raise their hand to be called on. Children who call out your name should be ignored—be consistent.

16. **What signal will you use to get the group's attention?**

16. Have a signal that cues students to start or stop an activity. This could be a bell, a timer, a finger at the lips, turning off the lights, or standing in a certain part of the room. You must teach the proper response to the cue, and consistently require appropriate behavior.

17. **How will the children know their assignments?**

17. Each morning put the day's schedule on the blackboard and explain it at the beginning of the school day. Third graders may also have requirement sheets.

18. **When will you give instructions for assignments?**

18. Give instructions during a class meeting on the rug, explaining what they will do at each of the areas. Third graders may receive an assignment sheet from a monitor after the instructions have been given.

19. **How will you give out papers and supplies?**

19. Appoint a monitor to give out paper and supplies. Corrected papers can also be handed back in each area. Long waits for supplies can lead to disruptions.

20. **How will you give out books?**

20. Give younger students something to do while you are giving out books, like a dot-to-dot or puzzle. With third graders, have their books for the day ready on their desks.

21. **Where will children put their completed work?**

21. After explaining the finished-paper basket, always keep it in the same place. You can collect the papers at the end of the day and use a class list to check off who handed in work.

22. **How soon will you return corrected work?**

22. It is important for students to know how they are doing with their work, so get corrected work back as soon as possible. It is ideal for the teacher or aide to be able to help a student who is having trouble on the spot while the subject is fresh in the child's mind. Finished papers can be stapled into a packet to take home each week.

23. **What rules do you have for moving around the room?**

23. Children should move around the room quickly, quietly, and without disruption. Set up rules and follow through.

24. **How can you help the children clean up on time?**

24. Set a timer to go off five minutes before they are to go to the next area and let them know it is time to clean up. Demonstrate cleaning up before you begin the program.

25. **What will you do the first twenty minutes of school?**

25. Say the Pledge of Allegiance, take attendance, discuss birthdays and important events. This helps get chatter out of the way and gets children ready for work.

26. **What will you do at the end of the day?**

26. Summarize the day's activities, discuss homework assignments, and give children something to look forward to for the next day. If some children must leave early, have an activity such as a puzzle or a game of hangman for the remaining students.

27. **How do children behave when there is a visitor in the classroom?**

27. Children are to be courteous to a visitor. If a person is visiting the teacher, students should continue with their task, and find an independent activity when they are done.

28. **How will you select the class monitor or helper?**

28. Have a helper's chart with a slot for a child's name next to each duty. Change the children assigned to each duty at the beginning of the week.

SUMMARY

In preparing for a new school year, remember that the forms your curriculum and classroom take should follow their function: teaching children. Begin your planning by considering the big issues of the grade level you are teaching and what your goals are for the school year. Be sure that you are familiar with the curriculum and collect materials that you think will be helpful. Remember that teaching is a dynamic profession, and keep yourself educated and involved through classes, books, and literature. Carefully consider the function and ease of use of each area in both the first and second academic hour of the school day, as well as the flow of traffic through the room. The time and energy you invest in this advance planning will really pay off on the first day of school and throughout the school year. What do you do the first day of school? We'll talk about it in Chapter 3.

Chapter
3

The First Day of School

Begin at the Beginning

Let us watch well over beginnings,
and results will manage themselves.

— Alexander Clark
American clergyman (1834–1879)

elcome to the new school year! Because you have been so thorough in your preparations, the classroom is ready to go when you arrive the first day. It is absolutely essential to arrive at school early every morning to ensure plenty of time to prepare and organize the day's work, but it's especially important the first day, when you will be greeting your new children and their parents.

Check over the schedule for the day on the board. Has anything been forgotten? Next, check to see that the areas are well-labeled, that the signs are visible and clear. Locate the class lists for taking attendance and review points to be stressed, adding thoughts you may have had the night before at home.

49

Sit back, take a deep breath, look around the room with confidence, and know that everything is ready. The anticipation of seeing the new, eager faces that go with the new names on the class list is thrilling, but try to avoid confusion. Your calmness and self-assurance will help to allay the nervous and frightened feelings of the children, some of whom may be coming to school or meeting each other for the first time. If the teacher is calm, the children will be calm. Jitters, loudness, and anxiety are contagious in a classroom, and there is nothing worse than a roomful of keyed-up people. Experiencing a simple, orderly, calm, smooth first day will go a long way toward easing some of their tensions and will help ensure a relaxed, positive atmosphere every day of the year.

Greet the children and their parents as they arrive. Be certain to have eye contact and to say something to each child and parent as you greet them. Some will be there early, others might show up at the last moment. The student teacher or aide can show the children where to put their lunches and coats and tell them to wait on the meeting rug until it is time to start. The beginning of the first day may be taken up with answering questions and talking to parents. It is important to try to answer as many questions as possible now, so the parents can go home with a feeling of assurance and trust. They will feel better knowing you have listened carefully about their special child and her needs. Some parents of kindergarten children will have a difficult time leaving. Elicit the help of your principal to hold a coffee meeting with the new kindergarten parents when the bell rings for school to start.

WALKING THROUGH THE FIRST DAY

Let's walk through the first day. The following schedule (see Figure 3.1) was specific to my school, so keep in mind your daily schedule may be slightly different.

8:55 a.m. Attendance

Gather the new class on the rug area. You may need to go outside to call in stragglers (make sure there is someone with your class, of course; I've had to take them along to the playground when there's been no aide). Give out name tags as you call the roll. When the attendance is complete, send it to the office immediately, with a student who is familiar with the school or with an aide. Introduce the children to the aide and/or student teacher, and tell them something about yourself and your family.

Figure 3.1 FIRST DAY SCHEDULE

8:55	Name Tags, Attendance, Fire Drill
9:30	Tour the school
10:00	Back on the rug, Bathroom procedures, Color groups
10:15	Snacks
10:20–10:40	Recess
10:45–10:50	Storytime
10:50–11:10	First Area rotation
11:10–11:15	Back to the rug
11:15–11:35	Second Area rotation
11:35–11:40	Back to the rug
11:40–11:55	Third Area rotation
11:55–12:00	Back to the rug, Dismissal
12;00–12:45	Lunch
12:45–1:00	Storytime
1:00–1:20	Game
1:20–1:30	Discussion
1:30–1:45	Art
1:45–2:00	Discussion, Dismissal

Agenda:

It is of the utmost importance to start school letting the children know in a kind, caring manner that you are in charge. Explain the behaviors expected of them in the room: that they must walk slowly, speak with soft voices, listen when they're on the rug, keep hands to themselves, and so forth. (From now on, be sure to reinforce the children's positive behavior by noticing and commenting on it.) Read the school rules. Walk around the room while the children remain seated and give them a mini-tour. "These are your cubbies; there's one with your name on it somewhere. The A's start over here. This is where you can keep things you bring from home and papers you will take home. This is my desk, and the door behind it opens to the next classroom." Make sure you open all closet doors to allay any fears of what might be behind a closed door.

Carefully explain the procedures for a fire drill. At this point during the first day, conduct a practice fire drill, taking the children out of the building and then returning to the meeting rug. Praise them for remembering the procedures and how to behave. It is best to conduct the drill before you tour the school. You can discuss the school tour after the fire drill.

On a large piece of newsprint, make a list of the children's suggestions for proper behavior while they are touring the school. Remind them that the goal is to not disturb other classes and administrators.

9:30 a.m. School Tour

First visit the library, introducing the children to the librarian and explaining that they will have a certain day when it is the class's turn to check out books. Stop next at the school office, so they can meet the secretary and the principal, who will welcome them to the school. This should go a long way toward demystifying the principal's office. Explain briefly that the duty of the attendance monitor is to give the attendance folder to the secretary. You can give each child a turn during the year to be the attendance monitor.

Most important is a bathroom stop. Explain it is a school rule to play on the playground and not in the bathrooms during recess. Tell them you will explain the procedure for going to the bathroom when you return to the classroom.

The sight of the nearest drinking fountain, of course, makes them all thirsty. This is a good time to have them line up behind each fountain. Notice whether they are keeping their hands to themselves and not pushing. Once again, be sure to positively reinforce good behavior. When they have had their drinks, show them the place where they will gather to meet you when the bell rings at the end of recess. Let them know that if the teacher or aide cannot come for some reason, someone will come to meet them.

The next location to visit is the outdoor eating area for the children's snacks at recess, if you have such a place in your school. Remind the children to sit down on the benches and eat, and to place all trash (don't throw it!) in the nearby trash containers.

Take a look at the playground and the area where they will play at recess, pointing out how to use the equipment safely, the necessity of boundaries, and what to do if a ball goes outside the yard. Review the school playground rules.

Take the children to the lunchroom and show them their assigned lunch table or area. Discuss appropriate lunch-time behavior and include, again, instructions about placing their trash in the waste containers.

10:00–10:20 a.m. Bathroom Procedures, Color Groups, Snack

Upon returning to the classroom, mention that you noticed how quiet the children were and how proud they must be of themselves as a class. Reinforce this compliment by reviewing their suggestions for proper behavior, remarking that they did remember to follow each suggestion.

Now is the time to answer any questions. Someone will certainly ask about the bathroom, but if they don't, remember to bring it up. Show them the OUT sign on the blackboard near the door where they can sign out when they leave the classroom to go to the bathroom. Explain that only one boy and one girl may sign out to go to the bathroom at a time. For example, you might say: "If a name is on the board, you need to wait until that person returns. We need to come back from the bathroom as soon as we can so the next person will not have to wait too long. When you return, erase your name. The next person may then sign out and leave." Explain the importance of their names on the board if someone needs to find them.

Explain to the children that you have grouped them all in color groups that coincide with the color on their name tag, and read off the names in each group. As each entire group has been read, dismiss that group to the yard for snacks (dismissal by small groups of six to nine children makes for a calmer, more orderly exit). A teacher's aide can take them to the snack area with apples and graham crackers for the children who come without snacks. Be particularly prepared for this the first week of school. Not only do the children forget to bring a snack, but also they seem extra hungry and thirsty. After they have finished their snack, they may play in the playground until the end of the recess period.

10:20–10:40 a.m. Recess

On the first day, it is wise to stay with the children at recess (with a short bathroom break for you) to give the new students assurance that someone they know is nearby. Tell them the name of the person on yard duty, and point her out. Explain that she will be there for the rest of the week, to talk to if there are problems or if someone gets hurt.

10:45 a.m. Storytime

Be prompt! When the recess bell rings, meet the children immediately. When the remainder of the classes have gone into their classrooms, long unsupervised waits in line for the teacher only mean disruption and fights. Walk together to the classroom. Remind them to practice their quiet voices as they are coming in the door. Gather the children together on the rug to hear a familiar short story (*Curious George*, *The Cat in the Hat*, or *Clifford the Big Red Dog* are a sure thing for the first day). It is best to plan a quiet time following an active time. Two active times back to back are too stimulating. Be authoritative and in charge. You must let them know you are serious about their being quiet while they are listening on the meeting rug.

10:50 a.m. First Group Areas

Now it's time to begin to teach them the structure of the class day. After the story explain the different learning areas. Describe the areas and their various activities slowly and simply as in the following examples.

Reading Area

"When you are in the Reading Area, find a book to look at or read. If you need help, raise your hand. No talking because people are reading. When the timer bell rings, put your book in the box for your color group (point out the boxes underneath the blackboard) so you will know where to find it tomorrow. If you have finished your book, put it back on the shelf carefully when the bell rings. This way, not on top of other books. Stay in the rug area when you are reading. Make yourself comfortable.

"The yellow group stays in the Reading Area. Look at your name tag. If it is yellow, then you are in the yellow group. (See Figure 3.2.) The yellow color is under the picture of the children reading."

Listening Area

"When you go to the Listening Area, remember to walk slowly and quietly. Put on your earphones and wait for the record chairman to start the record. If you

Figure 3.2 ROTATION DIAGRAM

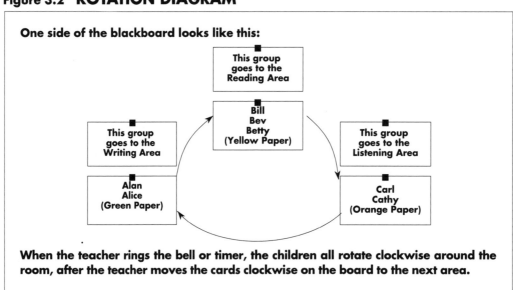

One side of the blackboard looks like this:

This group goes to the Reading Area

Bill
Bev
Betty
(Yellow Paper)

This group goes to the Writing Area

This group goes to the Listening Area

Alan
Alice
(Green Paper)

Carl
Cathy
(Orange Paper)

When the teacher rings the bell or timer, the children all rotate clockwise around the room, after the teacher moves the cards clockwise on the board to the next area.

can't find your place in the book or if your earphone plug falls out, raise your hand. Listen. Keep your hands to yourself. Leave the earphones plugged in." Show the children the book they will hear.

"In the Listening Area only the record or tape chairman touches the record or tape player." Ask for volunteers. For the first day, the record or tape chairman can be a child helper who has had experience, perhaps last year, with the record player or tape recorder. If there are several volunteers, choose someone in alphabetical order from the list under the picture of earphones on the blackboard. New students are reminded to watch the chairman so they will know the proper procedure when it is their turn. If you have a class of kindergartners, tell them to wait until you come and change the record or tape, and do not appoint a chairman until they are familiar with the equipment.

"The orange group goes to the Listening Area. The color orange is under the picture of the earphones on the blackboard. If you are in the orange group, your name tag is written in orange."

Needless to say, in the Listening Area the children are expected to listen. If there is a problem with the record, the chairman will tell one of the teachers by raising a hand. I tell the children, "If you cannot find the page in the book where the record is playing, then raise your hand and one of us will come and help you. I will be walking around the room in order to help people. The earphones are to stay plugged in. If you unplug your earphones, you are telling us that you do not want to listen, and you need to leave the Listening Area. One of the teachers will make this decision." Remind them, "When the record or tape has finished playing and the timer bell rings, please leave your books and earphones on the table in front of you for the next group. Come wait on the rug."

"The last group to go to the Listening Area cleans up and puts everything away. They collect the books and give them to the record chairman. The chairman then will put the books and records or tapes in the proper envelopes. Does anyone know what color group will be at the Listening Area last?"

Choose a record or tape that is not longer than ten minutes for the first day, remembering that you want to keep the program short, simple, and interesting. Keep the children busy by moving promptly from one activity to the next.

Writing Area

"The green group goes to the Writing Area. Look at your name tag. If it is written in green ink, you go to the Writing Area. At the Writing Area the teacher's aide will help you." Lined papers with children's first names printed correctly are prepared ahead of time for kindergarten and first grade classes. The first assignment the children will receive is to practice printing their first name. Show examples of the paper. They are reminded that this is something they will use many times on their papers and that their name must be printed clearly in order to tell the teacher it is their paper. The aide will be able to help each child form his letters. Be certain to have available examples of ways to form the letters in the alphabet.

Because there are usually conversations between the children as they work in this area, they need to be reminded to use soft voices so that other children can continue reading or listening. "Walk slowly and quietly to the Writing Area. You can talk *softly* in the Writing Area. If you have a problem or a question, raise your hand and Mrs. Jones, the teacher's aide, will help you. Do you think that it helps to yell 'Teacher! Teacher!'? That's right, it doesn't. She will not help you until you are quiet and your hand is raised."

"When you are finished put your paper in the finished paper basket (show them the basket and where it will be placed) and then go back to your chair and clean up by putting your pencil and eraser away. If your paper is not finished when the bell rings, give your paper to Mrs. Jones. Come back to the rug."

Have the aide date-stamp the papers, and save them for parent conferences. It's interesting for them to see the dramatic improvements their children make from the first day.

Always Check for Understanding!

Before the children go to their next area, review what is expected of them at each one, demonstrating whenever it is appropriate.

Review the rules of the class and types of behavior expected, including:

> Walk to your area
> Keep hands to yourself
> Get right to your task
> Talk in soft voices
> Finish your work
> Clean up

It's important to check for understanding about how to go from area to area. One way to do this is to ask specific questions. How do they go to their areas? "Right, walk to your area." "Yes, hands to yourself." What do they do when they get there? "Get right to work? Yes!" "Talk in a soft voice in the Writing Area? Yes!" The children are dismissed, one color group at a time, never all at one time, to go to their first area.

"Those of you who have green tags on, stand up. You go to the Writing Area. Where does the green group go? Right! To the Writing Area."

"Where does the orange group go? Right! The Listening Area. Those of you who have orange tags on stand up and go to the Listening Area. What do you do when the record is over? Put the earphones on the desk and come to the rug, that's right!"

"Where does the yellow group go? Right! The Reading Area. Those of you with yellow tags are to stay here on the rug and look at or read a book."

This may take some time to discuss. If so, adjust the time at each teaching area and be prepared to answer question after question and repeat and repeat and repeat for the first few days.

When the groups get settled, set the timer for ten minutes.

11:15–11:35 a.m. The Second Rotation

When the timer bell rings, tell the children to come to the Meeting/Rug Area. This is necessary only for the first few days until they become accustomed to rotating from one area to another. Later on, transitions take only about two minutes when they go smoothly, so you can increase the time at each area to fifteen and then to twenty minutes.

Move the colored papers on the blackboard with the children's names on them clockwise to the picture of the next area. If each learning area is clean, direct the children to the next area. If it is not clean, the group that was there needs to return and straighten it up.

In the second period, the green group stays in the Reading Area. The yellow group goes to the Listening Area, and the orange group to the Writing Area. Dismiss them by color groups, checking for understanding. Set the timer for another ten minutes.

While the children are in their areas, you will be "floating" around the room, observing the children at work, helping things to go smoothly.

After a few days of rotating to each area, they will know exactly where to go and what to do at each area.

11:40–11:55 a.m. The Third Rotation

When the timer bell rings signaling the end of the second rotation, the children again come to the Meeting/Rug Area. After glancing at each area from your place by the blackboard to be certain the areas were left clean, rotate the colored papers on the blackboard. Explain the rotation of their groups clockwise on the board and around the room. The yellow group now goes to the Writing Area, the orange group stays in the Reading Area, and the green group goes to the Listening Area.

ROTATION OF THE AREAS. FOLLOW BEV TO EACH AREA.

The First Period. Bev is in the Reading Area.

This group goes to the Reading Area

Bill
Bev
Betty
(Yellow Paper)

This group goes to the Writing Area

This group goes to the Listening Area

Alan
Alice
(Green Paper)

Carl
Cathy
(Orange Paper)

The Second Period. Bev is in the Listening Area.

This group goes to the Reading Area

Alan
Alice
(Green Paper)

This group goes to the Writing Area

This group goes to the Listening Area

Carl
Cathy
(Orange Paper)

Bill
Bev
Betty
(Yellow Paper)

The Third Period. Bev is in the Writing Area.

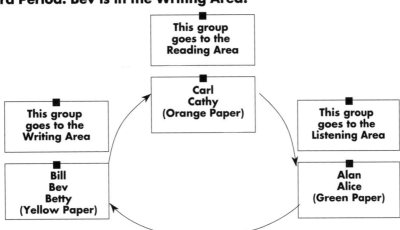

11:55 a.m. Dismissal for Lunch

When the timer-bell rings signaling the end of the third period, the children will gather at the Meeting Area. After checking that each area is clean, you may dismiss them for lunch. Walk to the cafeteria with the children or to the lunch table, planning to relinquish some of your own lunch hour the first day to be certain all of the children know what to do during and after lunch. Tell them you will stay on campus during lunch to eat. This can save upsets and tears for the young ones and give them a feeling of security.

Review the lunch rules as they come up. "Remember how we talked about cleaning up after ourselves? Where are the trash cans?" When a child has finished eating, she will be dismissed by the lunch monitor. Walk with them to the playground to show the new students where to go. Point out the person on yard duty.

12:00–12:45 p.m. Lunch Recess

When the children go off to recess, it's your chance to relax. This is your time, so develop your own rituals. You don't have to eat in the faculty room; you may eat in your room or (after the first week) take a walk to let go of any morning's hassles. You can lie on the sofa in the Meeting Area if you're tired. If you do choose to eat in the faculty room, beware of negativity. I never wanted to go to the faculty room the first day lest some teacher warn me of a "terror" in my class. I prefer to come to my own conclusions. If you want to talk to another teacher, find one who also has a good attitude about his job.

Come back a few minutes early to the classroom to set out supplies for the afternoon. (It's best if you prepared these the night before.) You'll need a book for storytime and paper and crayons set out at the tables.

12:45–1:00 p.m. Storytime

When the yard bell rings, the children gather at the designated place. Again, meet them promptly. Walk with them into the classroom and to the Meeting Area for any discussion or questions and then a familiar story. You can begin to introduce new books after the first day; the librarian is a perfect resource for new books; she also knows which books are best liked by different grades.

1:00–1:20 p.m. Game

Explain the procedure for playing a simple, popular game, such as Dodge Ball, Steal the Bacon, or Parachute. Discuss how to go out to the playground and how to return to the classroom. Remind the children they will be going by other classrooms on their way. One procedure for dismissal of the class can be by color groups to the classroom door. Place three pieces of paper matching the colors of the groups in a box. The child who is the messenger for the first week draws a paper out of the box. The first color drawn indicates the group of children in that color group should go to the door to wait. When all of the colors have been drawn, everyone walks out to the playground together. No one will ever accuse you of always choosing the yellow group first this way! When the game is over, the children should line up and walk back to the classroom.

1:20–1:55 p.m. Class Activities

Return to the classroom and the Meeting Area. Hold up a vacation picture about one of the things they might have done this summer. Then explain to the children that they can share with the class their favorite summer activity by drawing a picture and later telling the class about it. Explain, "This will help us to get to know each other. Some of you have probably told your friends about your summer, but not all of us have heard about it. When you finish your picture, you are to put your crayons back in the basket, put your picture in your cubby, and come to the rug to read or look at a book while you wait for the others to finish." Tell the children that they will be dismissed by color groups and direct them to the proper table for each group.

Again, check for understanding. "What are you going to draw today?" "Where do you sit?" "How do you go to your tables?" "Where do you put your finished picture?" "What do you do if you have finished and the others have not?" Again, the messenger draws the pieces of colored paper from the box to determine which color group moves first to their designated area.

At about 1:45 p.m., or after they have been working for fifteen minutes, go to each group of tables and quietly tell them they have about five minutes before it is time to clean up. If they have not completed their picture when they hear the bell, tell them to give the picture to you. The finished pictures are put in their cubbies. (When the entire class brings their pictures to the rug area at once, too much time is spent asking the children not to flap or wave their pictures while someone else is talking.)

Ring the bell, or call the children together in an orderly manner. After the children have cleaned the tables, have them sit in a circle on the rug. Ask for volunteers to talk about their pictures. As each child is called on, she walks to her cubby to get her picture, remains standing, and tells the class about her summer. If things are going smoothly, have two or three children at a time get their pictures and wait while one person is talking. Ask if anyone who has not finished her picture would like to share it anyway.

2:00 p.m. Dismissal

Before they are dismissed, tell them that they will learn something new and exciting the next day. Always try to have something for them to look forward to the next day: a film, a continuous story, a surprise, or doing something new. Keep them excited about coming back. Dismiss the children by drawing individual names (from a cut-up class list) which have been placed in a box. Before they leave the rug, ask them to share with the class one thing they liked best, or one thing they learned in the classroom that day.

Cleaning Up

After the children have left for the day, sort unfinished pictures into folders for each group color. The next day when a child has finished his work, and before he chooses another activity, the aide can check in the folder to see if an unfinished picture is there from the previous afternoon.

Look through the finished-paper basket, watching for papers that show that a child is having a difficult time writing his name, or forming certain letters. Sort papers with problems into another set of color group folders. These folders will hold all unfinished work from the previous day that needs corrections or extra help. The aide or student teacher should be instructed to check this file and provide instruction for the child before he begins a new task.

On Fridays, I would schedule the Writing Area for completing or correcting unfinished papers, devoting the entire writing period to this. Those children who had no papers in the file could choose a favorite quiet activity from the independent activity shelf.

There will be some children who consistently have unfinished papers. Positive reinforcement works best. Whenever they finally do finish a paper, be sure to notice their accomplishment. If they do not complete their work frequently, ask yourself if the work is too difficult or frustrating for them. Make a note in your book to watch these children while they are working on a particular writing assignment. If your observation proves to be true, adjust the requirements and work for these children. Do this even before the test results are complete and available to you, which is usually about four weeks after class starts. Four weeks is too long for a child to be frustrated!

Assessing the First Day

After the first day of school, before going home, sit down and mentally review the results of the day. What needs to be changed? If possible, discuss different children with the aide or student teacher. In what ways do certain children need help? How can they be helped to become more comfortable and have a better understanding of the program? Are more visual aids needed? Do the rules need to be written down? Was there enough review? Was there any part of the program that just didn't work? Remember, a weekly program is not set in concrete. It's important to have a plan, but it is even more important to make it work for your class. You can change your plan every day, if necessary, to fit the needs of your class.

Jot down things in your notebook that you forgot to discuss or points that you want to reemphasize. List these things on the board under the word "AGENDA." The children will become very curious and want to know about the agenda. Later in the school year they can put things on the agenda that they wish to talk about.

After each name on your class list or in your class notebook, record your impressions of each child. Does Suzy need extra help with writing? Does Jim squint? Does Basia not understand verbal directions? Brad is very active, Maria is very aware and likes to take charge, Todd needs to be given extra jobs. Write these things down. Record events or conversations with certain children if they trouble you.

Preparing for the Second Day

For the second day, again schedule short times for the area periods, to give yourself time to review the rules for the classroom and discuss what happens in each area. Allow for movement between areas and clean-up afterwards. Find a record or tape that is about ten minutes long for the Listening Area, and place the books and a plugged-in earphone at each place.

In the Writing Area, children will start writing or dictations for their journals. (See Chapter 9 for writing exercises.) These, of course, will have to be prepared ahead of time, and it is good to have three cans of sharpened pencils ready. Make sure there are enough crayon baskets and marking pens on the Writing Area desks to avoid arguments. Check the Reading Area. Did each child put her book in the colored bin? If so, make a note to congratulate the class tomorrow.

Schedule easy and fun activities for the second morning hour (from 11:00 a.m. to noon), like a dot-to-dot paper which builds counting or alphabet skills, or a puzzle area, where each child can choose an individual puzzle from a nearby shelf, or an art area with paper and crayons. Near your chair you will need samples to demonstrate and explain crayons and felt tip pens, a journal, an alphabet book, a dot-to-dot paper, a puzzle, and the finished-paper basket. Choose the stories you will read to them. Have activities from the Peabody Kit ready along with Sponges for those extra few minutes. Keeping the program simple and easy and delaying teaching academics or forming group projects or thematic teaching until the class is established will help you form a calm, smoothly functioning classroom.

The Second Day

Come early to school to have plenty of time to take care of things you thought of the night before!

After the class discussion, review the Reading Area activities and procedures with such questions as "What do you do when the bell rings at the end of the area time?" "Yes, that's right. Put your book in the box with your color on it or, if you finished it, back on the shelf."

A review of the Listening Area activities may include such questions as "Who puts the needle on the record?" "Where do you keep your hands?" "Why are you there?" "What do you do when the record stops playing?"

Checking for understanding and reviewing what you have told the children about journals may be accomplished by asking, for example, "What do you do if you need help?" "What if the aide is busy?" (Color your picture.) "If you need a word in your alphabet book, what do you do?" (Turn to the page of the letter that the word begins with and raise your hand or put a card in front of you.) "What do you do when the bell rings?" (Put pencils, crayons, and pens away. Put journals and alphabet books in cubbies.)

Read the children a short, familiar story after recess. After the story, explain the area activities for the next hour.

The children should be doing quiet, individual tasks. It is best to start the year by directing the children to work quietly, keep their hands to themselves, clean up, and use soft voices. After they have learned these behaviors, and a routine has been established, a program can be developed that requires them to work together. By getting the children to feel comfortable with the routine, you have done much to lay the groundwork for the learning that will now take place.

SUMMARY

The key to a successful first day of school is advance planning. Have every minute planned, and be prepared for potential problems. Children are excited and nervous on the first day, and you should try to put them at ease. This is your opportunity to get them enthusiastic about the school year. It is also the time to let them know what will be expected from them in the classroom. Clearly explain the class rules, and get their input. Let them know what color group they will be in, and show them the different learning areas and how they will move from one to another. At the beginning of the school year the teacher should emphasize routine and behavior over academics. If children start out knowing what is expected of them they will have a measure of confidence that will help them all year.

Chapter
4

Planning and Organization

Order means light and peace, inward liberty and free command over one's self; order is power.

—Henri Frederic Amiel
Swiss philosopher (1821–1881)

Perhaps the most formidable task a new teacher faces is the actual planning of classes and organization of material. Even with a well-developed curriculum in place, the novice instructor has to decide:

- ◆ What activities should I plan for this day, and what should I leave out?
- ◆ How shall I teach each lesson to ensure understanding?
- ◆ How do I know how much time to allot for each activity?
- ◆ How can I keep students interested and make sure they learn?
- ◆ How can I organize my records and materials for maximum efficiency?

65

As teachers, we have to plan classes so that they help meet curricular objectives and individual student learning needs, while keeping ourselves stimulated. In this chapter I offer some helpful hints for planning and organizing classes based on research findings and my own experience.

PLANNING

In planning your lessons each day, try to have an active program followed by a quiet activity. If the children come into the classroom excited and keyed up, have a quiet time to settle them down.

Remember to overplan. Always prepare for more activities than will fit into a day, and never allow a lapse when there is nothing to do. It is imperative to plan every single minute and more. Improvising might be an adventure once in a while, but don't get in the habit.

If you have an activity left over on a particular day, save it in a special place, such as your plan book, to be used when you need it. You can keep a list of activities you have not used to refer to when you write your lesson plans each Friday.

For peace of mind, make it a habit never to leave on Friday until you plan the lessons for the following week. Take a list home of things you need to prepare for Monday and what supplies will be needed for art, science, or math.

Some teachers plan a whole year at once. If you keep your goals and the required course of study in mind, you can maintain a more flexible and creative program when you plan a week at a time. The class's level of interest can help to guide you in planning. Continue ideas they like which require more time, or introduce themes that they suggest. Conversely, if a discussion or lesson falls flat, go on to something else. Be flexible. If something inside you says, "They need to do something else," then change. Don't ever feel obliged to stay with a program or lesson because that is what you have planned. Your plans are not carved in stone.

Evaluation of Each Lesson

At the end of each day, evaluate the results of the lessons for that day. If possible, ask the student teacher or aide for their observations and suggestions. Are the children confused about the program? Do they seem relaxed or frustrated? How can we help the children that need extra help? Are the children motivated? Are more visual aids needed? Are they ready for longer than fifteen-minute periods?

The children can also help evaluate the program. They can tell you what they liked and didn't like, and what types of activities they would enjoy.

Classroom Preparation

A hectic and rushed morning is virtually guaranteed if your preparations the night before were neglected. Make a commitment never to leave your classroom at the end of the day without setting up for the next day. Put the schedule on the blackboard; put the area pictures up; organize materials and duplicated papers for each area; determine what needs to be brought from home; complete preparations for a lesson; write the day and date on the board behind the Writing Area so the children can refer to it when needed:

**Today is (day)
Month, date, and year**

In the first week of school, the time spent at each area should be very short. The children tire easily and are not into a routine. They have spent the summer in an unscheduled environment. They are excited about the first days of school. A demanding, exciting program leads to bedlam. When the children are excited and tired, give them a quiet and more structured program. Make fewer demands of them. For example, if they are hungry by ten o'clock, take time for snacks outside. This kind of flexibility pays off.

Five-Step Lesson Planning

The secret of success is constancy to purpose.

— Benjamin Disraeli
English statesman (1804–1881)

In planning any lesson to teach a skill, it is important for the teacher to have a systematic procedure to ensure that children will thoroughly understand and internalize what is being taught. Madeline Hunter's five-step plan[1] is a useful guide. This system can be used for most lessons, but I outline it here using the example of teaching a small group of children to use a ruler. (Condensed and reproduced by permission of the Teachers' Learning Cooperative, Marin County Office of Education, San Rafael, California.)

This lesson is best explained in small skill groups.

1. Anticipatory Set. First, focus the class on the subject you are about to teach by asking a leading question. "I am five feet six inches tall. How tall are you?" After the children have had a chance to respond, tell them what they are going to learn. "Today we are going to learn to measure things." Let them know why it is important to learn this. "We are going to study the length of things, and knowing how to use a ruler will be a big help." Establish connections with any relevant past lessons. The anticipatory step sets the stage for the lesson by focusing the children's attention on the subject and letting them know what they are going to learn.

2. **Instruction.** Provide the children with information they will need for the lesson. "This is called a ruler. The little marks on the ruler divide it into inches. There are twelve inches on this ruler." Point to the one inch and four-inch marks while counting to four. Then show the class what they are going to do. "I am going to measure this line on the blackboard. By holding the ruler up to it, I see that it is five inches long." Finally, be sure that each child understands what you did by asking them to explain it back to you. The instruction phase provides children with the knowledge base they will need to perform the lesson on their own.

3. **Guided Practice.** Have the children practice as a group under your guidance. Give each child a ruler with only inches marked off. "Point to the mark that is three inches. That's right!" Be sure that each child in the class shows that they understand the lesson.

4. **Closure.** Review the material covered in the lesson and make sure the class understands what you have taught. "What is this? Right, it's a ruler. How many inches is this? Yes, it's six inches."

5. **Independent Practice.** Have each child do an exercise using the information in the lesson on her own. Give the children papers with lines drawn on them to measure. Monitor their answers carefully. Work with any children who are having problems with the lesson, and let them know when they are successful. Have an answer key available so children can check the results of their work.

Birdwalking

Birdwalking is when a speaker wanders from the main topic. He may start talking about unrelated facts and ideas and tell a long irrelevant story.

When a teacher birdwalks the children become confused, do not understand the concept, and miss the main point only to remember an unrelated fact. Children may tend to birdwalk but can be directed back to their purpose for speaking by directed questions from the teacher.

Being aware of when you are birdwalking is an important part of organizing your thoughts. The five-step lesson plan is a helpful guide to giving clear "on the track" directions.

Giving Directions

Giving clear, precise directions will go a long way toward creating an orderly, disciplined class. (See Box 4.1.) Before you give directions, take a moment to plan your most effective communication to the class. Never give young children more than three separate directions at once; they won't be able to remember more.

Box 4.1 GIVING DIRECTIONS

1. Planning

  A. How Many

    ◆ General rule: never more than three at one time.

    ◆ Only one new direction at a time.

  B. Sequence

    ◆ In the order to be followed.

    ◆ Use fingers to make it graphic.

  C. Written or Oral

    ◆ Use both kinds (both skills are important.)

    ◆ Use written directions when directions are long or complicated.

  D. Timing

    ◆ Just before the activity is to be performed.

  E. Individualizing

    ◆ Some students need extra assistance, as in math or reading.

2. Implementation

  A. Attention

    ◆ Use a signal or Sponge to get everyone's attention.

    ◆ Don't compete with a distractor.

  B. Give Directions

    ◆ Give in a way that reflects your conscious planning.

Box 4.1 (continued)

C. Check for Understanding
- ◆ Get feedback from the group.
- ◆ Model, if appropriate.

D. Translate to Action
- ◆ Release students so it's possible for them to efficiently perform.

E. Remediate (if necessary)
- ◆ Monitor and check to see if there are those that need help.

Reprinted with permission of Teachers' Learning Cooperative, Marin County Office of Education, San Rafael, California.

And if you are changing a familiar procedure, change only one aspect of it. For example, if the children usually write in their journals on Mondays in the Writing Area but this week they will be writing Mother's Day cards, make sure writing in their journal takes place the following Monday.

Be sure your directions are broken into clear, easy-to-understand steps. The class should be able to understand what they are to do first, second, and third. Use your fingers to illustrate the numbers if necessary. Tell them, "First, write your name at the top of the paper. Second, do the math problems. Third, turn the paper in to the finished-paper basket."

Give directions both orally and in writing. The children can learn to recognize both kinds of communication. Especially if the instructions are complicated, be sure that the children can see them in writing for reference if they forget a step. Write the directions on a large paper and post the paper in the area where they are working.

Be certain to give directions for an activity just before they will be performing it. If you give directions too far in advance, you will be flooded with questions from children who have forgotten what to do next. Make sure the class understands the directions before you send them to their activities. Be aware that a few children may need further clarification of your directions and be patient in your explanations. These children need to feel that their questions are not stupid, and by calmly answering them you will give them self-confidence and build trust.

When the time comes to give the directions, get the attention of the class by using a signal such as counting to five, clapping, or ringing a bell. Do not talk until you have everyone's attention. If one or two children are distracting the others, wait until they are quiet. Give your directions clearly and in sequence, then check for understanding. You may want to have a child volunteer to demonstrate the activity to the class. Then send the children to their activities, but be available to check the children's work and to answer questions. It is more meaningful to explain something to a child while it is fresh than to hand them a corrected paper the next day.

Managing Student Work

A part of good planning is having clear procedures and policies prepared before school starts. If you don't have your rules established in your own mind, the children may feel confused or angry at what seem like arbitrary or contradictory instructions.

Answer the questions in Figure 4.1 to clarify your own preferences for policies and procedures.

ORGANIZATION

Set all things in their own peculiar place, and know
that order is the greatest grace.

—John Dryden
English poet (1631–1700)

Good organization both of classroom materials and your own records will make your life immeasurably easier. The following is an overview of how I organized my files; you can adapt these suggestions for your own classroom.

Filing System

Store boxed files on a shelf in the room's supply closet. You can use open files or file folders to save examples of the children's work, to file their completed journals, and to file pictures you have collected to use for each month, season, or theme.

Figure 4.1

Teacher
Decisions: **MANAGING STUDENT WORK**

Question	Your Answer
1. What is your policy regarding: a. Heading papers b. Writing on back of paper c. Coloring or drawing on paper d. Use of manuscript or cursive e. Use of pen or pencil f. Late work g. Incomplete work	
1. How do you intend to a. Post assignments b. Explain assignments to your various groups c. Keep students working from one assignment to another	
1. For effective monitoring of work, how and when will you a. Make sure you get around to ALL the students, not just the distracting or demanding ones. b. Look carefully enough at students' work-in-progress to catch errors.	

Figure 4.1 (continued)

Question	**Your Answer**

4. How do you want students to turn in work?
   a. Where should they put it?
   b. How should they pass papers in?
   c. How will you keep track of whose work is and is not turned in?	

5. What will be your policy regarding
   a. Checking for turned in work
   b. Work not turned in
     1. on time
     2. by the end of the day
   c. Specific feedback
     a. Grades
     b. Written comments
     c. Graded by student or teacher
     d. Criteria for displayed work
     e. How and when to return papers to student
     f. Having students correct own papers
     g. Checking and returning corrections.	

Source: Teachers' Learning Cooperative, Marin County Office of Education, San Rafael, California.

Individual Files

Create a file for each child in the class, and have separate sections for each curricular area. These files will be useful during parent conferences and Open House. Be sure the papers that go into the file are *dated* as a visual example for children and parents of the improvement made over the course of the school year.

Reading Conference Files

Keep alphabetical files in open posting tubs at the Reading Conference Table containing a conference card for each child listing the names of the books they have read, notes you have made pertaining to their reading skills and comprehension, their reading O.A.T. test scores (see Chapter 6), and a class list in front of the first file to use as a check off sheet to record the children who read to you each day.

Posting Tubs

Put posting tubs in each of the three main learning areas in the classroom. These open tubs offer easy access to papers filed in them. They can store packets of progressive worksheets, reading and math skill sheets, children's papers behind alphabetized cards, and unfinished papers.

By the Teacher's Desk

I liked to keep the following confidential items locked inside my desk.

- Confidential information about the child and her family
- Children's state-adopted test results and tests
- Observations of the children's behavior
- Folders about meetings and notes about educationally handicapped children and children with severe discipline problems
- Notes I wrote about each parent conference
- Confidential notes from the parent, nurse, principal, or counselor
- Notes taken during staff meetings
- Handouts given during staff development courses
- School policies and procedures
- District course of study
- School district adoptions of tests, textbooks, and curriculum

◆ Notes from committees I was serving on

Keep your notebooks here; either a secretarial notebook for taking notes or spiral-bound 3" x 5" cards, with pages alphabetized. I kept two notebooks. One was my own personal plan book, where I would jot things down day-to-day, make my lists, store my thoughts, and make notes. The other was a notebook for the class. It had a class list in it plus a page with each child's name on it and their birthdate beside the name. This was then noted in my plan book. Here I kept observations on each child, so that I could keep track of their learning and personal growth. Pay attention to details when you observe a child, and date each entry:

◆ Is today his birthday?

◆ Does she squint, move lips, or use fingers when reading silently?

◆ Does he behave detrimentally to the other children's work?

◆ Does he interact in a positive way with other children?

◆ How does she hold a pencil?

◆ How does she attack her assignment?

◆ What are his work habits?

◆ Is her emotional behavior frustrated, sad, happy, depressed?

◆ In what areas does he need to be more confident?

◆ Does he participate in class discussions?

◆ Does she take an active or passive role in class activities?

◆ Is he a leader or a follower?

◆ What are her strengths?

◆ What does she need that would help her overcome any problems?

It's important to keep anecdotal notes on children, especially the ones you have difficulty with. Eighty percent of the children you will have in your classes will have few or no problems. Fifteen percent will act out in class in one way or another. Five percent of children have severe problems and need counseling. Your notes (i.e. "Today the teacher on yard duty reported that John spent five minutes banging his head against the bars on the jungle gym") will help with a referral. For the five percent of the class who have severe behavior problems, it is important to keep dated anecdotal records of:

- Verbal exchanges between you and the child
- What the child did physically to other children or you on the playground or in the classroom
- Your reactions to the unacceptable behavior
- Days the child's behavior was acceptable, what was happening?
- Days of the child's worst behavior, noting any patterns
- What was discussed at meetings with the parents, counselor, principal, and committee
- Suggestions from the counselor, school psychologist, or child's psychiatrist
- Copies of any notes and letters regarding the child
- Reactions of other people in contact with this child
- Any successes you have had modifying the child's behavior
- The Student Assessment Team's recommendations: What is to be done to help the child and when

Class Lists

In addition to using class lists for future color group assignments, you can check off the name of:

- who has contributed to the class discussions
- who has returned school notices
- who has participated in a reading conference with the teacher that week
- who has been given a turn to speak (this is a real eye opener as to who is being chosen time after time and who you need to choose, in order that everyone has a turn)
- who needs extra help (noting the letters, numerals, and other items that a child needs extra help with)
- who has received a packet of duplicated materials
- who takes a ball out to recess

Lists can also be cut up into strips for names to draw when choosing a child.

Choosing Children

It is hard to choose only three or four children from a group of twelve volunteers and it goes without saying that a teacher must have no favorites in the classroom. Instead of choosing a child, draw names. Otherwise there is a tendency to choose the more assertive personalities when it is the ones who are shy who need the enjoyable, easy jobs to do as well as the attention.

Take two deep boxes or containers and mark one "IN" and the other one "OUT." Cut up a class list and put the strips of names in the "IN" box. When you choose volunteers, take a name from the "IN" box, call the child's name and put that name in the "OUT" box when that child volunteers. When the "OUT" box is full, put all of the names back into the "IN" box.

Where to Find Materials

School supply catalogs are an excellent resource for teaching materials. The larger teachers' stores also have a wide assortment. Shop at these stores looking for products that help children to think and discover, and that don't just involve drill and repetition. For instance, the children are eager to work a math problem at their level when given math worksheets that contain a hidden message or code.

You will need open-ended worksheets for the first two weeks of your program. This is the period before the children are tested, and you do not know what concepts each child knows. Therefore, everyone will have the same page, preferably an enjoyable one such as a dot-to-dot or a color-in-the-numbers project.

Preparing these worksheets before school starts will ensure a smoother running classroom. Prepare several sheets and staple them in a packet for each child. Then, when a child completes his work faster than the others, he can proceed to the next pages. Eight pages per packet seems to work well. Number each packet in sequence and place the number of the packet the child is working on next to his name on the class list. You can easily eliminate pages in the worksheet packet if they prove to be too difficult for certain children. If you know you will be giving the level entry math test for the adopted math workbook for your grade or grades, prepare these tests before school starts.

Lesson Plan Book

Your lesson plan book could contain notes or lists of:

◆ subjects you have taught each week. I knew immediately if I was not including a subject by the lack of check marks. (See Figure 4.2.)

Figure 4.2 CHECK SHEETS FOR SUBJECTS TAUGHT

Month_____	Week of 9–13	Week of 16–20	Week of 23–27
Following Directions	✓	✓	
Cursive Writing	✓✓✓		✓
Math Paper	✓✓	✓✓	✓
Reading Paper	✓		✓
Reading Codes	✓	✓	
Crossword Puzzle	✓		
Sight Word Search	✓	✓	
English	✓✓	✓	
Health		✓	
Social Studies		✓✓✓	
Science			✓✓
Mapping		✓	
Alphabetizing	✓		
Creative Writing	✓	✓✓	✓
Math Book	✓✓✓		✓
Art	✓	✓	✓
Spelling	✓		
Reading Puzzle	✓		
Punctuation	✓		✓
Vocabulary			✓
Dictionary Skills			✓

- class list with the children's birthdates.
- class list with the children's phone numbers and addresses.
- dates of meetings to attend after school.
- the school district's calendar of holidays and meetings.
- the children who attend after school.
- the children who ride the bus.
- the latchkey children.

Ideas on Organization

- Have children learn their address and phone number. Otherwise, have the emergency cards or school directory handy.
- Have containers for each group of desks to hold common items such as felt pens, crayons, and erasers.
- Put a dictionary, thesaurus, records, tapes, and books on a convenient shelf so a monitor can easily retrieve them when necessary.
- Keep all your old lesson plan books for when you need ideas.
- Keep all the slips for movies you have ordered. They come in handy when you can't remember the name of that perfect movie for a certain grade level.
- Use an overhead projector as a teaching tool, especially for the third grade. It is easier to see than the blackboard.
- Use small self-adhesive papers to put in your lesson book to remind yourself of meetings and activities.
- Keep two reading books in each third grader's desk: one for reading lessons and the other for recreational reading.
- Take pictures of your bulletin boards for ideas in future years.
- Make squares on the bulletin board from brightly colored yarn or tape. Have each child responsible for a "brag square" featuring their journals, papers, art, and other work.
- When a child is absent, write her name on a piece of paper and staple that day's papers together with it and put the packet in the child's cubby or desk.
- Have a folder for each child containing seven or eight pages of

puzzles, handwriting activities, easy math, and other worksheets to work on when they have nothing else to do.

♦ Have a folder prepared for a substitute with three days of plans not related to what you are teaching now. That way when you are sick you will know that things are being attended to and you will feel less guilty.

WHO TO GET TO KNOW AT YOUR NEW SCHOOL

The Teacher Next Door

Establish a support system on campus, especially with the teacher next door. In an emergency, you can ask her to watch your class while you take a child to the office. This is usually not a problem; hopefully your class will be so involved in their areas they won't even notice your absence.

The Custodian

Get to know the custodian. He can help you find furniture and books stored away, be there when you need a clean up after a sick child, and tell you what is going on in the district and in other schools.

A Trusted Friend

Develop a bond of trust with a fellow teacher, so you have a person with whom it is safe to vent your feelings about an upset with a child, a parent, a fellow teacher, or the principal. It's best to keep these things as low-key as possible, yet you need to discuss problems so you can get some perspective. If you have a close friend or colleague you can avoid the gossip of the faculty-staff room.

The faculty-staff room is the place I least like to be. All sorts of negativity can brew here. Teachers often use this room to vent their anger and frustrations. Whole families are discussed, gossiped about, and can be torn apart insensitively. Children are labeled and given reputations that follow them throughout their attendance at that school. I was caught up in this negativity one day and talked about one of my children. I was sorry I did; I went back to the class feeling resentful, negative, and exhausted. After that I vowed never to discuss a child or family in the faculty room. I made an effort to make personal friends in whom I could confide and was greatly rewarded by it.

The Principal

Make your principal your ally. Tell her what you are doing with your class and show her some examples of the children's work. Share funny incidents and anecdotes about your class, but keep in mind that the principal is your evaluator and be careful about what you say that might be misconstrued as something to lower your esteem in her eyes.

The Librarian

This resource person can be helpful when you need books about a theme or unit you are studying. I've known librarians who would gather all of the books I needed and deliver them to my classroom. He may bring newly purchased library books to the class. The librarian may have a certain time each week to have your class come to the library to hear him read a story or to check out books. (See Chapter 12 for a discussion of the management of this time.)

The Secretary

The secretary knows where the supplies are, how to work the xerox, fax, and other office machines, and when the principal will be in her office. She can tell you about calls from parents that need to be relayed to their child. She is a wonderful source of information and help.

This is the person to give you information about forms needed for:

- getting credit for a course given by your district or local university
- repairs in your room
- a special study of a child (after conferring with your principal)
- taking children on a field trip
- ordering supplies
- state and district tests to give to children
- a referral to the school nurse
- a referral to the school psychologist (after discussing this with your principal)

The Nurse

She is usually on the committee that studies a child, from your referral, for difficulties with school work. She is a resource for doctor's medications and keeps prescribed medicine in her office to give to certain children. She is very interested in each child's physical health and will give eye tests when you request them. She alerts you and families to an outbreak of contagious diseases in your class. She is a bridge between the school and the child's personal physician.

The Teacher's Aide

Incorporate your aide into your program and treat him as a colleague. Ideally, he will be in your room daily, and he needs to be kept informed about the program, your ideas, and any changes. When something slips your mind an aide is invaluable as a person to remind you and fill in the gaps. He can offer some innovative ideas and suggestions for activities.

It helps the aide if you place a slip of paper where he sits to inform him of what duties he will have and if you have made any changes. My aide always came early to listen to me explain to the children the program and what I expected for the day, while she filed, corrected papers, or organized materials for me. The aide is another pair of eyes and can offer her observations about the children and the lessons. Find her strengths; they could be in math, creative writing, or handwriting, and make the most of them.

The Counselor

My school was fortunate enough to have a counselor who was always available to listen to an upset child. She scheduled circle meetings that dealt with emotions and behavior problems with my class and me. Through my observations of these circle meetings and with our counselor's training, I was able to conduct circle meetings of my own. She was available as a confidential listener when I needed advice or to talk about a child. Often she offered suggestions to modify the behaviors of that child. Our counselor was so valued that a parent would occasionally send a note to me asking: "May Johnny see Elenya today?"

SUMMARY

Effective planning and organization are important keys to a successful, smooth-running class. Plan each minute of every day, and always have extra activities planned just in case. Have all the materials you will need for each activity ready by your side. This much planning may seem time-consuming but it will pay off. If children have to wait for you to find the papers you need or to think up an activity to fill extra time, they will become bored and disruptive and you will lose their attention. Understand the best ways to present a lesson and to give directions, and you will have a confident, focused group of students.

Starting the school year with a good plan for the organization of class materials and your own records and files means saving yourself a lot of confusion later on. The extra time it takes to set up an effective system to manage your time and materials in the classroom will prove to be worthwhile. Get to know other staff members; they will prove to be valuable allies. Planning and organization are the cornerstones to calm, successful teaching.

SOURCE

1. Hunter, Madeline. 1982. *Mastery Teaching*. TIP Publications: El Segundo, California.

BIBLIOGRAPHY

Lakein, Alan. 1974. *How to Get Control of Your Time and Your Life*. New American Library, A Signet Book: New York.

Olson, Ken. 1974. *The Art of Hanging Loose in an Uptight World*. A Fawcett Crest Book: Greenwich, Connecticut.

Chapter

5

Setting the Stage for Stars

Forming Relationships with the Children

The teacher who is attempting to teach
without inspiring the pupil
with a desire to learn is hammering on cold iron.

— Horace Mann
American educator (1796–1859)

or the first few weeks your objective as a teacher should be to teach the types of behavior that you expect in the classroom, rather than immediately beginning to teach academic subjects. Teaching an academic subject during the first days or weeks of school is like putting the cart before the horse. The children do not know the program, schedule, or what type of behavior is expected in school, and until they are comfortable with your expectations of them, they will not learn the academics. Once the school year is

under way, the children can be guided toward ever greater independence in learning.

Consider the following four types of programs and their consequences.

Figure 5.1

PROGRESSION FROM DEPENDENT TO INDEPENDENT STAGES[1]

Type I: More Dependent   *Teacher:* Decides/assigns
                                Children: Do

Type II: Less Dependent   *Teacher:* Decides options
                                Children: Select choices

Type III: Less Independent *Teacher and Children:* Suggest options
                                Children: Select
                                For example, "I would like you to do...
                                What would you like to do?"

Type IV: More Independent   *Children:* Suggest and select options
                                Teacher: Provides resources

Problems can arise when you ask a child to do a Type IV program when he is still dependent and needs more guidance. A Type I program would serve this child better. If the class starts a Type III program before they are ready, the result will be a loss of discipline. Young children must progress from Type I, going to Type II only when they are ready to become less dependent. A teacher can usually sense if a class is ready for more independence by the children's remarks and behavior. I learned while teaching third grade that my program needed to have two or three types of plans in order to fulfill the children's individual needs. Thus the independent children could make selections and not be held in the dependent level by the few children who needed it. Appendix B discusses the organization of such a program.

These plans of action follow a natural progression, moving from dependence to independence. The children move from needing the approval and guidance of adults to becoming more autonomous and morally responsible.

MAKING YOURSELF AWARE
Floating

By freeing yourself to be able to move or "float" around the room, you will be more aware of the feelings of the class and you can immediately help a student or intercept a disruption from the beginning of the school year. This sets the mood of the classroom as a learning, involved environment. Go quietly from area to area, trying not to interrupt or talk too much. Set a tone of quiet conversation and concentration. Give a quiet pat on the back and a smile to those who are reading or looking at a book quietly.

A glance in the Listening Area will tell you whether everyone is following the page that goes with the place on the record, and who needs help. Give an O.K. sign and a smile to show them your support.

Quietly go to the Writing Area, being careful not to interrupt the children's thoughts. They will be overjoyed to see your interest in what they are writing. The helper may have many children waiting to be helped and so welcome your assistance. Keep in mind that the goal is to help the children to learn to trust themselves.

While floating, pick up the feeling of the class. Some classes are able to adjust to areas faster than other classes. Some can move without coming to the rug after each time period, while others need two or three weeks of this routine before going directly from one area to the other.

It is easy to tell if a majority of the children are confused. Take longer to teach them if this is the case. *It is never wise to rush into teaching academics before the class is ready.* It takes longer to reteach them and get the class back together again.

If someone raises her hand, or attempts by means of some other agreed-upon signal to get the attention of the aide or helper, acknowledge this behavior with a pat or eye contact with a smile or a nod. When children talk in a soft voice, give them a smile. When they shout the aide's name or your name, do not recognize this behavior. Their classmates will tell them to raise their hands, and they soon learn that their questions will only be answered when they raise their hands quietly.

Helping

In the Reading Area, stop to help someone find a book to look at or to read. You could quietly ask what he is interested in and then direct him to the correct area in the class library to find a book. Go with the child and locate five books from which he can choose one. It sometimes takes three to five minutes to help a few children each day, but it is needed and important, it shows you are interested in having them look at or read a book they will really enjoy.

Observing

Notice the dependent children; they are the ones who need extra help and reassurance. Keep a notepad with the children's names listed alphabetically to write your observations about each child's needs. Dependent children are often passive and don't get involved in classroom activities. They need strokes or a pat on the back, and now and then, a hug. They want to be near you and gain your attention and seek help for a task. They have more anxiety if given too many choices; you can reduce their anxiety by physical proximity and encouragement.

INTRODUCING USE OF MATERIALS

I am satisfied that we are less convinced
by what we hear than what we see.

—Herodotus
Greek historian (484–425 B.C.)

Demonstrate

Never put out new materials—such as puzzles or pattern blocks—without explaining their proper use.

Explain how the materials are to be used and how to care for them. Demonstrate the difference between the noise level of dumping the blocks or puzzle pieces on the table and taking the pieces out one by one. Find a puzzle piece that has been misused and is chipped by such handling. Then show them what little time is needed to take the pieces out a few at a time and lay them on the desk. Showing what you mean is worth a thousand words. Also, demonstrate how to put these puzzles and blocks back on the proper shelf neatly.

If you notice the class library in the Reading Area is in disarray, put the word "Library" on the agenda on the blackboard, and demonstrate how to put the books back on the shelves upright, not on top of each other. Show the children what would happen if the books were thrown in. Talk about how to clean up again. Almost immediately you will have many volunteers who wish to put the books in their proper order.

Show the children the containers for the pencils, erasers, and crayons. Demonstrate the difference between throwing crayons in containers and slowly placing each one carefully away, and how to push the lids tightly on the felt pens.

Teach the new students how to use the record player in order to give them a turn to be record chairman. Sometimes it is helpful to write the directions on a piece of paper and post them.

1. Look at the earphones. Are they plugged in?
2. Turn the record player switch to "ON."
3. Turn the volume down if it is too loud.

BEHAVIOR

He that has found a way to keep a child's spirit easy, active,
and free, and yet at the same time to restrain him from many things he
has a mind to, and to draw him to things that are uneasy to him,
has, in my opinion, got the true secret of education.

—John Locke
English philosopher (1632–1704)

A code of classroom behavior should be created, understood, and generally enforced by all members of the classroom. Post the rules needed to maintain a learning environment on a strip of tagboard with the name of the child who suggested the rule. Rules are needed to teach children to behave properly so that they and others can learn effectively and not be a hindrance to each other. Nonetheless, every class will have a child or two who is a problem and does not act according to agreed-upon norms. Children who need to be disciplined must be dealt with creatively and effectively.

Children Who Need Extra Help

Early in the year you may observe children who are loud, aggressive, and disruptive and who aren't functioning well in the classroom. Always view these disruptive children with the attitude that they will become less disruptive and learn, eventually, to work within a group. Sometimes it is difficult not to label a child a troublemaker but remember, a child will become what you think he is. View the child as someone you can help.

Disruptive children must learn to function in a quiet, nonplayful atmosphere. They may need to work by themselves for a while, completing their work at a separate desk near the aide in their learning area. When their color group changes learning areas, they move to another desk near the next area .

Recognize them for working quietly and keeping their hands to themselves. Some might take home cards checked with the number of times they stayed in their seat, completed their work, kept their hands to themselves, used a soft voice, and asked for help in the established way.

Discuss problem behaviors with them in private, using plenty of eye contact. Elicit their ideas not only as to what is disruptive in the class, but also as to what is appropriate behavior. As they suggest these behaviors, write them on a card to be used as a reminder for them at their desk (see Figure 5.2). Whenever they improve, recognize them by a pat on the back and a comment about how quietly they are working. These children can also be given a checklist of the tasks they are to accomplish by the end of the period at their desks (see Figure 5.3). If they complete these tasks, they are given stars.

Figure 5.2 Behavior Modification Chart used at a child's desk. A mark is entered each time a child is doing the behaviors for five minutes.

	9:30 to 10:25	11:00 to 12:00	1:00 to 2:00	Totals
Monday				
	On Task On Task	On Task On Task	On Task On Task	
	In Seat In Seat	In Seat In Seat	In Seat In Seat	
Tuesday				
	On Task On Task	On Task On Task	On Task On Task	
	In Seat In Seat	In Seat In Seat	In Seat In Seat	
Sent home on Tuesday	**Task Complete**	**Task Complete**	**Task Complete**	
	Homework/Notes Returned			
			Grand Total	

Points ☐	Parent's signature _____
Reward ☐	Teacher's signature _____
Total Points ☐	Student's signature _____

When the child shows she is able to work alone at a desk and be less disruptive, bring her back into the group. Tell the children "Nina is going to be with us today. We will have a discussion after lunch. I want you all to find something that she did to make your morning with her enjoyable." Helping this child function with her classmates and be accepted is your goal.

Figure 5.3 Tasks to be completed by a child at an individual desk

Name_____ **Date**_____

Day_____

1. Read your book for 10 minutes. ☐

2. Listen to a record/story quietly. ☐

3. Write about Things I Do Over and Over. ☐

Recess

1. Do one page in my math book. ☐

2. Study and draw a mealworm. ☐

3. Complete one pattern blocks page. ☐

Total Stars ☐

The Star System

　　If your class needs additional reinforcement or encouragement to work, put all of their names on the blackboard under headings for each color group like this:

YELLOW GROUP	GREEN GROUP	ORANGE GROUP
1. Cari*	1. Arthur*	1. Adam
2. Cynthia*	2. Ava	2. Aden
3. Dale	3. Barbara	3. Alice
4. Doris*	4. Barry	4. Alison
5. Edna	5. Bert	5. Alan
6. Elmo	6. Bertha	6. Alam
	7. Blair	7. Andrew

Put the following instructions on the blackboard below the names:

Each star means one minute early to recess.
Up to five minutes can be earned. To earn a star you must:

1. Walk directly to the learning area
2. Keep your hands to yourself
3. Get right to work
4. Use a soft voice
5. Finish your work
6. Clean up

If you or your aide see someone setting a good example in all behaviors listed on the board, put a star next to their name immediately. If you can't get to the board right away, notice that they remembered what to do and write their name and the star on a paper. Then, when you are finished helping a child, be sure to give the deserving person a star on the board. Or you can give them permission to put a star up for themselves.

Continue to keep the rules clear in a firm, consistent manner. A posted chart helps the children to remember these rules. When desired behaviors are recognized, children learn them quickly, and will be able to function responsibly in an involved learning environment.

Try to find times when you can give each child a star so that they all may have some successes. This also sets good behavior in the classroom as the norm. After two or three months, you will probably not need this behavior chart any longer. The times I have used this chart have been very brief; soon the children worked together and the burdensome star chart was removed from the blackboard without the children being aware that it was no longer being used. I had the class come to the rug, and announced that since they had all worked so hard and quietly, everyone could go out to recess five minutes early. The star system is not necessary for all classrooms. Use it only when several people or more need a boost.

Caring and Closeness

If when talking to a child about his problematic behavior, the child says "I don't care," what you really are hearing is that the child cares very much and is really hurting. Ask what behavior he thinks needs working on. List the behaviors he suggests. If he can't think of any, ask "Do you think you are kind to your friends?"

No teacher should be afraid of closeness. A teacher who develops a close relationship with a problem child may be providing that child the first love and warmth he has experienced in a while, and the results will certainly be beneficial to both the teacher and the student.

Dr. William Glasser believes we must reject the idea that it is good to be objective with people.[2] Objectivity is good when working on problem behavior, but we must be careful not to treat the children themselves as objects. Conversely, if you can separate the person from the behavior, the behavior can be seen in an objective light by teacher and student alike.

Children at all ages respond to unconditional caring. When a child has an upsetting day, be sure that you erase the slate in your mind that night and greet him fresh the next day with a new beginning.

Touch

Touch has proven to be very soothing to some children. One boy was always wiggling when we sat in the circle for discussions. Eventually, I had the boy sit next to me and I would gently put my hand on the top of his leg when he'd start to squirm. He seemed to suddenly melt and all of the tension in his wiggling limbs was gone.

I found that a gentle hand on a child's shoulder while the child was working would bring a smile to that child's face. It is what we call a "warm fuzzy." Many times as I walked along outside talking to the children, I couldn't resist letting them know I loved them by giving them a hug.

Once when I visited my old school, after being away for three years, I stopped to say hello to the children I had taught. They were playing volleyball at noon recess and were now sixth graders. They all stopped playing when they saw me and the girls came over to hug me as I hugged them back. Soon the big boys came over for a hug and then they were sending boys I didn't even know to me for a hug! I floated on air the remainder of the day. When you give you receive!

A Success Story

I had a student who, according to his former teacher, would be sent to a school for emotionally handicapped children if he didn't make it with me that year. I heard all of the terrible things this child did from his former teacher. After all this negative input about him, I sat in my rocker and thought about how this boy must be feeling. I asked myself how could I help him without disrupting the rest of the class.

I explained to him that people were not for hurting and that whenever he pinched or hit someone, he would have to be moved. I tried to reinforce him positively whenever I could. There were days when his constant pinching and hitting during discussion times were more than I could take. I would abruptly say, "Pete, go to a desk away from the group."

I thought about the attention he was getting. I decided his behavior was not going to get better. I met with the boy privately before school. I told him I loved him as a person, but did not like or approve of his behavior with his school-mates. I asked him what he thought we could do to improve his behavior. He said,

"No one likes me." I told him I did not agree. He was liked as a person, but no one liked his behavior. What could we do to improve his behavior? He said he did not like it when I would say, in an angry voice, "Pete, go to a desk." I said I didn't like it either and that was why I was talking to him now.

I told him that his behavior seemed to be keeping him from getting what he wanted: friends. Therefore, we must work on his behavior. I asked him what behaviors he thought he needed to change in order to have friends. He listed the behaviors that were bothersome to the class. I said I would no longer tell him to go to a desk, but I could not tolerate the rest of the children being hurt. What could we do?

This boy's mother was also very concerned about his behavior. He was seeing a psychiatrist. I had talked to the psychiatrist and his mother. I wanted to give him more positive feedback, and I knew the mother and the psychiatrist were in full agreement. The boy also knew I had talked to his mother and his psychiatrist. I told him that I had an idea, but that I needed his mother's help.

Figure 5.4

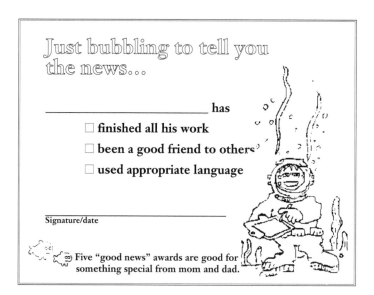

Source: News Gram TREND Enterprises, Inc. Reprinted with permission.

I told him that my idea was to give him a slip of paper each day (see Figure 5.4). On the paper were the good behaviors we had listed. If he did all of the behaviors, he would take the paper home.

I talked to his mother about what she would do to recognize his good behavior. She was more than willing to be informed when her son was behaving right for a change.

We agreed that if he came home with three papers out of five for the first two weeks, he would get a treat from her such as going to the ice cream parlor. The next two weeks, four out of five papers were needed for a treat. If he ever came home with five out of five, he got a present. We also agreed that on the days he did not bring home a paper, no reprimand, uproar, or attention was to be given. It was to be his disappointment, not his mother's.

After two weeks, he started getting papers. By one and a half months, he had five every week. Then I mentioned to the class that the principal thought that Pete was waiting for the bus so well that he didn't have to wait in the office anymore. I asked if there was anything they had noticed.

A flood of appreciative remarks came to him from his classmates, and he glowed. It was the first time I had seen him smile since he came to my class. We then had an appreciation day for everyone. Even the children who are well behaved need to have a pat on the back!

The Child Who Needs Discipline

When a child is a serious discipline problem, get help immediately. Talk to the principal or have a parent conference with the principal, counselor, or psychologist present. Include people who work with the child or can help solve the problem. If you want to have a psychological study done, you must have the permission of the child's parents.

Problem children are crying for help. Do not give up. Let go of your own anger and you will be more successful. Create a safe environment through procedures and rules.

Classmates usually know what is going on. They can cooperate and help a disruptive member of the class learn. You can overlook some problems and not mention them to the class. But if you have a child who is upsetting the classroom, it does not help to keep it private between yourself and the child. The class knows what is happening; they are being bothered, too. They need to be brought in on the discussion and talk out their frustrations. The child needs honest feedback. A discussion of their frustrations and anger will lessen the whispering and taking sides. Tell your class, "We can all help this person. I love all of you, including this person. I do not like this person's actions. I want to help her."

A strong positive attitude on your part makes an immeasurable difference. It adds to your energy and enjoyment levels. If you catch yourself thinking negatively at the end of the day as you are reflecting on the plan for the next day, ask yourself how you can transform the negative way you reacted to a situation or child into a positive way. Try to erase the actions of the child and greet him with a new start each day. Catch yourself and say "Hey, watch out. I'm getting caught up on negative thinking. I love teaching and children too much not to enjoy each day."

Child Abuse

A teacher is sometimes exposed to the terrible fact that a child in her class is being abused at home. I have discovered this several times. During a one-to-one reading conference one day, when my attention was entirely on one child, I noticed bruises and the child seemed nervous. Another time I intercepted a note from one child to another, and discovered a drawing the child had done of adult sexual acts from beginning to end.

It is the law that a teacher must report any suspected acts of violence or sexual abuse. I notified the principal, who in turn consulted the school psychologist. These matters are crucial and can then be handled by children's protection agencies.

HANDLING AN UPSET

The following excerpt is from Elenya Stephan's book, *Stir Until Clear.*[3]

There seems to be an ideal and yet natural process through which many upsets pass. Notice how the process naturally follows the awareness-responsibility-change pattern. First there is a blaming time, then an awareness that the relationship may be damaged or rendered inefficient or an awareness of boredom or exhaustion. Next there is a willingness to let the upset go, and finally there is a clarity about one's own contribution to the upset, along with a reaffirming of the relationship or perhaps the making of new agreements. Sometimes this process takes many days to be completed. The following procedure may assist the facilitator and participants to speed the process along, particularly when there is a true willingness to let the upset go.

When members of the group feel unwilling to let the upset go, it may be appropriate to let them know of the possible consequences. They may, for example, get to continue feeling upset. Or the upset person may be asked not to present himself at school until he can let go of it (insofar as we have agreed to keep the school a safe place...).

Responsibility, different from blame, is nonjudgmental, and reflects simple ownership of behavior. Approaches that attempt to determine a person to blame, and then implicitly, an "innocent victim," make it unsafe for those involved to acknowledge their contribution to the upset. Such an approach is not only ineffective, but reflects the misconception that there is a victim.

Once youngsters have experienced this process a few times, perhaps during a group meeting time or privately with a facilitator, they will begin to see the sense of orderliness about it.

Shaping Attitudes and Behaviors

Alvyn M. Freed claims a "warm fuzzy" is when you do something nice for someone.[4] It can be a smile, pat on the back, or someone saying "Hi." A warm fuzzy feels good. A cold prickle feels bad. A cold prickle is being ignored, hit, or yelled at.

When there is unkindness to others, clear the air by letting the children know that you do not condone it. People are not for hurting. Make a note to teach kindness to others. It may be a part of the social studies curriculum for home and school. Give warm fuzzies. Ask them how they feel when they get a warm fuzzy and how they feel when they get a cold prickle. If a child says to you, "You are a nice teacher," acknowledge the compliment by saying, "That warm fuzzy made me feel good. Thank you!" (See the appendix at the end of the chapter for a list of films and books about feelings.)

Recess Upsets

Recess is a time to observe the children at play, but it can sometimes seem overwhelming. You need to keep a few things in mind:

- ◆ Tattling will get to you if you don't find a way to handle it. One way is to use active listening (see discussion later in this chapter) and to repeat back to the child what you have heard her say.

- ◆ Very often after fights or disagreements the children will be friends again within five minutes.

- ◆ Some children just want attention.

- ◆ It is difficult to judge who is at fault if you did not witness an incident.

- ◆ Try not to get emotionally involved and side with one child over another; it usually takes two to fight.

- ◆ If someone reports an injury, investigate immediately!

Yard upsets are best handled if you remain calm and nonjudgmental. I often wondered if there was a way to break up a fist fight between sixth graders other than pulling them apart and risking getting punched or kicked. I found my answer when a student teacher was helping me with yard duty. A fight broke out and he simply walked over to these two boys and yelled, in a firm voice, "It's over." To my amazement the fight stopped. I was given the chance to practice this after the student teacher graduated. A bloody fight erupted while I was on yard duty. I mustered up my courage and self-confidence and yelled, "It's over!" A look of shock must have crossed my face as the two boys stopped. It was almost too simple a solution to believe.

Kindness Works

One boy in my class especially needed kindness. He was the scapegoat, ridiculed by most of the children. A large, lovable boy who never fought back, my heart went out to him from the first day of school for the hurt he must have been feeling.

My coming to his defense did not seem to be the answer. It would be Nick and me against the rest of the class. Lecturing to the other children about their behavior would not help either. Rather, I decided to study kindness—for the rest of the year if necessary! I showed movies on kindness, we had discussions on kindness, we talked about kindness to animals, family members, new people we meet, and friends. I decided to reinforce these discussions by my example. When appropriate, I would put my hand on Nick's shoulder. I recognized him when he did something well, and encouraged him to show the class how to do it. For instance, he was especially good at kicking a ball. Another child needed a kicker because of a hurt foot, and Nick kicked for him. I was careful not to overdo the attention and cause the children to have jealous or resentful feelings toward Nick. I also made sure to recognize each of them when it was appropriate to do so. Rather than lecture, I simply said I did not tolerate ridicule in the classroom. The firmness in my voice was evidence that I meant business. I noticed any act of kindness given to Nick and other children in the class. It took a while, but when the children realized they were not getting attention from me for hurting someone, they stopped.

CLASSROOM DISCIPLINE

Discipline in the classroom begins with the teacher being in charge and stating her expectations and goals. Her goals are to help the children learn and for the children to make it their own goal to learn. A teacher can best reach these goals by letting the children have a voice in the discussion, and in setting the rules needed in the class to obtain their goals. Cultivate a positive attitude by catching the children remembering a rule or helping one another. This is generally the best way to help the child who is a severe behavior problem, without giving this child too much attention. Give the child reasons to behave in an acceptable manner. Know that underneath the tough exterior is a child that you love.

Punishments are best not dealt out too often; they focus attention on problems and distract from positive behavior. A meeting with a child before school is a good way to halt a problem, and a class discussion about it as it comes up is often even better. Immediate eye contact with the child, without a word spoken by the teacher, is often enough to head trouble off. (See Chapter 5's appendix for an excellent list of suggestions for classroom discipline.)

Consistency

Being honest with the children will develop their trust of you. If you promise to do something you must carry it out. Consistency can be hard to develop, but if a teacher becomes aware of her inconsistency she slowly changes. Be consistent maintaining rules and applying those rules to everyone. Children remember what you said or did.

Example

You state the rule, "Walk in the classroom," but one day two girls run to the door just to be the first in line for recess. If you overlook this infraction you are not consistent, but if you have the girls go back to where they started and then walk to the door you are furthering the use of the rules.

Getting Attention

How do you get your class's attention? You can announce, "I would like your attention." You can ring a bell, or establish some other signal that the class will respond to, like a squeaky toy hammer from the dime store. It is good to set up your expectations early in the year. Tell the children that by the count of five you expect them to finish talking and be ready to listen.

For kindergartners, you can play a chord on the piano, sing down the scale, say "Please listen to me," or count to five holding a finger up for each count. Make up your own games and signals. Change them from time to time for variety. Stay calm and in control.

Sayings That Can Lead to Disaster

Think before you speak. The following, often said in haste by well-meaning teachers, can result in classroom chaos.

Do you want to finish your work?

Everyone may go home.

Everyone stand up and go outside.

I will meet you at the library.

Who did it?

You hit him?

Dismissal

Have a list of tricks and games to dismiss the children at recess and lunch, to learning areas, or at the end of the day. This keeps order in the classroom, keeps the children paying attention, and keeps them thinking and enjoying themselves. These are some of my favorites.

- Whisper. If the teacher uses a soft voice, or whispers, the class will begin to pay attention. Whisper the name of a child who is quiet, "Katie may leave." Other children will notice some children leaving and wonder how they were dismissed. They can see your lips moving and must be quiet in order to hear.
- Dismiss by color of eyes, clothing type or color of shoes, month of birthday, beginning letter of first or last name. "Everyone with red socks may walk to recess."
- Draw slips of paper with the children's names on them from a box for dismissal.
- Dismiss children by their initials, "M.C. may leave."
- Guess who? Describe someone in the class, "She has blue eyes, brown hair, a friendly smile. She may leave for recess."
- "The person who has a birthday today may leave."

Again, make up your own games. Have fun with this.

PAYING ATTENTION

> *To teach listening, notice when the children are*
> *listening. To teach the children not to listen, mention*
> *and notice that they are not good listeners.*
>
> —Mary Coons

The best way to teach listening is to notice listening. By shouting to a noisy room, "You are not listening to me!" you are giving plenty of attention for not listening. Be sure to notice when all the children listen without talking out of turn for, perhaps, five minutes. "That is a record; you listened for five minutes," you might say. Then the next time, when they are listening quietly for even a longer period of time, you might comment, "You sat for twenty minutes without talking. Good for you!"

Draw attention to good listening. "Did you all notice how quiet everyone was while Jane was talking?" When they listen, tell them, "You people know how to listen." Some students in my classes have proudly told the principal, "We are good listeners." One of my students wrote a book about good listeners.

Listening not only means being quiet while someone is talking and not interrupting, but also understanding and focusing on what is being said. Listening can be taught by example and in other fun and interesting ways.

You can:

- Have the children repeat what the child who just spoke said before they tell their news.

- Sing a popular song using "Loo" instead of words. Have the children guess what the song is.

- At the beginning of the school year, when the children are in a circle meeting, go around the circle and have each child name the person sitting next to him or her.

- Clap out syllables, using one, two, and three syllable words.

- List three words in a group

(1)	(2)	(3)
apple	house	hen
grass	street	cluck
peach	road	pig
orange	highway	robin

and ask: "Which one does not belong?" (They have a song for this on Sesame Street.)

♦ Play records and tapes containing sounds for the children to identify.

♦ Play "Simon Says."

♦ The teacher can start a story, and the next person must repeat what the teacher said and add to the story.

♦ In a very low voice, have them signal with thumbs up if they have heard a question.

Active Listening

Of the many ways to teach children how to listen, the most important is for you to be a good listener. A boy I'll call Hugh helped me many years ago to be an active listener.

Just before lunch one day Hugh was so mad he headed for the door with the intention of running home. Why, I didn't know. I asked the aide to take the children to lunch while I stayed in the room with Hugh. Instead of persuading him to stay in school and listing all of the consequences that would occur if he left the school grounds, I merely said, "You are very mad. You're feeling upset. You want to go home," echoing his feelings. Sure enough, it worked. By the end of the lunch hour Hugh was calm. He verbalized to me that he was mad at a friend who refused to play with him at lunch time. We decided that he could resolve the situation by using either of two solutions: talking to his friend or finding another friend. The happy ending of Hugh's not running home was well worth my lunch hour.

Active listening is the term given to the process of working to accept another person. It takes participation and effort on both sides, particularly that of the listener. Following is a summary of Thomas Gordon's ideas about the basic process:

♦ The receiver (teacher) tries to understand what it is the sender is feeling or what his message means.

♦ Then the teacher puts his understanding into his own words (code) and feeds it back for the child's verification.

♦ The teacher does not send a message of his own, such as, an evaluation, opinion, advice, logic analysis, or question.

♦ The teacher feeds back only what he feels the sender's message meant![5]

I believe, as Gordon does, that active listening is an important skill we can develop to help children work through their problems. Active listening gives back to the child some responsibility for his own learning and facilitates personal growth, self-confidence, and independence.[6]

In order to give your full attention to listening to someone you need to put aside any paper, notes, or pens, look at the person, think about what the person is saying, and not judge or get angry at what is being said. A person feels listened to if you look at her, smile or nod your head, and do not interrupt before the person has finished talking.

When the other person has completed his ideas, ask questions to clarify your understanding and try to get the main idea. Do not give examples of such an experience you might have had. Try not to get caught up in the person's emotions but concentrate on and react to what was said. Note in your mind what the person did not say or avoids discussing, but do not try to think ahead of the person. Do not judge or become angry at what is said, and do not assume anything. Find out all of the facts; when you have heard all of the facts try to relate these back to the person you are listening to, along with your understanding of the way the person feels.

The attitude of accepting another person makes active listening work so well, and is very important. A teacher should be able to say the following things to the child:

- ◆ "You have a right to feel the way you do."
- ◆ "I respect you as a person with your own ideas and feelings."
- ◆ "I really want to hear your point of view."
- ◆ "I am not judging you—I am neither agreeing nor disagreeing."
- ◆ "Your feelings belong to you."
- ◆ "I trust you to handle your feelings, to work out your problems."

These statements convey an attitude of acceptance, which:

- ◆ Makes the child feel that the teacher is not trying to change him and forms a closer relationship.
- ◆ Encourages the child to continue communicating—to say more, to share his feelings, and not be afraid of his own emotions.
- ◆ Facilitates self-direction, self-responsibility, independence.
- ◆ Promotes a relationship of warmth and closeness.
- ◆ Facilitates problem-solving in the child. It helps the child think out loud and work it through.

◆ Encourages the child to be more open to the teacher's thoughts and ideas.

◆ Helps the child be more willing to listen to the teacher when the teacher listens to him.

There are times, however, when active listening is not appropriate. Active listening should not be a method of manipulating the child into feeling or behaving the way the teacher thinks he should. Active listening facilitates self-directed change—change in a direction chosen by the child. Active listening should not be used when the teacher does not have time to hear the child out completely. It should not be used to get the child to expose his feelings, after which the teacher moves in with evaluation, judgment, punishment. This process should also not be used when the child needs some other kind of help from the teacher, for example, when a child needs some information. When Suzy asks where the bathroom is, you merely need to tell her where it is. And of course, do not use active listening when you're really not very interested.

Use active listening, rather, when a child needs self-discovery and understanding, when a child is confused, or when more difficult or personal answers are sought. Active listening should be used:

◆ When a child is expressing feelings: "I feel terrible."

◆ When a child indicates he has a problem: "What am I going to do?"

◆ When a child is sending messages that are coded in ways that make you uncertain what is going on inside the child: "Will my parents ever be happily married?"

◆ When your own feelings are not too involved—when you can be separate from the child.

◆ When you are feeling accepting—you don't need to change the child.

Here are some pointers to remember when using active listening:

◆ Don't give up too soon—don't interrupt the other person.

◆ Concentrate on what she is saying, focus on her words, ideas, and feelings.

◆ Look at the other person.

♦ Smile and nod appropriately—don't overdo.

♦ Control your anger—your anger at what she is saying may prevent you from understanding her words and meaning.

♦ Get rid of distractions—put down papers and pencils.

♦ Share responsibility for communication—try to understand and if you don't, ask for clarification.

♦ React to ideas, not to the person—her ideas may be good.

♦ Avoid hasty judgment—wait until all the facts are in.[7]

Effective Listening

We all can tell, on some level, when we are not really being paid attention to, and sometimes children will act out until they are heard. Often it only takes a little attention to acknowledge that a child is a human being in the process of learning how to live, and we can acknowledge their feelings with our responses. There are two basic ways to respond to a child's feelings: with an open response or a closed response.

Closed Response: Ignores students' feelings, demonstrates the teacher's unwillingness to accept and understand.

Open Response: Acknowledges students' right to their feelings by demonstrating that the teacher accepts what they feel as well as what they say. Indicates that the teacher understands.

Compare these responses to student's remarks:

Student's Remark	Closed Response	Open Response
(crying) My parents are getting a divorce.	Ah, gee, that's too bad, honey.	Are you feeling sad?
Mrs. Lorenzo, Tom copied from my paper!	Well, I'll take care of him!	Sounds like you're really angry about Tom's cheating.
I'm going to get to go to camp this summer!	That's nice—please sit down so we can get to work.	That sounds exciting!

| You're the meanest teacher in the world! | Don't you dare talk to me like that! | You're very angry with me. |

(Used with permission from the Teachers' Learning Cooperative, Marin County Office of Education, San Rafael, California.)

Listening for Feedback

Be aware of complaints from more than one child about a program or activity. If several children say that they did not like what the class did, lead this remark into a discussion and get their input. If it is something that is necessary for the children to learn before they reach the next grade, you should tell them this. However, ask them what could be done to make whatever it was they didn't like more enjoyable. Write down their suggestions, but first warn them that you will only hear sensible suggestions and that silly ones are not acceptable. Explain you want to help them learn. Write any worthwhile suggestions on a large piece of paper stored near the blackboard and clip it to the blackboard with large magnetic clips where they can all see it. Read the suggestions over together with the children, and tell them that you are going to prepare their lessons for tomorrow and will try to use some of their suggestions.

Most of the time these suggestions are very helpful. A slight change the next day, using one of their suggestions, may be all that it takes to improve the activity for them. The children seem to feel better about the subject, and the complaining diminishes.

If they give you several good suggestions, tell them you will write them in your lesson plan book on Friday for the following week's lessons—that there were so many good suggestions, they can't all be used at once.

Ask the children, from time to time, with the same warning—only sensible suggestions—what is their favorite activity? Ask if there is anything the class hasn't done that they would like to do? Are there other subjects they would like to study? Write these on a sheet of paper, clip it to the board, and read it over with them. Copy the ideas into your plan book and use them when appropriate.

Always have handy many large sheets of paper with two heavy magnetic clips and colored pens near the blackboard—just in case a discussion starts.

CLASS DISCUSSIONS

Class discussions are part of learning how to listen. They are one way I have found to get children to listen to each other. When the children have learned how to listen and take turns talking, use the time after lunch, after recess, or the first thing in the morning for discussion in a circle on the rug area. You can meet to discuss all manner of things.

In the first few days and weeks it's a good idea to begin meeting as a class to get to know each other, to start learning how to listen, and to begin to address problems as they come up. After two months or more when you sense a trust and cohesion within the group, you can begin talking about values and feelings, and scheduling activities such as topic discussions and interviews with each child. Do not begin to discuss feelings and values until after the class has gotten to know each other. I've found that the best time for these discussions is after lunch.

Time spent with the children in a group, talking on the rug, is valuable. By learning about each child in a caring manner, you are building a trusting, cohesive group. Use active listening during these times, and never let judgments enter your discussions with the children. Discussion times are when the class becomes a unit, and individuals come to accept their differences and appreciate their uniqueness.

Ground Rules

Set rules for discussions, and involve the entire class in their enforcement. The most basic rule is that everyone listens to each other and does not interrupt. Be gentle and firm in teaching these rules. For example, if a child starts talking while you are talking, stop. Explain that everyone takes turns talking, so you will wait until it is quiet before you continue. The children around the talking child soon tell him to be quiet.

Encourage the children to make statements about how they feel, but let them know they must stay away from accusations if they have a problem to discuss involving another person in the class. Before you start a discussion of a problem, let the children know exactly what your ground rules are:

- If someone has a problem, they are to talk about the problem and not use names.
- If they want to talk to a person about a problem, they are to talk to that person by saying "you." They are not to say "he." That is tattling.
- They are not to call anyone names. They are to tell the person how they feel or felt when something was done to them.
- Only helpful suggestions. Silly ones tell us they do not want to be in the group.
- We are here to help one another.

Do not dwell on one particular method for discussions but put many ideas together and use what is natural for you.

There are two ways to ask questions. You can ask convergent questions, which require a specific answer, or you can ask divergent questions, which encourage the other to give their own answers. Examples of divergent questions are: "Have you thought about…?" "What might others have done in the same situation?" "How might you find the answer to your problem?" "What is your opinion on …" or, "What do you think about…?"

Problem Solving

Discussions will vary depending upon the class. Sometimes it may be necessary for you to initiate a discussion to fulfill your needs, such as reviewing behavior, or controlling the noise level. If you do not approve of something, it is best to discuss it immediately. Make a note to teach skills that will facilitate class communication. For instance, you may note that the children are not listening while on the rug; therefore, you will want to teach listening.

Present information in the form of "I" statements: "I feel frustrated when I am talking and someone else is talking, too." Use "I" messages frequently. By saying, "I get angry when people are ridiculed unfairly," you give a more informative, personal, and direct impression than if you say, "You should never ridicule people."

Remind children to avoid accusations. In the end, they will feel better. Fewer fights will occur because they have not accused one another. No one will get defensive. Ask the quarrelers how they think they both could have done things differently to avoid hurting or upsetting one another. If no solution is given, ask the class for suggestions.

Be careful not to let discussions degenerate into someone being heckled by the class. Ask the remainder of the class how they would handle a certain upsetting situation described by the child and accept only helpful suggestions, explaining that silly suggestions such as "Hit her," are not appreciated and will be ignored.

Try to end each child's discussion with a summary of his problems. This shows that you are listening. If appropriate, you might ask, "Why do you people think Dick is acting this way?" The answer usually is "To get attention." Follow this by "How can we help give him attention?"

I particularly enjoyed one discussion time. Candy had a problem. I knew that her father was a professor at the nearby theological seminary. Candy said she had always wanted to say some swear words and couldn't we have Mondays from 1:00-1:15 for swearing? I wanted to let her know my needs. I told her I realized she would like to say these words, but to me swear words are offensive. However, we all helped her solve her problem so as to not offend anyone. Candy could check out of the room if she felt like swearing and go over to a tree and swear to the tree. The tree wouldn't be offended. I always smiled whenever I saw Candy looking up at a tree.

Also use discussion time to give the children positive feedback about themselves as students. For example, you might say, "You people worked so hard last week. You remembered the rules and didn't play. You went right to work. I can tell you are here to learn." Above all, strive for class unity. Try to teach positive attitudes by example, accepting every child in a caring manner.

Voting

Voting can be a simple and rapid means for each child to publicly and easily affirm their opinions and values. This is a good way to start conversations, giving the children time to gain confidence to be able to orally state their views. By doing this, they realize others often see issues quite differently than they. This is helpful for the egocentric younger children, and also gives the shy children a chance to be more secure in their opinions. I used the thumbs up and thumbs down procedure of voting.

Values Clarification

There are two levels of questions during a discussion time. One is the kind that encourages a child to gain insight to her feelings. The other level of questioning is what Simon, Howe, and Kirchenbaum call *Values Clarification*.[8] They are exercises for the children to express their values or choices in a particular situation.

Each day, throughout our whole lives, we must make choices. Practice in choosing among alternatives and publicly stating, explaining, or defending their choices exposes children to the fact that many issues require thoughtful consideration.

Make up some questions that begin with "How many of you...?" Those who vote yes put their thumbs up, those who vote no put thumbs down, and those who do not wish to vote keep their hands in their laps. Discussion can follow after the list of questions is completed.

First you can ask broad questions, that most of the class will answer affirmatively: "How many of you...

> like to go to the movies?"
> like to go on picnics?"
> have a favorite rock group?"
> think teachers are helpful?"
> like to play with your brother or sister?"

can throw a ball?"
sometimes tell on your brother or sister?"
have a secret wish?"
would like to have your own room?"
have a job at home?"

Another exercise is to give the children three choices and ask them to think seriously about what choice they would make. The children are then called on to give a response. Children may say "I pass." A class discussion may follow, with the children who spoke or who didn't speak giving the reasons for their choices.

For example: "What would you rather do for a summer vacation?"
fish in the mountains?
swim at the beach?
stay at home with your friends?

Or "What kind of pet would you like most to have?"
a dog that's bigger than you?
a dog that's smaller than you?
a cat?

For further values clarification questions, refer to the book *Values Clarification* by Sidney B. Simon, Leland W. Howe, and Howard Kirschenbaum. New York, Hart Publishing Company, Inc., 1972.

Circle Meetings

Circle Meetings are good for discussion of certain topics which involve all of the children. For example, you might discuss why they are at school and their goals for the school year. They have been told by their parents that they are in school to learn. You might tell them, "I am learning from you." "You are given opportunities to learn from the things the aide and I give you." This can dovetail with a discussion of class disruptions, and an explanation of your motives as a teacher. "If you take learning time from other people, then you are telling me to move you away from the rest of the class. You will come back to the class when you can allow everyone to learn."

Below is a list of topics used in my school. These may seem a little deep for primary graders, and perhaps for kindergartners they are, but first and second graders responded to them thoughtfully and with great interest. Have a Circle Meeting on Circle Meeting topics to get ideas. Consider doing this after having led several meetings with topics of your choice.

- Have you ever been afraid of being teased? What makes people tease? Are there other ways of feeling good about yourself without it being at another's expense?
- What is the best thing you do for yourself?
- What is the worst thing you do for yourself? What does doing this do for you?
- What is competition? What's it for?
- How does it feel to lose?
- What is love? What's it for? What does it feel like? Do you feel it?

There are more of these questions under *Circle Meeting Topic Suggestions* in Chapter 5's appendix.

INSPIRATION

Specific Suggestions for Motivating Children

A teacher's concern for and awareness of each child is an important aspect of motivation for students. Take time on a one-to-one basis to learn about each child and her attitudes about school and the subjects she studies. Find out how the child is feeling, ask about the child's interests, family, what she does after school, on weekends, her favorite activity, and the names of her playmates and friends. The better you know your students, the easier it is to motivate them. You can become intimately acquainted with each child during a one-to-one reading conference.

Consider what type of thinkers they are. An introverted child needs a few moments to think before she responds. Give her time after a question. Reflective children may look like daydreamers but they're not. Be patient. The majority of children are extroverts. They need to talk, they need to brainstorm.

Likewise, the more your children know about you, the better they respond to you. The children need to know something about you. They need to see you as a real person with feelings of anger, sadness, and happiness, not as a teacher who never experiences the emotions they feel or the mistakes they make.

Start the year by stating your expectations of each child's behavior, and tell them that you know each of them can learn. Work to remove anxieties from a child who wonders what you want and whether he will learn.

Being alert to signs of boredom and restlessness when a lesson is in progress can signal to you that the class is losing interest. A wise teacher will change or shorten the lesson in this case, or acknowledge that the class seems restless, and ask for their opinions and ideas for changes. Children who are encouraged to give input into the content of their lessons are in turn interested in those lessons. Their active participation makes them feel involved, teaches active listening to complaints and problems, and develops feelings of trust, respect, and adventure between teacher and class. Allow students to make as many choices and decisions as possible.

Along with your enthusiasm for teaching, you need to bring something new to the classroom and to vary the program. Use guest speakers, change the room arrangements, and change the groupings of children every six weeks or so. Use various visual methods to present lessons, like overhead projectors or bulletin boards. Have a board featuring a classmate of the week, a joke, cartoon, news, sports TV program, or class project. Display photographs of the class at its various activities. Always incorporate student interests into your lessons (sports, TV, pop music, animals, dinosaurs, toys), as well as school activities, places and events that are familiar to students.

Vary the routine by going on field trips. Eat lunch together in the local park, walk to the library, visit the local merchants, go to the park or school lawn for a story. After the young children are familiar with school, and things have become routine, make a point of being spontaneous, enthusiastic, and unpredictable. Use novelty or gimmicks for dramatic impact to liven up a dull lesson. Keep surprises up your sleeve. The use of three different activities during a regular period breaks up the dull routine that can be experienced when the same subject is presented for a long time.

Be reasonable in your expectations. Use active participation devices when teaching new material or when holding discussions so that students are not allowed to be mere passive listeners. When a student seems to be apathetic, direct your questions to her: "I am going to call on you, Maria, in one minute, be ready to tell me what you think." Give them some perspective: "It's important to know this before we can go on to the next step." Remember to keep them excited about their own learning process: "Your teachers next year will really be surprised that you know this!"

Motivation and Reinforcement

You can praise and encourage a child in ways that teach him not to be motivated by pleasing others, but to learn to do things for his own good. Reflect on your classroom attitude toward each child with your teacher's aide or student teacher. Assess whether you are encouraging self-motivation. Inspire children to learn with encouraging, positive words and do not dwell too long on the negative. Lead a child to think he is right or doing a good job. If you bribe or threaten a child, you take the responsibility of learning away from the child and put it on yourself.

You can encourage whatever behavior you want to teach with the words you use with a child. "You mean to say you are completely finished, so soon? It's hard to believe!" "I can tell you are here to learn by the way you are working." "You're a fast learner." "Wow! You know it all! I just can't catch you!" "You are such a good thinker. You complete your work on time." You will be surprised at how well enthusiasm works. (For a list of do's and don't's see Chapter 5's appendix.)

Encourage a child to progress at his own rate. Have kind words for the child as he progresses in his work; do not always wait until after the work is completed. Teacher-pleasing sayings motivate the child to progress for the teacher and not for his self-motivation. Avoid teacher-pleasing by saying:

"I like the way you came in."

"I'm pleased, you finished this on time."

"Look at how straight Jim is sitting and ready to listen."

Instead you can say, "I see five people ready to go to recess."

CONCLUSION

Behavior, attitudes, and discipline go hand in hand. You will deal with them each day. The more positive your attitude and examples, the more you read and learn about this aspect of your teaching responsibility, the easier these problems will be to handle.

You must keep several ideas in mind in order to have a climate in the classroom of calmness, cooperation, and eagerness to learn. In summarizing the things I think are most important for a teacher to keep in mind, I would say that children need:

1. Love, and people to show an interest in them

2. Clear and consistent limits

3. Democracy—feeling that their ideas and opinions are worthy of discussion and respect

4. Your full attention when being listened to

5. Independence, which allows them to do for themselves and encourage their curiosity

Always remember these three cardinal rules for teachers:

1. Giving answers yourself ends thinking for pupils.

2. Asking open-ended, divergent questions stimulates curiosity and thinking and helps children discover their own ideas.

3. Helping children plan, carry out, and evaluate projects provides experience and builds self-confidence, creative thinking, cooperative learning.

SOURCES

1. Collins, Mary Reiss. 1972. Instructor, California State University, Sonoma. Presently: Assistant Superintendent of Schools, Instruction, Petaluma, California, 1992.

2. Glasser, William, 1965. *Reality Therapy, A New Approach to Psychiatry*. New York: Harper Collins, p. 158.

3. Stephan, Elenya. 1982. *Stir Until Clear: A Handbook on the Counseling Relationship in the Schools*. R. and E. Research Associates: Palo Alto, California, p. 115.

4. Freed, Alvyn M., 1973. *T.A. for Tots (And Other Prizes)*. Jalmar Press: Sacramento, p. 10.

5. Gordon, Thomas. 1974. *T.E.T. Teacher Effectiveness Training*, Peter H. Wyden Publisher: New York, p. 74.

6. Ibid., p. 123.

7. Ibid., pp. 75–76.

8. Simon, Sidney B., Leland W. Howe, and Howard Kirschenbaum. 1972. *Values Clarification*. Hart Publishing Company, Inc.: New York.

Chapter 5 Appendix

A LIST OF SUGGESTIONS FOR CLASSROOM DISCIPLINE

Be Consistent. If you punish Emily one day for hitting Sarah, you should also punish her the next day for hitting Seth. Otherwise she gets confused: Is it all right to hit or isn't it? She may be tempted to hit again just to see what will happen this time.

Play Fair. A day of no bike-riding is a reasonable punishment if your student misused the bike. Taking the bike away for six months is not reasonable.

Make It Clear. One of the main purposes of discipline is to teach children how to behave; therefore, you have to explain clearly why certain behavior is acceptable and other behavior is not. Being clear also means being as specific as possible. Telling a child not to wander "too far" is vague. "Stay in the playground" is easier to understand. "Stay in the playground or you'll have to stay inside" is even better.

Act Promptly. Children should be punished (or rewarded) very soon after their bad (or good) behavior takes place. Don't expect them to remember what they did wrong hours after the event.

Be Honest. If you smile gently at your student while berating him for something, you'll probably confuse him. The same thing is true if you assure him that you're not angry while forcing your words out through clenched teeth. We often send confusing signals to our children when we ourselves are confused. Sort out your feelings first and then try to be straight with the student.

Delay Complaints. In order to reduce tattling it's a good idea to have a problem box where children can write down their complaints or problems. These can then be addressed at the weekly school meeting. Often by this time the students have been able to work the problems out for themselves. In the meantime the teacher has avoided being pulled into every minor dispute and the children have learned something about delaying gratification.

Catch Them Being Good. We have all heard this a million times. However, despite our best intentions, we don't always do this. Remember to give yourself a little bit of time each day to focus on good behavior.

Use Childrens' Negative Behavior in Positive Ways. Have the class "talker" read aloud to the class. Keep the "wiggler" busy with hands-on jobs; change tasks often. Make a student who is motivated by power the class president.

Give a Choice of an Appropriate Consequence. For example, a student may choose between running around the track, or writing out an apology or explanation.

Remember if You Lose Your Temper to Not Dwell on Guilt. Figure out what didn't work and make the needed correction so it won't happen again.

Remember to Counteract "Whiners." When they say "I don't want to do this," consistently saying, "You *get* to do this," can stop them cold.

Remember That There Are Limits to the Teacher's Responsibility. Feeling that you are supposed to be responsible for a student's development in all areas is likely to make you feel too frazzled to be able to begin to address a student's needs. Remember that education is a team effort and that the educational system, the students, the parents and the teachers share this job.

(Used with permission from the Teachers' Learning Cooperative, Marin County Office of Education, San Rafael, California.)

COMMUNICATION: LISTENING AND SENDING MESSAGES

Situations in which the teacher determines problem ownership and then decides whether to listen reflectively or to send an I-message.

Situation	Problem Owner	Reflective Listening	I-Message
Student crying about low report card.	Student	You feel very sad because you didn't get the grades you wanted.	
Teacher returns to the room and finds several students throwing paper wads.	Teacher		When I have to leave the room and return to find things like this happening, I feel very disappointed because I thought we had an agreement on how you would conduct yourselves in my absence.
Student tells teacher she feels sorry because she and a friend had a fight and she called the friend a name.	Student	Sounds like you feel terrible because you think you hurt your friend's feelings.	
Student leaning back on chair as if he might fall over.	Teacher		When you lean back in your seat, I get scared because you might fall and hurt yourself.
Student tells you her mother is in the hospital for surgery.	Student	You're very worried about your mother.	

(Used with permission of the Teachers' Learning Cooperative, Marin County Office of Education, San Rafael, California.)

CIRCLE MEETING TOPIC SUGGESTIONS

- ◆ What bores you? An important aspect to encourage here, if it comes up, is how we bore ourselves by not choosing to make a personal investment in whatever it is. What are our resistances to such an investment?

- ◆ What do you worry about most?

- ◆ How do you react when peers (friends), school mates pressure you to do what they want? Can suggest keeping a tally of the number of times we sell ourselves out to avoid the "little death" of losing the attention or love of a friend or parent. Be sure the tally has the other side to it—the times we stayed with our position out of self-respect, and/or respect for the other.

- ◆ What bothers you most about adults? Have you taken responsibility for expressing these feelings with those involved?

- ◆ What's a teacher? Do teachers understand you? How? How not? Describe a teacher you felt especially good about (omit names). What if teachers got tired of "helping"? Are teachers responsible for you?

- ◆ What is jealousy? What's it for? What does it feel like?

- ◆ What's divorce? What's it for? What does it feel like to you?

- ◆ What does it mean to be dependent?

- ◆ I have two tickets to Disneyland in my pocket. How can I fairly decide who should go? How does it feel to lose? (This is a good topic to precede the one on competition.)

- ◆ Where is happiness? Start this with what is happiness and lead into where.

- ◆ How do you get to be popular? A question which evolved from this spoken by a student was, "How does somebody get to be the 'class creep'?"

- ◆ Go around circle with: "The most important person in my life now is...because...." It's sometimes most valuable to go around with "The three most important people..." With sophisticated students you can see about going into what it means to be dependent.

◆ What does "good" mean? What does "bad" mean? You may find the discussion naturally beginning with very specific examples of "good" and "bad," which with some guidance can be led into some interesting generalizations about "good" and "bad" for the students.

(Reprinted with permission from *Stir Until Clear: A Handbook on the Counseling Relationship in the School,* by Elenya Stephan. To order, write to R. and E. Publishers P.O. Box 2008, Saratoga, CA 95070. This book is full of good information.)

DO'S AND DON'T'S IN USING MOTIVATION

"DO'S"	"DON'T'S"
Do *build a learner's productive concern about her learning task.*	***Don't*** *build so much concern the learner can't concentrate on the task.*
"Let's see if you can beat your yesterday's record." "I'll be back in a minute to see how you're doing." "We'll come back to it later to see if you remember."	"If you don't get them all right, you'll have to stay after school." "This is the last chance you'll have for help." "Your whole grade depends on this."
Do *use pleasant feeling tone.*	***Don't*** *use pleasant feeling tone when it isn't working.*
"I'll bet you can learn them." "You're really a fast learner."	"Even though you're not trying very hard, I'm here to help you." "You're fun to teach."
Do *make examples interesting and meaningful.*	***Don't*** *make things so vivid the learner thinks more about them than he does about learning.*
"Suppose you made five home runs every day for four days, how many home runs would you have made?" "Suppose you got three times $5 from your grandmother. What are all the things you'd like to buy?" "I'll time you with a stopwatch. Have you ever seen a stopwatch work?"	"Suppose three monsters came in your room every night until Friday and hid under your bed, how many would there be?" "If you got $5 for your birthday and your grandmother said, 'I'll give you three times that much,' how much money would your grandmother give you?"

Do *see that a learner experiences success.*

"Let's count how many new words you've learned." "You see you got them all right." "I just can't catch you."

Don't *have the job so hard he can't possibly do it or so easy he doesn't have to try.*

"I know you've never done one this hard, but try to figure it out." "You always get these right. Let's do them again." "How much money would your mother give you?"

Do *give the learner specific knowledge of results.*

"Your spelling is correct but be careful, i's don't look like e's." "The surprise ending made your story just great."

Don't *give only general information.*

"I put a check on your paper to show you I've seen it." "It's a 'B' paper."

Do *use extrinsic motivation when the learner has no intrinsic motivation to learn a particular thing.*

"If you do this, I will…" "Your dad will be so… to find you know this."

Don't *negotiate or bribe to get a child to learn.*

"Finish this so you can…" "Finish it so you can be one of the first out to recess."

The former tempts a child to consider whether she will put forth the effort. The latter makes it clear the job is to be done, but there will be pleasant consequences. After successful learning, many things become intrinsically motivated.

(Reprinted with permission of the Teachers' Learning Cooperative, Marin County Office of Education, San Rafael, California.)

DO'S AND DON'T'S IN USING REINFORCEMENT

"DO'S"

Do *let a child know when he is really trying, that what he is doing is worthy of note.*

"DON'T'S"

Don't *praise a child for things which are easy for him and take little or no effort on his part.*

"You remembered to put your name on your paper so I'd know whose good work it was."

Do *let a child know she is making progress even though the work is not perfect.*

"That's getting better." "It's getting easier for you, isn't it?" "That's coming." "Pretty soon you'll have it finished." "You're really trying hard."

When a child is learning something new, or something that is hard for him, **do** *reinforce him for each part he does.*

"That's right, now what will you do?" "You did the first one right, now try the next one." "That's a good start, go ahead."

Do *vary the words you use.*

"That's just right." "You're absolutely correct." "You got them all." "That's excellent work."

Do *follow a negative reinforcer with a positive one as soon as possible.*

"Look at this once again. Good, I knew you'd find your mistake." "No, look carefully and you'll get it." "Why am I stopping you from doing that? Good, I knew you'd know."

Do *ignore, if possible, behavior that is merely attention getting.*

"You did a good job of putting your name on the paper" *(when a child has been doing it for years).*

Don't *say something is really good when it isn't. Children know when they're off and can see through insincere praise.*

"That's great" *(when she hasn't really tried).* "You know it perfectly" *(when there are errors or halting responses).*

Don't *wait until he is completely finished with a difficult task before you give him some reinforcement.*

"I won't look at it until you're through." "Let me see it after it's all finished."

Don't *use the same words for everything.*

"Perfect, perfect." "Very good, very good." "Right, right, right."

Don't *leave a child with a negative reinforcer.*

"That's wrong." "You missed five." "No, that's not quite right."

Don't *make a "federal case" out of every little incident.*

Ignore the "blurter outer": call on someone who raised her hand *(if that's what you asked the students to do).*

"Now just what did you mean by that rude remark?"

Do *remember to reinforce every time when new behavior is being learned.*

"That's great Bill, you remember to wait every time until I call on you."

Don't *be inconsistent with your reinforcement when new behavior is being learned.*

"I know you're trying to remember to raise your hand but I just can't call on you every time."

Do *be specific when you reinforce a behavior.*

"Good job, you're finished right on time." "Good for you, you remembered to come the first time I called you." "That's just right, you have finished every problem on the page."

Don't *be so general that the reinforcer is ineffective, ignored or "tuned out."*

"Good for you!" "That's great." "Fine." "Good job."

Do *state the reinforcer as a recognition of achieving the expectation that was set.*

"Good for you, you remembered to come in and go right to work." "You finished all those problems in time to go to recess, just as you said you would."

Don't *promote "teacher pleasing" with a reinforcer that is a personal value judgement.*

"I like the way you came in and went right to work this morning." "I'm pleased you finished in time to go to recess."

Do *determine what is a positive reinforcer for each child or group.*

"You've all been such good help getting the room cleaned up, take time for another inning in your baseball game."

Don't *choose an inappropriate reinforcer for individuals or groups.*

"Since you finished all the questions on this page, here's another set of questions to do."

*If children want attention, **do** give it to them privately or quietly as the group leaves for the playground.*

"Jim, you were a good listener and remembered to raise your hand every time you had something to say." "Jane, you listened so well during the story."

Don't *choose inappropriate teacher attention.*

"Look at how straight Jim is sitting and ready to listen and discuss the story" *(when the last thing Jim wants is to be the center of attention).*

(Reprinted with permission of the Teachers' Learning Cooperative, Marin County Office of Education, San Rafael, California.)

HANDLING AN UPSET INVOLVING SEVERAL PEOPLE

A W A R E N E S S

Blaming...

Awareness of possibility of damaging the relationship or rendering it inefficient

Feeling bored or exhausted from the tension ...

Willingness to let the upset go ...

1) Have each person acknowledge what happened from his own point of view. Do not let the others interrupt. This clearly defines the problem or upset, and may include blaming, if it doesn't get out of hand.

2) Have each person acknowledge willingness or unwillingness, truthfully, to let go of the upset. If at this point anyone is unwilling to let go of the upset, have them acknowledge this explicitly. Let any unwillingness be okay. Sometimes individuals may still be so upset that they may want to hold on to it. Eventually, they may tire of it and then be willing to let go.

R E S P O N S I B I L I T Y

Clarity about one's own contribution to the upset situation ...

3) Have each person acknowledge what he or she did that may have contributed to the situation. Have them speak only in the first person, and include even the most obvious contributions, for example, "I was in the area" was significant. Have them limit themselves to speaking only of their own contributions. If a group member is having a difficult time remembering his contribution, and others do not feel clear about this, they can "remind" him if he would like. Avoid blame. No contribution needs to be seen as either negative or positive for this process to work. Such judgments will in fact interfere.

This process softens and clears feelings, and gives each participant the opportunity to experience the satisfaction that can come from accepting responsibility for their part in an event.

C H A N G E

Reaffirming the relationship and/or making new agreements.

4) Have each person, as appropriate, make an agreement with each other person with whom this is needed. This agreement may be in two parts:
A: What I want from you ... and
B: What I will do for you...
Sometimes asking those involved what they think it would take to clear up the upset can be helpful with this.

(Reprinted with permission from *Stir Until Clear* by Elenya Stephan.)

RESOURCES FOR TEACHING VALUES AND FEELINGS

The teaching of values and exploring the different emotions everyone experiences can be incorporated with the study of families, friends, home, and school for a social studies unit. Books and films that deal with values and feelings are extremely helpful and loved by children. An excellent reference for books to read is Jim Trelease's, *The Read Aloud Handbook*.

Films

What To Do About Your Upset Feelings
The Magic Tree
Putting Together the Rules
Pigeon That Worked a Miracle
Why We Have Laws
Kindness to Others
Let's Have Respect
Getting Along With Others, Tell Me About It
Walter The Lazy Mouse
Your Job, Going To School
The Red Balloon
Guidance: What's Right
What Makes a Friend Special? Tell Me About It
Hopscotch
Mario and the Marvelous Gift
Let's Pretend, Getting Even
The Crying Red Giant
Guidance, The Fence
Your Table Manners

Books About Values and Feelings

Allard, Harry and James Marshall. 1977. *Miss Nelson Is Missing*. Scholastic Book Services: New York.

Beim, Jenold. 1955. *Laugh and Cry, Your Emotions and How They Work*. William Morrow: New York.

Brown, Margaret W. 1947. *Goodnight Moon*. Scholastic Book Services: New York.

Carlson, Bernice Wells. 1973. *Let's Pretend It Happened To You*. Scholastic Book Services: New York.

Davidson, Margaret. 1969. *Helen Keller*. Scholastic Book Services: New York.

Drexler, Carol Joan. 1970. *Young Helen Keller*. Educational Reading Services: Mahwah, New Jersey.

Frost, Erica. 1975. *I Can Read About Good Manners.* Troll Associates: Mahwah, New Jersey.

Gantos, Jack. 1976. *Rotten Ralph.* Scholastic Book Services: New York.

Guilfoile, Elizabeth. 1957. *Nobody Listens to Andrew.* Follett Publishing Company: New York.

Heide, Florence Pany. 1969. *Some Things Are Scary.* Scholastic Book Services: New York.

Hoban, Russell. 1969. *Best Friends For Frances.* Scholastic Book Services: New York.

Holland, Marion. 1977. *The Christmas Tree Crisis.* Scholastic Book Services: New York.

Keats, Ezra Jack. 1975. *Louie.* Scholastic Book Services: New York.

Lexau, Joan. 1969. *The Christmas Secret.* Scholastic Book Services: New York.

MacDonald, Betty. 1949. *Mrs. Piggle-Wiggle's Magic.* Young Readers Press, Inc.: Katonah, New York.

Mayer, Mercer. 1968. *There's A Nightmare In My Closet.* The Dial Press: New York.

McGovern, Ann. 1965 *"Wanted Dead or Alive," The True Story of Harriet Tubman.* Scholastic Book Services: New York.

Trelease, Jim. 1985. *The Read Aloud Handbook.* Penguin Books: New York.

Vreeken, Elizabeth. 1959. *The Boy Who Would Not Say His Name.* Follett Publishing Company: Chicago.

Waber, Bernard. 1971. *Nobody is Perfick.* Scholastic Book Services: New York.

Watson, Jane Werner, Robert E. Switzer, M.D., and J. Cotter Hirschberg, M.D. 1971. *Sometimes I'm Afraid.* Golden Press: New York.

Watson, Jane Werner, Robert E. Switzer, M.D., and J. Cotter Hirschberg, M.D. 1971. *Sometimes I Get Angry.* Golden Press: New York.

Zolotow, Charlotte. 1969. *The Hating Book.* Scholastic Book Services: New York.

Books About Self-Esteem

Gesell, Arnold and Frances Ilg. 1946. *The Child From Five to Ten.* Harper: New York.

Glasser, William, 1990. *The Quality School.* Harper & Row: New York.

Gordon, Thomas, 1970. *Teacher Effectiveness Training.* Wyden: New York.

Hart, Louise. 1987. *The Winning Family.* Lifeskills: Oakland.

Chapter
6

Testing and Teaching for Skills

Most teachers loathe the idea of testing children. Yet those despised tests are valuable tools and can be used to your advantage. Tests give a teacher information as to what skills need to be taught to each child. A test is the pivot point for lesson planning, especially when teaching individually. Imagine test results as a road map for each child's education; you can refer to them when you want to know where you are and where you should be going.

Tests administered to primary students can vary. Usually, primary children are given tests the second week of a new school year to determine their grade level in reading and math and their knowledge of the basic skills in these two areas. The children are tested again about four to six weeks before the school year ends to determine their growth. Another test is given to determine if they have learned the basic skills they need to learn. These test results are often published in the local paper and/or nationwide.

127

OPERATIONAL ASSESSMENT TOOL

The Operational Assessment Tool (O.A.T.) is an individual testing device that was adopted by my school district as a supplementary test to be used after the mandatory state tests are given to determine reading and language skills in the primary grades. It is used throughout the year to assess reading, language, spelling, and encoding and decoding phonetic skills. You may have a similar test or series of tests in your own school district. You can use these tests to form skills groups and choose books for your students.

Begin testing only after everyone understands the routine. Do the testing when the children are at their learning areas. Once you have tested everyone with the O.A.T., you can use this time slot for reading conferences, which will continue throughout the year. Use a desk where you sit side-by-side with the child being tested; do not use your own desk. This test should be seen as a regular part of the daily routine, not as a cause for stress in any way.

Presenting the Concept

Children can learn to hate tests early in school. The surprise of unanticipated questions and fear of failure, however, can be mitigated by an easygoing attitude on the teacher's part.

After about the first three weeks of school, when things are running smoothly, tell your class that you will be talking to each of them individually, in order to determine what you need to teach them. Tell them you will be giving them a test, different than the group test they had earlier but assure them that you do not expect them to know all the answers. After all, if they knew all the answers, then you would have nothing left to teach them!

Explain that while you are talking to one person, you will need help from everyone else in the class, since they will be left on their own for a little while. The aide will be in the Writing Area, but you will no longer be floating around the class, and you do not want to be disturbed. Review with them what they can do if no one is in an area to help them. If they are in the Reading Area and need help with a word while reading silently, they can quietly ask a friend for help. Ask for volunteers from each color group who will offer help if needed. Remind them not to talk unless receiving help; they will be breaking a rule! You might offer them a "carrot" for their cooperation: if you are able to talk to one person at a time without interruption, the class will be able to go out to recess five minutes early.

If during the testing period the class becomes disorderly, stop testing immediately and go back to floating. Wait two full days before you test again. Review the rules and tell them you know they can help.

Begin the Testing

Now the moment of truth has arrived. You will learn if the class is ready to function without you. You will also get to know each student and her personal needs for learning. For this reason, it is a good idea to give the O.A.T. yourself, and not assign this to a parent or an aide. You can pick up subtle problems, or note who needs extra help and you can take care of some of the skills right away. For example, when you notice that a child knows most of the words and only misses words with the "ph" sound, you can teach that skill during the test.

Some examples of the types of questions used in the O.A.T. Reading/Spelling Criterion Phonic Decoding Test are: The child is asked if she knows what you mean when you say two words rhyme with each other. The child listens as you rhyme several groups of words, for example, *cat, fat, sat*. Then you have the child say a rhyming word to a word you pronounce. Each time you note in the booklet whether the child was able to rhyme. If not then you stop testing. The child who can continue might be asked to read the words in the booklet. Some words are real and some are not. For example, the child would be asked to read *chat* and *shum*.

The Reading/Spelling Criterion Phonic Encoding Test was used in my class to determine the language and visual perception abilities of pre-readers. For example, figures are drawn on the page and the child is given a pencil and instructed to put an X below the tree. If the child was reading, I used this test to coincide with my skills group and individual spelling books (see Chapter 10) for the second graders. An example from the test could be the letters *f_t* on the page. The child is given a pencil and asked to add a letter to make the word say *fat*.

The children should be relaxed about testing. If they start to miss many words because they do not know the answers, stop testing. They will be less likely to become frustrated. A little diplomacy goes a long way toward not making anyone feel dumb. You might exclaim "Oh, good! Now you have given me something to teach you!"

Test the children in a quiet place, out of earshot of the rest of the class. They should not have to worry about other children hearing them. Each child takes but a short time to test, five to ten minutes. If you give only one test during each area rotation, which by now should take up a full twenty minutes, you will still be able to float around the classroom and help in the Reading Area for the remainder of each period. Upon reviewing each test, you can determine if a child is ready to read by noting whether the child has learned the basic skills.

Analyzing Skill Needs

Buy a stamp-collector's page and put the name of the skill at the top. Papers with the children's names who need to be taught that particular skill are placed in the slot below. When a child has mastered the skill, move the paper with his name to the next skill to be learned. (See Figure 6.1.)

Figure 6.1

OATS. READING	
3 Letter Blends	**Long Vowels**
Nowa	Ivan
Nan	Don
Seaton	Janice
James	Fran
	Joy
	Grace

It is important for you to also review the results of the district-adopted test.

Figure 6.2

Word Recognition	Symbol/ Sound	Word Matching	Word Meaning
Joe Pete	Jane Hope	Bill Pete	Alan Bruce Jill

In the chart in Figure 6.2, the skill is listed at the top. Beneath is a list of the names of the children who did not pass that section of the test. From this summary, you can determine which group of children is ready to read, and exactly what skills you need to teach each group.

These test results usually are the same as the O.A.T. but give broader information. Keep this chart and your chart from the O.A.T. test in your reading conference file. (Chapter 8 discusses how you use these during reading conferences.)

Reading Skill Grouping

Grouping the children so that you can instruct them according to their individual needs is tricky, and scheduling a time for skill groups to meet takes foresight and organization. I was frustrated by the schedule my school used. Half the students in my class arrived at nine and left at two and the other half came at ten and went home at three. The first group had an hour of skill-building in the morning and the second group learned new skills in the afternoon. The class was together from ten until two, yet it was never quite one unit, since it was divided into two groups that could look on themselves as better or worse than the other group. The best learning hours for the group that came in at ten would be wasted on TV. The students were further divided in these two groups, so that half would be taught skills while the other half did busywork, wasting their time. I found this system wasteful, confusing, and tiring and so I devised a simple, flexible schedule that would work throughout the school year and would keep the class energy high and unified.

I formed groups of seven or fewer children, homogeneously according to their skill needs. All the students came to school at 9 a.m., which made working parents happy, challenged all the children equally, and kept the class feeling like one unit. One afternoon each week was usually scheduled for a teacher's in-service class, which left four days for skill groups to meet from 2:10 until 3:10 pm. One day could be a reading readiness skill group. Another day could be a two-letter blends skill group, a short vowels skill group, a vowel diagraphs skill group, or a prefixes, suffixes, and irregular words skill group. (See Figure 6.3.)

Figure 6.3

Monday One Group	Tuesday One Group	Thursday One Group	Friday One Group
Long Vowels	**Short Vowels**	**Rhyming**	**2 Letter Blends**
1. Alice 2. Bill 3. Sue 4. Steve 5. June	1. Hope 2. Sam 3. Trudy 4. Steve 5. Lisa 6. Mary 7. Pete	1. Harry 2. Ned 3. Frank 4. Patty 5. Grace 6. Joan	1. Phil 2. Jack 3. Clara 4. Able 5. Joe 6. Candy 7. Ann

You will find that you can give a small group of six or seven children more attention if you don't have two different groups on the same day. You will have plenty of energy and time for the instruction areas, the class time in the afternoon, when children are tired and sleepy will be short, and the whole day will be more productive. Each afternoon you will see new faces and get to spend time concentrating on their individual learning. Spend each skill group hour productively: in the first twenty minutes, teach a lesson, then for the rest of the time present skill-building individual tasks, such as games, puzzles, and cutting and pasting, while you retest each student one by one. The routine is similar enough to the regular daily ritual that the children behave naturally.

Some students will move through the skill groups rather quickly, others will stay in one group for a long time before moving on. It all depends on the individual. If one student is learning skills before the others in his group, it's time to move that child to a group that is learning the skill to which he has progressed.

TEACHING READING SKILLS

Organizing Materials

Organize teaching materials as soon as you can, perhaps by creating a reading box. On 8" x 5" cards keep a list of ideas on how to teach each skill, and list words that contain the skill to be taught. For example, on the card for two-letter blends for the beginning "bl" sound, list such words as *blue, blend, blanket, blossom, blouse.* Another card might contain a list of games to play that pertain to two-letter blends. (At the end of this chapter you'll find a list of resource books on teaching reading skills.)

If you are fortunate enough to have some teachers interested in organizing materials with you, get together and each of you research one skill. Put your methods, games, and follow-up on enough cards for each teacher. You will each have a list of the procedures for all of the skills. Look for books that have lists of words and ideas for games. File your worksheets for each skill in a cabinet under titles such as Compound Words, Short A, Blends, and you will have skill sheets ready when the need arises.

Your school library may have skills-related games to check out. Games are also available as a bonus from the Scholastic Book Club.

Effective Teaching of Skills

When teaching skills in the early grades, try to avoid prodding a child to advance. Ask yourself whether the child is really ready. Time and patience are important when teaching reading skills to the beginning reader, particularly since the discouraged or intimidated child will often give up and lose the initiative to learn.

Teach reading skills using the different modalities of learning, letting the child see the symbol or word (visual), say it (auditory), and write it (kinetic).

I have found that children have about a ten to fifteen minute attention span for instruction and review. Then they like to apply themselves to a fun cut-and-paste page or two as another approach to the skill just taught. Next, they may choose among a number of games that will reinforce the skill, like pin-the-tail-on-the-elephant or blend bingo.

If you participate in a game with the children, you will get an insight into who needs further instruction. As each skill group learns to function smoothly, you can have a chairperson or resource person for each game. This person should be committed to learning the game and teaching it to the other children. They will internalize their learning when they are responsible for teaching others.

Maintaining Interest

Always look for different ways to keep the pace going and to make this learning process interesting. Make books with word families, like the "an" book (*fan, tan, ban, pan*, etc.) with words and pictures, which are just as important as phonics in seeing relationships within words. Cut words out of newspapers, or make a collage of words. Workbooks are available that have cut-and-paste activities. (See the list at the end of the chapter.) Intersperse cutting and pasting with written activities.

Keep a list of the words the children miss in reading conferences and use these words in a word game. Also use abstract words (*this, that, the, where, what*) in a word bingo game.

You could set up a treasure hunt of words the children have learned that day; hide words around the room for them to find. Or, if the children seem to be ready for such an activity, have them make up their own games.

Make a class composite of a book about different language concepts such as *big, little, tall, short*, with pages made by each child. The big book, of course, would have pictures of big things, the little book would have pictures and words of things that are little. Later, this can go into the class library.

Some children are not interested in visual symbols and the alphabet letters are too abstract for them. Don't push the slow starters into learning the phonic symbols too soon. Instead, give them language development with the Peabody Kit, and Ruth French's Multi-Sensory Reading. Language development is something they should enjoy. If they don't know the alphabet, use teaching aids such as Talking Alphabet Records, which come with accompanying cardboard illustrations with raised letters.

Time Out from Skills

When you feel that the children have been inundated with words and skills, take an afternoon field trip to the public library. The children will be introduced to a wide choice of books and have an opportunity to receive a library card.

Take the children for walks so that they may experience what they will read about later. With the whole class, or with a small group developing their language skills, visit a gas station and then come back to the classroom and have a language development period. Study a big picture of the gas station and ask them questions about what they saw. When their language vocabulary has grown, they will be able to dictate more stories and understand more words. Also give them listening- and following-directions games. Being able to listen and follow directions is an important prerequisite to reading.

Pantomimes, Puppets, Plays, and Dramatization

Pantomimes, puppet plays, and dramatization are rewarding and fun activities when used during a small reading skill group. With the children reading at the same grade level they feel relaxed and enjoy this play acting.

Puppet play is an excellent activity to include each year. The children can make their own puppets and develop their own play by retelling a story such as "The Three Billy Goats Gruff." They enjoy performing. You might have the dress rehearsal for the others in the class during the 1:00 to 2:00 p.m. hour and then an actual performance for their parents.

Some children who find talking very difficult may express themselves very well through a puppet. One girl in my class would not talk above a low whisper. During her reading skills group we were having puppet plays. She became very interested and excited. I asked her if she would like to choose a friend and make up their own play. She was delighted. Later, I heard talking from the portable puppet theater. This can't be Sue, I thought. Having never heard her voice, I was curious. I tiptoed up to the theater and signaled to the five members of the audience to be quiet. Peeking over I saw Sue talking in a normal voice, so absorbed in her part she didn't notice me. She spoke in a normal voice from then on.

If they dramatize an easy book, like one from the Follet series, the children will have good practice sequencing a story from beginning to end in the proper order. They do not need to read directly from the book, but can retell the story in their own words.

A good source for children who are reading is the book *A Dozen Little Plays* selected from *Little Plays for Little People* from Scholastic Book Services. It is helpful if each child has his own copy of the play to read.

...And Test Again

When it becomes apparent that the children have learned a particular skill, retest with their individual O.A.T. or another test. If they've spurted ahead, it's time to move the children to different groups. Those who are progressing faster than the rest can be moved to the group that is studying the more advanced skill to which the child has progressed.

Time is usually set aside by the school district to give the children the state adopted tests in May. These tests determine how much the children have learned since September. Before you give the tests to the children in May, take five to ten minutes for all of you to breathe deeply and relax. Have everyone close their eyes and tell them slowly and calmly, "You are all well prepared. See yourself calm, relaxed, and answering the questions." This is one good way to take the anxiety out of the test-taking procedure. They seem to think more clearly when they (and you) are relaxed.

SUMMARY

You may not like the idea of testing children, but this is the best way for you to find out their strengths and weaknesses so that you can design a reading program most suited to each child. Set up a testing area that is private but allows you to keep an eye on the rest of the class, testing the children throughout the year. Explain the testing procedure to the child and try to put her at ease about the process. After the test or during a reading conference, if you notice that a student needs a mini-lesson, you can give it to her on the spot. If a child is consistently missing one kind of skill, make a note of it and stop testing at that point. When all the tests have been conducted, group the children homogeneously into reading skills groups. These groups meet once a week and feature lessons teaching that skill. Retest children periodically to keep track of their growth. When a child has learned a skill before the others she may leave that skill group and move to a new one.

LIST OF SOURCE BOOKS

Some of the most valuable materials came from the following publishers and manufacturers.

Workbooks to Use in Supplementing the Teaching of Reading Skills

Creative Teaching Press, Educational Insights, Media Materials, Frank Schaffer, Good Apple, and Incentive Publications.

Further Reading on Teaching Skills

Bloomfield, Leonard and Charles Barnhart. 1961. *Let's Read, A Linguistic Approach*. Wayne State University Press: Detroit.

Durkin, Dolores. 1980. *Teaching Young Children To Read*. Allyn and Bacon: Boston.

French, Ruth A. 1975. *Multisensory Reading:The Child's Way of Learning*. Frank Adam Products: Sacramento.

Heilman, Arthur W. 1968. *Phonics in Proper Perspective*. Charles E. Merrill: Columbus, Ohio.

Hiskes, Dolores G. 1990. *Phonics Pathways*. Dorbooks: Livermore, California.

Spache, Evelyn B. 1972. *Reading Activities for Child Involvement*. Allyn and Bacon: Boston.

Veatch, Jeannette. 1966. *Reading in the Elementary School*. The Ronald Press: New York.

Chapter 7

Many Ways to Teach Reading

To waken interest and kindle enthusiasm is the sure way to teach easily and successfully.

—Tryon Edwards
American theologian (1809–1894)

There are many tried-and-true methods of teaching reading, and you will teach best if you do not subscribe to only one of them. I developed my own method of teaching reading to the beginning reader as I became aware of the different needs and learning styles of each child. I noticed that only a few of the children learned well when I taught from the teacher's guide that accompanied the basal readers. The children who did not learn so easily taught me to be more creative as a teacher. I have learned to try several methods with the child who is having difficulty learning to read, and the reward comes when I finally hit on the right approach for this child and see her suddenly blossom into a reader.

Researching the various methods and tools, I found that even though all the teachers in one school may teach the same material, their methods of presenting them vary greatly from room to room. One needs to be knowledgeable about the many options to be able to try different approaches and select the ones that are suitable to the task at hand and the desired outcome.

Here is a sampling of what I've found to be the more accepted and well-known methods of teaching reading. I researched a number of sources for this topic and refer to them throughout my descriptions. You'll find these sources listed at the end of this chapter.

METHODS OF TEACHING READING

Basal Readers

The most widely used materials for reading instruction are the basal readers. Sometimes they are the only materials a teacher uses. A typical series includes tests, workbooks, readers, and a teacher's manual for each grade level; some also include additional materials such as flash cards, filmstrips, and progress charts. Basal readers can be a comforting and practical approach for a beginning teacher because they offer a complete program. The teacher can follow the manual and the children can follow their workbooks, page by page.

A typical teacher's manual contains an explanation of the reading program and its objectives, specific instructions for each major unit and story in the pupil's copy, and a copy of the pupil's text. First the teacher administers entry-level tests to determine the reading level of each child in the class (pre-primer, primer, low first, middle first, high first, and so on). Next the teacher groups the children according to their reading levels, usually assigning these groups names such as "bluebirds" rather than "low first." Then the teacher reads the lesson plans for each level and gathers or prepares whatever materials the manual prescribes. During the week the teacher prepares the children for that week's story, teaching necessary words and skills and working up enthusiasm. Finally the children read the story by taking turns reading aloud, progressing around the semicircle of children. During guided reading, the teacher asks the child reading many questions to check her comprehension. Then the students take worksheets or workbooks to their seats to make sure they have understood what they have read. Many series include supplementary workbooks for children who are having trouble.

After the child has completed the book on her reading level, she is given a test before she can progress to the next level. If she does not pass, she is given a supplementary book by the same publisher.

Basal readers are not for all children. They provide a useful structure for beginning teachers, but they have many drawbacks. For one thing, they do not meet the varying needs of students. Children with better reading skills are bored, while the lessons can go over the heads of other students. Basal readers put children into a single category. Stronger readers cannot be given the basal reader for the next grade level, as the teacher they will have next year needs to use this book when they are in her class. And they can't read the next story until the teacher has introduced the lesson. Basal readers also take the act of learning away from the children, leaving the responsibility for learning entirely with the teacher. When I used basal readers children didn't enjoy the books, so they didn't internalize or retain it.

I am also skeptical of the emphasis basal readers place on oral reading. Most children who are first learning to read do not like to read unfamiliar passages aloud to their peers, and it is not clear that they gain anything from the experience. Many children simply memorize the one sentence they are to read when it is their turn, which is not a learning activity.

Reading Aloud

In round robin reading, children take turns reading aloud, usually reading one sentence at a time. When I first became a teacher, I practiced having the children read aloud and in a round robin manner, until I experienced the trauma my son, who is dyslexic, had when he was called on to read aloud in the first grade. I learned that scars from this practice can shape a beginning reader's attitude about reading and his self-esteem and confidence. From then on, I vowed never to humiliate a child by making reading aloud mandatory. It serves no educational purpose.

The Word Method

The word method teaches children to recognize the entire word instead of taking it apart phonically. It is a very popular method and I myself believe that word recognition is a necessary skill but should not be taught in isolation. In my opinion, good reading instruction combines written language word recognition, phonics, and the linguistic method.

The word method does seem to be used in the basal reader. I found new words were introduced with no pattern or apparent reason, except that they were the words a second grader should know. Since some of the words were too difficult for the children to learn, this meant they had to memorize them only to forget these words the next day.

The Sounding Approach

Most sounding systems teach children to recognize printed words using phonics. They emphasize teaching specific consonant and vowel sounds and tend to minimize the importance of recognizing whole words by sight.

The way characteristics of the sounding approach are combined with actual reading exercises can vary greatly. Some approaches include reading from actual books as well as performing phonic drills. Other approaches teach children to sound out individual letters (and certain groups of letters) but do not have them read whole words. After the children are familiar with this approach, they are supposed to be able to combine the sounds to make actual words.

Personally, I do not see the value of using the sounding approach when teaching reading. In my experience, the children's reading became haltingly painful as they tried to sound out each difficult word.

The Phonic Approach

Like the sounding approach, the phonic approach can be used in isolation or in combination with other approaches. Rote memory drills are relied on to teach the phonic elements and phonic rules in a phonic-only program. The phonic approach is often used within the context of a more developmental program. Before being taught specific phonic rules and relationships, the children are taught to discover the sound-symbol relationship within words. Many educators feel that the phonic approach should be used only with other methods.

I do not use the phonic approach in isolation. It is best used with a variety of approaches, since each child learns differently. I have used the phonic approach during small homogeneous reading skill groups, but never during a reading conference. I feel if the children are taught to sound out each letter and never the whole word they will not read the word smoothly. When learning the word in isolation, then sounding out is necessary. After sounding out the word, have the children say the word several times. The children should not be made to sound out words too difficult for them while they are reading to you, but be given the pronunciation of the word immediately.

The Linguistic Method

According to the linguistic method developed by Leonard Bloomfield and Clarence Barnhart, the child is first taught to associate letters and sounds with different patterns and with no regard to deriving their meaning. Then a child can convert a new word to sound and thus meaning.

Phonemes are the individual sounds that make up words. The word *fit*, for instance, contains three phonemes, and in this case each phoneme is represented by a single letter. Some languages have as few as fifteen phonemes, while others have as many as fifty. There is a written character for each phoneme of a language and with these characters one can write down any word of that language. With alphabetic writing even nonsense words can be pronounced (words such as *pid*, for instance).

I have used the linguistic method myself and have found that this method makes sense to the children. They can pronounce a word more easily using this method than with most others, which means that they begin reading sooner and have more reading successes early on. Because the linguistic method teaches children a whole list of words that are similar, a child can start reading many words in a row at an earlier stage of development. In traditional readers there is no pattern; words are not presented in families (such as the "-at" family). Instead, children have to struggle with each different word. A sentence like "The house is on the hill" has too many different sounds and requires too many different skills. This frustrates the children and discourages them.

Drawbacks to the Linguistic Method

The linguistic method has at least two major drawbacks. The first has to do with the irregular spelling of many words in the English language. Much of the English language follows conventional rules of writing which are not phonetic. The verb *knit* and the noun *nit*, for instance. However, teachers can teach irregular words as spelling units as described in Chapter 10 of this book.

In my experience, irregular spelling does not appear until fairly late in the progression of skills (high second or third grade). The main drawback I encountered was the lack of good materials for the linguistic method. The available readers, such as Lippincott, were not very exciting to read. It was hard to find good books that used words in families. The pre-primer books I finally found were *Stories from Sounds* (Educators Publishing Service) and *A Pig Can Jig* (Science Research Association).

First Materials for Linguistic Reading

First, the child must master the letters of the alphabet and be able to read them from left to right in upper and lower case. The linguistic readers give first readers two- and three-letter words containing short vowels and fifteen consonants b, c, d, f, g, h, n, p, r, s, t, v, w, y, z, and use only the hard values of these consonants (c as in cat, f as in fan, g as in get, y as in yes).

Bloomfield and Barnhart maintain that this approach will establish and reaffirm a pattern in the child's mind as she discovers the relationship between specific letters and specific sounds. But they claim there is no point in explaining that similar spelling indicates a similar sound to a child who may not know when he looks at words such as *can* and *fan* that they are similar in sound. In this way the linguistic method is different from the phonic method. The important thing, they state, is to establish a pattern for the child to recognize and then not upset that pattern. In other words, the repetition of the pattern should not be upset by presenting letters that are different (such as teaching three-letter words that end in *at* along with those that end in *an*).

Kits and Programmed Instruction

Unlike basal readers, kits and programmed instruction provide the student with a self-guided program for acquiring reading skills. The student studies independently and at his own pace.

One common kit is the Science Research Association (S.R.A.) kit. It consists of a box full of color-coded cards with short readings on one side and comprehension questions on the other. Children progress from one color to another and record their progress on a special sheet. They answer the comprehension questions on a separate sheet and correct their own answers, thereby getting immediate feedback.

When I used S.R.A. I found that it had certain drawbacks. Some children tried to progress too rapidly in order to brag about how far they'd gotten. ("I'm up to the red!") And it is difficult for the teacher to monitor how a child's skills are developing or when a child needs instruction to learn the next skill.

I also used the Sullivan Program. This is a series of self-guided workbooks in which children supply the missing word in a sentence by choosing from a multiple choice list. The choices of words are linguistically related, such as *fan, tan, can*. The answers are on the right-hand side of the page and the child keeps them covered with a long card until he is ready to check his answers. The Sullivan Program can be a fun and useful place to start, but by first grade my children already found it boring.

The Content Method

Teachers often assume that the reason many older students and adults do not understand what they read is that they were not properly taught to read. Adults can grasp the meaning of a passage while barely noticing individual words or letters, but children are less practiced readers. When the passage the child is reading is so difficult that the child must puzzle over a word slowly, by the time he reaches the end of the sentence he has forgotten the beginning and he cannot grasp the content. The child only gets the content when the teacher reads a story out loud or when she knows all of the words she is reading.

I believe the content method teaches an important skill when the child can read all of the words but should not be used exclusively. The main reason I gave my students worksheets that had a paragraph to read and questions to answer about what they had read was to prepare them for a required standardized test with the same format.

Informal Reading Inventory and Miscue Analysis

The Informal Reading Inventory (I.R.I.) program prescribes a special notation for recording children's errors as they read an unfamiliar passage aloud. The kit contains a double-spaced version of each story for the teacher to use to record the special codes that indicate the specific errors a child is making while he is reading. The teacher later reviews these codes (cues) when the children are absent in order to diagnose each child's problems. Taping the child's reading may alleviate some of the child's anxiety, as the teacher can review the tape later and mark mistakes out of the child's presence.

Miscue Analysis uses the same method of identifying miscues as I.R.I., by having the child read an unfamiliar passage, and having the errors marked on a separate sheet at that time or later by the teacher. Miscue Analysis kits also provide a teacher's manual explaining worksheets for children who are having specific difficulties.

I feel that both the I.R.I. and the Miscue Analysis methods are too prescriptive. They focus too much attention on reading for mistakes. They make the teacher (and the children) overly aware of minor errors. The whole process of taping the child's reading from the reprinted material and then listening to the tape to mark the passage with the miscue notes is very time-consuming for a teacher and, in my opinion, not necessarily worth it.

Written Language Approaches

Written language approaches use the child's own words to teach her to read and write. Teachers generally start their students off with listening and speaking experiences, then move on to writing and reading experiences. Before a child can write, she dictates her stories or thoughts to her teacher (or teacher's assistant), who writes her words for her. The child becomes aware that reading is talk written down.

Written language approaches can be used with individuals (see the language-experience approach) or with groups (see experience charts).

Language-Experience Approach

With this approach, a child's first reading and writing experiences make use of his own vocabulary. The child first dictates, then learns to write down his own stories. His writing vocabulary is completely determined by his speaking vocabulary. The teacher keeps a list of the words each child uses in his dictated stories along with high frequency words such as *the*, *and*, *to*, and *on*. Later, the child can learn to write for himself using the words from his list.

I had children in small, heterogeneous groups write journals. This way they could use their own words and write about their own interests. I then used the journals as readers, having children read aloud from them in one-to-one conferences. Later, children would often want to read their journals to the class.

Another approach is to have the children draw pictures on large pieces of paper and then describe the pictures by writing down (or dictating) what the pictures are about.

Experience Charts

Experience charts use the children's interests, what they have just experienced, and their speaking vocabularies. They are a group effort, and so reflect the vocabularies and interests of many different children. For example, the class goes on a field trip and when they return the teacher asks what they saw, did, and said, writing down their responses on a large piece of paper, using a different color pen for each response, as the children take turns answering. Although a field trip usually precedes this activity, a teacher can discuss some other commonly shared experience with the children and then write down the story.

After the children's experiences are recorded on a big chart (or on the chalkboard), the teacher asks for volunteers to come up and read their sentence. Later the teacher can make "sentence strips" and ask the children to match the sentence on the strip to the one on the chart. The teacher can also have the children draw a picture to describe the sentence they dictated for the experience chart.

Key Vocabulary

The key vocabulary method was developed by Sylvia Ashton-Warner with Maori children in New Zealand. With Ashton-Warner's key vocabulary method, the children write in their own words about their own experiences and then read what they have written. Ashton-Warner believes that a child's own words carry an emotional and cultural meaning for the child when he reads words that are in his vocabulary about his own experiences.

Reading about Ashton-Warner's method inspired me to develop weekly journal writing. I feel children internalize their learning and enjoy learning when they are given the opportunity to be creative with something that is of their personal experience.

Literature-Based Learning

The reading of literature in the elementary schools has been gaining in popularity. The California Department of Education's publication, *Recommended Reading in Literature*, states, "the literature program is an essential part of the reading program and is as important as the developmental, basal reading materials."

The methods for teaching from these literature-based books varies. Some teachers in North Carolina use literature-based books at their grade level along with a copy of the same basal reader for every student. Some teachers in California use the Houghton-Mifflin Literacy Reading Series. They group the children into four homogeneous groups or the whole class reads the same story. The teacher introduces new words. As the group reads together, each child is called upon to read aloud. The teacher extends the study of the story through the children's writing, book reports, notebooks about the story, and journals, sometimes using the subject or theme of the story in all of the subjects taught in a thematic approach (as described in Chapter 10). Accompanying worksheets are used as a follow-up. The children may also be asked to read their stories three times to get to know the words or use choral or partner reading.

Lesson plan books (available at teachers' stores) that are designed for literature-based reading can be purchased. These books contain pages of literature-based activity ideas, lists of books, including Caldecott and Newberry award winners, and planning forms. In some approaches, children check out books overnight from a class box containing selections from the extended or recreational literature list.

As currently taught, the literature-based method seems to be similar to that used with the basal readers, where individual differences are not accounted for. However, I believe literature-based books could be used on an individual basis. For example, the children *could* choose from the books in a literature reading series, with each child reading a different story individually to the teacher. The California State Department of Education's *Recommended Readings in Literature Kindergarten Through Grade Eight* contains selections listed by grade level or span, cultural group, and type such as core, recreational, or extended reading. The thematic approach to literature-based reading requires the teacher to be creative and to spend time investigating ways to expand the story's main idea into the other subjects. While this method gives children a thorough understanding of literature and its relationship to other subjects it does not accommodate for the various reading levels of individuals.

Individualized Reading

Every teacher has a different approach to individualized reading although it usually involves one-to-one conferences with children to monitor their progress and provide guidance. (Many authorities recommend a minimum of 5 or 10 minutes with each child each week.) The children then read on their own and at their own pace. Some teachers direct their students to specific materials, while others let the children choose whatever appeals to them. Sometimes a teacher must try several different methods with a particular child before finding one that works. This is the beauty of individualized reading: that each child is given the chance to learn in a way that accommodates her unique abilities.

When a teacher decides there are several children who all need to learn a particular skill, the teacher may form a skill group to address their common need. (See Chapter 6.) Another feature of individualized reading is the heterogeneous grouping of children (even of different reading levels) who share their favorite books or passages with each other.

I strongly recommend individualized reading. It is highly rewarding to experience children getting excited about books. It gives the teacher a chance to be creative and not rely on a prepared lesson in a teacher's manual. The teacher forms a close relationship with each child, the child gets to choose books from within the range the teacher recommends, and each child can progress at his own rate. More advanced readers are not hindered by grade-level restrictions, and children who aren't doing well can focus on materials that are within their grasp. It also removes the embarrassment of reading aloud to their peers.

Advocates of individualized reading feel that the advantages are threefold: (1) a child is not held within a group instruction and can advance more rapidly, (2) the child is self-motivated when not compared with others, and (3) children enjoy reading and therefore read more extensively when they choose their own material.

However, a teacher must not allow a child too much freedom in choosing material for this can result in the child selecting a book at an unsuitable level, either too difficult or sometimes not challenging enough.

This is what scares many principals about individualized reading. They often see it as unstructured, and are afraid the teacher will not monitor a child's progress and endeavors.

Individualized reading is a difficult and time-consuming method to implement. Only seasoned teachers are really equipped to face the task. In addition to procuring a wide range of available materials, one must be familiar with them. Since individualized reading offers no prescribed lesson plans, you must be familiar with reading development patterns. You must also be well organized and keep careful records of the children's progress. A teacher also needs to have the courage of her convictions and a lot of confidence in this approach, because many people will be skeptical of it and will oppose its use.

MY METHOD OF TEACHING INDIVIDUALIZED READING

The best teacher is the one who suggests
rather than dogmatizes, and inspires his listener
with the wish to teach himself.
—Edward George Bulwer-Lytton
English novelist (1803–1873)

My method involves organizing the class into heterogeneous groupings of children for a smooth flowing curriculum, allowing for flexibility within these groups. Children develop their reading and language arts skills through a variety of activities. Daily writing periods enable the children to express their creative thoughts. When children write about their own experiences they see that writing is talk written down. Reading their own paper, they come to see the connections between talking, reading, and writing. The teacher holds individual reading conferences with each child once a week to track the progress of that child. The conference includes a time when the teacher and child together choose a book for the child to read. The children's reading skills are recorded and taught in a small homogeneous group after the remainder of the children have left for home. The skills are taught using various methods: visual, kinetic, and auditory. The listening period allows children to hear a book on tape while they follow along in their book. Children learn to spell by using words they encounter in their reading or writing. In addition, daily discussions of problems, values, and feelings encourage children to express opinions and to feel like a valued member of the classroom. The children are given the responsibility to learn in a positive environment.

ENGLISH SCHOOLS

The University of California at Berkeley offered a field study of the English schools in Bristol during the summer of 1979 and I was among the members of this field study. We were sent to observe Doris Nash's school and her approach to teaching reading through written language. Some classes I observed combined first, second, and third grades. Instead of sitting at assigned desks, children moved from table to table according to which activities appealed to them. The teacher usually moved about the room, too, advising on projects, listening to children read, asking questions. At the schools I visited children were permitted to talk freely. As a result, the rooms were fairly noisy.

At the beginning of each day, the teacher would announce what activities the children could choose from that day. The ground rules were that they must clean up when finished and mustn't bother other students. I noticed that teachers sometimes gave students assignments when they thought it was needed.

Joseph Featherstone studied similar schools. He noted the teachers used a variety of reading schemes with each child, with a tendency to abandon textbooks. Instead of buying forty sets of everything they bought six sets of each reading series along with single books at different levels, putting the responsibility on the teacher to be familiar with a wide variety of books in order to be able to meet each child's needs.

Formal reading or math was not emphasized. Featherstone learned that the teachers depended on the children learning from each other, especially in multiage classes. These seemed successful in the early grades, where older children helped younger ones in reading and classroom duties.

The older children learned by being teachers. Nonreaders learned about reading by watching others reading and looking at books, and teachers were able to provide children with individual attention.

On my visit, Doris Nash was extremely proud of one first grade teacher who did not even have to set up her paint area, the children did it all. I was impressed by the school's flexible approach to children's different personalities and abilities. Our field study class felt, however, that we were visiting the top income levels and the best schools in Bristol. We requested a day's visit to a school in the impoverished section of town, and the request was granted. This was a real eye-opener. The school was following the same theory of letting the children decide completely, and there was complete chaos. Children coming from unsettled homes need structure and guidance. Some of the children handled this open situation by acting up. I felt as if the school would someday explode. The children could not handle the additional looseness this school was giving them.

WAYS OF GROUPING CHILDREN

Homogeneous and Heterogeneous Grouping

Children in a single class can be grouped "homogeneously" or "heterogeneously." The more traditional approach is to group children homogeneously, according to their skill level. The "slow readers" are all placed in one group, the "advanced readers" are all placed in another. Homogeneous grouping is also known as tracking. A child's test scores and academic achievement determine her placement into one of three or four subdivisions within the class.

Grouping children this way certainly makes teaching easier, but it may not be the best learning situation. Children know which level they have been assigned to and internalize this judgment of their abilities. It is also a divisive force in the classroom; it encourages competition and discourages cooperation.

There is a current trend away from homogeneous groupings. The methods for determining a student's standing in a homogeneous class are being called into question. Many are not sure the tests we have can accurately or comprehensively measure a child's intelligence or potential. Realistically, even "homogeneous" groupings contain children with a range of skill levels.

More teachers and schools are choosing to organize their classes heterogeneously, placing children in groups that contain students of various levels of ability. They all work together, although they do not all do the same work or work at the same level.

Current opinion is that children actually learn better in heterogeneous classes. Heterogeneous groups avoid the labeling that leads to internalization of negative judgments. They challenge "slower" learners, whose performance shows a clear improvement in heterogeneous settings and, contrary to many fears, they do not appear to slow down the more "advanced" learners, who have the opportunity to act as tutors. Grouping children heterogeneously encourages them to reach as far as they can and achieve as much as they can. They are not restricted by the expectations a teacher has of the particular category to which they are assigned.

The heterogeneous classroom also tends to be more cohesive. The children work as a family; they tend to help each other rather than compete against each other. And since different children excel in different areas, almost everyone gets the chance to give as well as receive help.

I was lucky to have experienced both homogeneous and heterogeneous grouping of children. Without this experience I would not have realized fully the difference in these groups. The first year I taught, I was placed in a school in Salinas where each grade had two classrooms, one for the more advanced children and the other for the lower children. Somehow the two classrooms always seemed to be divided into the migrant farm laborers' children and the children of the owners of the farms where the laborers worked. I have reflected many times on what a loss that segregation meant. The children in each class could have learned from each other.

Another school I worked at developed levels for math instruction. At a given time each day the children from grades 1 to 6 moved to the teacher who taught the level they were assigned to. I was assigned levels 12 and 6. Children from various grades came to me. I gave them all a lesson from the same page. I never felt any enthusiasm for this type of teaching. These twenty-four children from every class but my own were like a sea of faces. I never felt close to them.

Heterogeneous grouping, which I discuss throughout this book, was the most satisfying and rewarding to me. The children became united, helping and caring and teaching each other.

Graded Schools

In graded schools a child is assigned to a specific grade and must perform certain tasks for that grade only. Children are grouped according to age (unless a child is kept back a grade). This system offers no flexibility and imposes one idea of what a child in a certain grade should be like. It does not allow for differences. It addresses the mass, not the individual, and apparently, it does not teach more effectively than non-graded schools.

Non-Graded Schools

Non-graded schools carry heterogeneous grouping a step further, placing children of different ages in the same classroom. They usually combine two or three grade levels, such as first and second grades or first, second, and third grades. Such grouping is designed to meet the needs of the individual. It is also designed to relate sequential development of subject matter more realistically to child-growth patterns. For this reason non-grading is sometimes called vertical organization, and there are different methods for advancing children or deciding when they are ready to move on to another class.

In non-graded schools children tend to be less concerned with competition. They are more interested in the act of learning than in surpassing other students. In non-graded schools a child is graded according to his own ability, not according to the norm for his age group.

Although I never taught in a non-graded school, I practiced the theory of non-grading in my classroom because I felt this was the approach a child needs when beginning school. Self-confidence and self-esteem are developed in a non-competitive environment. Telling a child that she must do all of these assignments and only these assignments because she is in this grade, is putting the child in a box. We all learn and grow differently.

Team Teaching

Although team teaching requires extensive coordination, many find it rewarding and stimulating. Having another teacher to talk to, confer with, and plan lessons with does away with some of the loneliness of teaching. Often when two teachers work on planning something together, one idea sparks another. The large classes (often twice as large) can be overwhelming though, and of course one must find two teachers with similar philosophies of teaching. The children are assigned to small groups and move to the various activities with the two teachers as resources.

CONCLUSION

Many experienced teachers and specialists accept no one method as best for teaching all beginning readers. Instead, you should consider all the methods with which you are familiar and decide which is most appropriate for each child.

Children can and do learn to read in a variety of ways. One method may be helpful for one child but not another. There are many kinds of techniques that will promote interest in reading and foster good reading habits and skills. A teacher needs to be aware of each child's learning style and individual needs.

In the next chapter, I explore how to work individually with each child in your classroom to determine the best ways for them to learn to read.

SOURCES

Ashton-Warner, Sylvia. 1964. *Spearpoint: Teacher in America*. Random House: New York.

Austin, Mary C. and Morrison Coleman. 1963. *The First R: The Harvard Report on Reading in Elementary Schools*. Macmillian: New York.

Beggs, David W. and Edward G. Buffie. 1967. *Nongraded Schools in Action*. Indiana University Press: Bloomington.

Bloomfield, Leonard and Clarence L. Barnhart. 1961. *Let's Read: A Linguistic Approach*. Wayne State University Press: Detroit.

Bond, Guy L. and Eva Wagner. 1966. *Teaching the Child to Read*. Macmillian: New York.

Durkin, Dolores. 1980. *Teaching Young Children to Read*. Allyn and Bacon: Boston.

Featherstone, Joseph. 1971. *Schools Where Children Learn*. Liveright: New York.

Flesch, Rudolf. 1981. *Why Johnny Still Can't Read*. Harper and Row: New York.

Gans, Roma. 1964. *Facts and Fiction About Phonics*. Bobbs-Merrill: New York.

Goodlad, John I. 1984. *A Place Called School*. McGraw-Hill: New York.

Goodman, Yetta M. and Carolyn L. Burke. 1971. *Reading Miscue Inventory*. Macmillan: New York.

Guszak, Frank J. 1978. *Diagnostic Reading Instruction in the Elementary School*. Harper and Row: New York.

Kohl, Herbert R. 1969. *The Open Classroom*. Random House: New York.

Park, Joe. 1963. *Bertrand Russell on Education*. Ohio State University Press: Athens, Ohio.

Postman, Neil and Charles Weingartner. 1973. *The School Book*. Delacorte Press: New York.

Chapter

Responding to Individual Reading Needs

What blockheads are those wise persons,
who think it necessary that a child should
comprehend everything it reads.

— Robert Southey
English poet laureate (1774–1843)

ne of your most valued times will be that spent with each child during a one-to-one reading conference. Only by checking in regularly with each student can you track their progress, note the skills they need, and direct them to the appropriate book for their interests and level of understanding. At the end of the first grade, children will range in reading level ability from pre-reading to the third grade. Third graders will range from first to eighth grade reading levels. I scheduled reading conferences during the first hour and a half of the language arts period, while the children were at their

tasks and the class was functioning smoothly. It is important not to start conferences until you are certain the children can function at the different areas and know what to do. If you start conferences before the children know the program, you will be constantly interrupted. Begin reading conferences after you've given the first round of individual reading tests.

Initial conferences will take from ten to fifteen minutes for each child, and you will meet with each child about once every three days. By the end of each conference, the folder should contain notes on what the child's interests are and anything else you observed that will help you select books for her, including what the child was taught or needs to be taught. This might include words the child did not know, blends discussed, or problems with short vowels. Occasionally you can use this time to test the child at the next level in the individual reading skills test. You should keep track of the book the student is reading, noting the date and page number.

Create a relaxed, quiet, cheerful environment during the reading time. Let the children know this is not the time for socializing, but time for reading. Everyone is to have a book in his hands. The children can relax on the rug or sit in one of the rockers or couches to read.

What kind of book they read doesn't matter. It can be comics, a Dr. Seuss book, a paperback, a science book, or a basal reader. When the nonreaders realize that books are to be enjoyed in school, they will relax and look forward to reading.

A child who is not comfortable with books will not naturally go near a book on her own. You must require that this child at least open a book. If she senses that she does not have to perform—just enjoy—she will soon become less frightened of reading. Seeing other children enjoying reading is extremely encouraging and will affect a child before you know it.

Have three special boxes marked with the color of each group. Instruct the children to put the books they have chosen in this box at the end of the reading period so they can find their book the next day.

There should be no talking unless someone is asking a resource person for a word he does not know. The resource people can be the children you may have had in your class last year, or any student volunteers. This should be a book-oriented, quiet period. No one has to read yet but they must have a book in their hands, look at the book, and not disturb others.

Build a positive attitude about books now. Books are to be enjoyed, used, and cared for. A child learns to enjoy books by becoming familiar and comfortable with them.

Suggest that the class gather ideas about how to choose a book and write their suggestions on a sign that hangs in your class library. It might read:

HOW DO YOU CHOOSE A BOOK?

◆ Cover Looks Good

◆ Not Too Long or Hard

◆ Pictures Are Pretty

◆ Something I Am Interested in Reading

Your class library should contain books at levels ranging from a grade below the lowest test score to two grades above the highest score.

CONDUCTING READING CONFERENCES
Preparing the Class for the Conference

During the first few weeks of school and throughout the school year, especially before conferences, discuss with the children why they are at school, what school is for, and why they think you, the teacher, are there. This will focus them on their goals as well as your own. Establish standards of acceptable social behavior. Acknowledge with words of praise when the class is listening, when they are working with soft voices, cleaning up after themselves, and helping others.

Don't rush into reading conferences. You may feel this urge, but keep reminding yourself that the "initial" period—your first few weeks of shaping the class—when you float about the room observing your students and offering help and support, is of prime importance and demands your full attention. With your constant reinforcement, the positive behavior you encourage will allow for a positive learning environment and classroom unity in the long run. Make this your goal before you begin to set your course for reading conferences.

When the class is functioning smoothly and the children know whom to go to for help, it's time to set up the conferences. The Language Arts/Reading period is now one and a half hours long, divided into three periods of twenty to twenty-five minutes. The reading conference time will be during each one of these periods.

By no means are the rest of the class members to interrupt a private conference, except for an emergency, of course. Be emphatic. "We must not be interrupted!" Tell them that you cannot help until the conference is over, and encourage them to use the aides available in the classroom or quietly ask their peers. However, you must be aware of what is going on in the classroom at all times so you can intervene if there is a situation that needs immediate attention.

Before you begin the first round of reading conferences, explain the process to them. Let them know that you will be calling them one by one to a reading conference.

Teacher Preparation

The initial goal of an individual reading conference is to build a friendly rapport. When the child feels comfortable, then evaluating, diagnosing, teaching, listening, and sharing can occur in a relaxed, nonthreatening environment. If the conference is held at a teacher's desk, the teacher towers over the child in a formal atmosphere. Having other children within earshot of the conference restricts the privacy of the conference and the reluctant or shy child (or the child not as able as the others) will become nervous and concerned. Hold the conference at a student-sized double desk, so the child can sit side-by-side with you. From this desk you should be able to see the complete class, in a place that offers privacy for the reader (see Figure 2.5 in Chapter 2).

On one side of your conference desk have an open posting tub containing the children's folders filed alphabetically by first name. Create a folder for each child that contains:

- The results of the individual reading skills test you use.

- Notes on the child's interests, and anything else you observed during the conference that will help you select books for her.

- Notes on words missed and skills taught or needed.

- A form to keep track of the book the child is reading, with the date and the last page number read to you, because occasionally the book marker falls from the book between conferences. (See Figure 8.1.)

Figure 8.1

INDIVIDUAL READING CONFERENCE FORM			
NAME		**AGE**	
AUTHOR	DATE	COMMENTS	PAGE#

Also have in the posting tub:

    ◆ A class list to check off names as each child reads to you (see Figure 8.2).

Figure 8.2

READING CONFERENCES					
	1/21	1/22	1/23	1/24	1/25
A. Quail	X				
Burt Smith	X				
Candy O'Shea		X			
Cass Roberts		X			
Curt Kanter			X		
Curry Crandall			X		
Dan Scott				X	
Frank Howard				X	
Helen Arrow	X				
Hilda Swartz	X				
Jack Gates		X			
Jean Southern		X			
Jemima Welsh			X		
Jerrold Baker			X		

    ◆ A chart of the results of reading and phonetics tests (see Chapter 6).

◆ Questions to ask after each story is read to you. (Some good questions can be found in *Reading in the Elementary School* by Jeannette Veatch, 1966. The Ronald Press: New York. pp. 142–150.)

◆ Pens, pencils, paper, extra conference sheets, a stapler, and an eraser.

◆ The Scholastic Book Company's kit containing cards in a box with grade level and questions to ask after a child has read a paperback from the kit.

Keep a small blackboard and an eraser handy for quick lessons, when a reading difficulty arises. Also keep your lesson-plan book handy to enter the name of the child who would like to read her book to the class. Set a timer for twenty or twenty-five minutes, to signal the end of each period.

For children who were in your class the year before, keep a list in their file of the books they read to you last year. Review this list to refresh your memory.

Decide how the children are going to come to the conference. Having the children sign up for a conference is not a good idea. It means one or two will always rush to the blackboard and the rest are rarely heard first.

Write the child's name on the blackboard next to the number in the order in which they will be heard. As you hear each child, erase her name from the blackboard and check her name off your class list. This functions as a quick reference for you to glance at the next day and schedule the children with no checks by their names for a reading conference. The children with names on the board are to have a story from their book selected and read through before they come to the conference. They will know their story and be well prepared. A child should not have to read to you something she has not first read to herself. A child does not read smoothly and fluently if the story is not familiar and this affects her self-confidence in her reading. Only the best reading a child is capable of need be checked. If you observe less than her best effort, you will have trouble finding the real and crucial difficulties in reading patterns. (See Box 8.1 for a check list to make sure you and your class are ready for reading conferences.)

The First Reading Conference

The first reading conference is to get to know each child. Talk to the child about his feelings about reading and what books he likes. It is essential to establish a relaxed setting so children are at ease when they come to the reading conference.

Box 8.1

BEFORE THE CONFERENCE ASK YOURSELF THESE QUESTIONS:

1. Is the class ready? Have all of the learning areas settled down and become involved in their work?

2. Is the file ready for each child with whom you will have a conference today?

3. Are the conference desks in a private place, where the child who reads to you will not be heard by other children?

4. Can you see all of the other areas and children in the room from the reading conference desk?

5. Are the children comfortable with the class routine? Do they know where to find supplies or more books? Do they know procedures for leaving the room, for completing their work? Do they know whom they may ask questions if they have problems?

6. Do you have questions prepared that you will ask during the conference, or do you know the next step to take with each child?

7. Do you have a plan to develop each child's interest in reading?

8. Are you aware of how the child is feeling before and during the times he's at the reading conference?

9. Are you ready to scrap all of your open-ended questions and listen?

10. Do you have each area supplied with all the necessary materials and aides?

During the first two or three weeks of school, the children have been reading or looking at books they have chosen. Some questions you could ask them during the conference are:

- What kind of books do you like to read or hear?
  (true stories, animals, baseball, science fiction)

- What kinds of things are you interested in?
  (cars, soccer, skiing, camping, fishing)

- ◆ How did you become interested in these things?
- ◆ What do you do well?
- ◆ What would you like to be better at?
- ◆ What's the easiest thing for you to do?
- ◆ What's the hardest thing for you to do?
- ◆ Who do you play with?
- ◆ What do you do after school?
- ◆ What do you do on weekends?
- ◆ What are you doing this weekend?

This time should be special and enjoyable. You are getting to know the children. Their faces light up as they talk about fishing with their father, learning to ride a bike, or a trip they have taken.

Write these things in their folders, and then read to them what you have written ("likes horses," "has a dog named Shadow," "doesn't like meat," "friend is Andy or Sue," "has two older sisters," "jobs around the house are to take out the garbage, make beds, set the table," "just went to the ball game"). Sometimes they will add a few more things they have forgotten.

After the children help you with this information, you can find books in the class, school, or public library about what they like. For instance, a picture book about baseball on how to throw the ball, a story about a famous baseball player, a fictional story about going to a baseball game, or the comic strip "Charlie Brown" about a baseball game. They can read or look at these while in the Reading Area, until you help them select a book during the second reading conference. These first reading conferences should take about fifteen minutes each, and the first round about two weeks to complete.

Helping a Child Select a Book

You need a starting place when helping a child find a suitable book. Study the chart of the district reading test results. Some test results give you the reading grade level of each child. Also note from the individual test what reading skills the child has. The skills a child knows tend to coincide with the grade level of most basal readers, although it is difficult to say precisely where the child can be placed. As a rule of thumb I found the following placement levels agreed with most basal readers.

Pre-reading
> rhyming
> letter recognition
> alphabet
> language concepts
> left to right

Primer
> consonants
> short vowels

First Grade
> two-letter blends
> consonant digraphs

Second Grade
> three-letter blends
> long vowels
> common inflectional endings
> r-controlled vowels
> second sound of *C, G, S*

Third Grade
> silent letters
> vowel digraphs
> irregular families
> syllabication
> roots and affixes
> common prefixes and suffixes

It takes time to become familiar with the levels of the basal readers. First, look in the back of the book for the grade level of the book and also the list of new words being introduced in the book. If most of the new words are ones the child could read on her test, then you have the correct book; it is at the child's recreational level. This is one method to evaluate books for grade levels.

Another method is to put the graded readers into six piles on your reading conference table. Keep in mind that some reading series do not coincide with each other in their graded difficulty; a child could read an easy first reader in one series and a hard first reader in another. Say to the child, "Find a book from this pile that you read best." Guide him to about the grade level he is reading. Tell the child, "Find a book you haven't read but is one you might like. When you have found the book, read it silently, then we will have a conference and you can read it aloud to me and we will talk about it."

Selecting a paperback book for a child is not so easy. But if you have color-coded the spines of the books in advance you are at an advantage. (See Chapter 2.) The Scholastic Book Company's kit of individualized paperback readers comes with cards in a box that give the reading grade level of each book; this makes for an easy reference guide. The California State Department of Education's *Recommended Reading in Literature, Kindergarten Through Grade Eight* lists books in categories such as Picture books, Folklore, Science Fiction and so on and gives a grade span for each book.

The Second Reading Conference

You'll spend a major part of the second reading conference in the Reading Area in front of the bookcases, while you choose four or five books of the correct reading level for the child. The child will then select one book to read.

Thus, the responsibility for learning is placed squarely on the child. She may seek help, but the obligation is hers. From the time she chooses her own book she makes a decision. One learns to make good decisions by making decisions. Each choice is a practice applied toward growing up.

Do not give a book to a child that she cannot read, or one in which she does not know a majority of the words. If, in selecting books for a child, you suggest one that is too easy (or too hard), the child will usually tell you during the next reading conference, thus building trust and confidence between you. Your objective at this point is to have the children read for enjoyment, therefore, the books must be at their power level. When a child has a difficult time reading and pronouncing the words in a book, he is not understanding what he reads and so getting a sense of failure.

A child's independent level or power level is the level at which children can read without help. Independent-level material gives the child a sense of power over his learning, fosters a good feeling about reading, and develops good learning habits.

While the child is deciding which of the books he wants to read, you can help the next child to choose four or five books. When the child has decided which book he will read, go to your conference table and note the name of the book chosen and the date. This process should take around five minutes for each child.

Before meeting with the next child, review her test results and reading grade level.

All of the children in the Reading Area must learn to wait quietly, looking at a book, until you are able to help them. Remind them to talk only when they need help with a word, and then only to their resource person. Be sure to let them know how much you appreciate this, that you are able to help more of them when they are quiet. The second round of reading conferences should also take about two weeks.

By the third or fourth conference week you will be ready to hold reading conferences that are truly informative and instructional.

Length of Reading Conferences

A conference can be as long as ten minutes, but it is sometimes difficult to stay within this limit. Teachers often take a longer time when first trying individual conferences, mostly because both teacher and child enjoy these sessions so much. Be sure you are aware of this and work to speed up things so that you can get to every child.

The reading conference soon becomes a time when the children may want more than ten minutes alone with you, but longer periods of time reduce the number of conferences you will be able to conduct. Reassure the child that you will hear him read again in two days. A child should be able to confer individually with you once every three school days. This means you need to be well prepared and sharpen your interviewing skills to get the best out of the ten or fifteen minute period.

Subsequent Conferences

Tell the children you are interested in hearing each of them read a story from the book they selected last week. When they see their name listed on the blackboard under Reading Conference, they are to read a story to you they have read first to themselves.

During a reading conference the child reads her familiar story. If she does not know a word, tell her the word immediately; do not make her sound out the word. This is not a lesson. While they read, never interrupt the story being read unless the book is too hard.

Check to see if the child can:

1. Read silently with little help.

2. Read the story aloud to you with ease.

3. Answer questions about the main idea of the story.

Note words missed on a chart you have set up for her skill group and in her folder. Every error has a good base. Note if there is a pattern of words missed. You can put these words in a game for the child to play during the skill lesson. Teach the skills needed during the afternoon skill group. Note the child's strengths as well as what she has missed. Read to the child at the end of the conference what you have noted about her reading, starting with the positive remarks and then explaining skills to learn.

ANALYZING READING SKILLS

While a child is reading to you, try to be alert as to how she is reading:

◆ Does she read with ease or difficulty?

◆ Is she missing many words? (Is the book too hard?)

◆ Is she missing words with two-letter blends?

◆ Is she missing contractions? (This is a teachable moment. Take your piece of blackboard out and teach contractions on the spot, after the story is finished. All the child needs is a short explanation of contractions. If a child misses blends or short vowels, save this lesson for a skill group.) Make a note on the class or skill group list that you have taught contractions to this child. Then, at the next reading conference or during the skill group, check to be certain that the contractions were learned.

◆ Is she substituting letters?

◆ Is she reversible reading, or saying "saw" for "was"? This is a common error. After the story is read, take out the blackboard and write "was" and "saw." Give the child a marker with a hole cut in it so only one word at a time is visible while reading her story.

◆ Is she missing beginning sounds?

◆ Is she following directions from the book?

Also listen for:

♦ How he sounds out words.

♦ If he substitutes words.

♦ Whether the child needs help in speech; if so, refer him to the speech specialist.

♦ How the child analyzes words.

Observe whether the child is:

♦ Squinting.

♦ Squirming (nervous or relaxed).

♦ Enjoying the book and reading.

♦ Looking tired or worried.

In this way you can determine whether the selected book is appropriate and any physical or emotional needs to be met.

Don't Do Too Much Checking

Checking *everything* about a child's reading prevents learning. It literally stops a child from reading. Many teachers do this because they think that the child needs to prove that he has read what he is reading to the teacher. Sometimes teachers insist students fill out worksheets after a story is read, quizzing them to prove they did the reading, but this shows a lack of confidence in children. Some teachers feel children must be forced to read and that checking is a measure of enforcement. This takes away the child's responsibility for his own learning. When a child has a stake in his own learning, enthusiasm, interest, and initiative follow naturally.

Whenever a child is interrupted while he is reading, the child's thoughts and flow of reading are stopped. The only time you should stop a child's reading is when the child is painfully struggling with the difficult words and missing about every other word. Then you might say, "This is an interesting book, but right now it is too difficult for you. It is all right to miss one or two words in order to learn new words, but there are too many hard words in this book. Let's find five other books for you to choose from. That will show what a fluent reader you are."

Conversely, if a child is reading a book that she brings to you and says, "I don't like the one we chose last week," and has swapped it for an easier book and doesn't miss one word, she needs guidance. The child who is not missing a word is telling you something. Let it go for a week or two. Let the child read the easier book while you try to determine if the child needs to feel more secure in a very easy book for a while. Sometimes a child just likes to read an easy book for a change.

When she has completed the book you might say, "You are such a good reader! That book was too easy for you, but I can tell you enjoyed it. Now, it's time to find one that you can learn something from. We all learn from our mistakes, and that's why you need to miss a few words in order to learn." Tell her that if she misses a few words, that is fine—she has a word or two to learn. If she doesn't miss any words, then she will not have anything to learn. A child needs to move away from reading very easy books to books on her instructional level.

If a child consistently chooses a short book and doesn't finish it, it is necessary to tell her that you expect her to read this book to the end before she may choose another one. Some children have difficulty focusing and staying with a task without external limits or rules.

Books without words are a good source for nonreaders, giving them experience in art, context clues, and sequencing. (See the list of books without words at the end of the chapter.) Find easy books with words under the pictures, such as the pre-primers. Sometimes you will want to read with these children during a reading conference, pointing to the words as you read. Children find *A Pig Can Jig* enjoyable and can read it with success if they are ready to learn short vowels. The Economy Press has short, interesting pre-primers that start with short vowels and progress to blends.

Offer encouragement constantly. Get excited if a child knows a word, just by body expression or a pleased look. Do this with every child. Let them know you enjoy hearing them read to you.

What grade a child is supposed to be in is not important. Take them where they are and let them know they are doing beautifully for their effort and interest in reading, not for what they accomplish in the way of advancing quickly or being at grade level. The less pressure and anxiety the children pick up from you, the more relaxed they will be about learning to read and the more open their minds will be to learning.

If as the year progresses, a few of the children are still either not reading fluently or not reading many books, remain relaxed and don't become anxious. Children will read when they are ready, but if you push and they feel something is wrong, they may lose interest in reading or feel like a failure and not want to read. Your goal should be to have them enjoy reading; pushing or forcing them at this time is the wrong approach. They can read their journals, books without words, the labels on their artwork, books with pictures labeled, and their dictionary books.

Yet you cannot ignore the few children with problems. Continue to look for various books that will hold their interest. Continue to write their dictated stories and, perhaps, label their pictures or make sentence strips to accompany the pictures and teach the skill they need to learn. The red-letter day will come when they are ready to read. They will bring a book up to you, and they will read the book. It just all of a sudden clicks. This is such an exciting day! They are so proud and they want to read! This can sometimes take a year and a half, and is another reward to teaching several grades at once, or having children in your class for more than one year. Having patience with children pays off.

Children pick up on anxiety, so you must try to remain calm. They read because they think they can. The few late starters do not need academics pushed on them, and they need to feel good about themselves. If they are not excelling in reading, then they can excel in art, sports, and so on. (One child in my class was the resource person for origami. She could fold paper and interpret the illustration. This child was having trouble reading at the time. She felt ten feet tall as she explained how to fold paper to her group.)

Be sure to relate this to the parents of these children during the parent/teacher conferences. Let them know their child is being challenged but not getting pressured at school.

Conversely, as some second grade children started reading at the fifth and sixth grade levels, I found they would branch out into many interests. One girl liked only to read about real people; another loved horses. One boy was interested only in science; another boy was interested in animals. These children were reading long stories and liked to see the growing list of books I kept on their conference sheets. They liked to look at this and say "Way back in November I didn't know elephants were mammals but now I know it," or "I have read fifteen books so far!" This list of books was a help to me because I could see a pattern and make notes: "Ben really likes *Dr. Seuss*—check out more from the school library; Sue likes riddle books, get more; Jane is into Pippi Longstocking; Mike likes nothing but whale books, find easy ones like *Watch the Whales Go By.*"

There are times when you should shift the emphasis away from a child's reading skills. By the way he looks, the child is telling you he is upset. After a short page is read to you, when you sense that something is wrong, quietly inquire how the child is feeling or what has happened in his life that might be upsetting. Active listening on your part is important when this happens.

You might ask, "How are things going?" or "How do you feel about reading today?" or "You must not feel like reading to me today." Sometimes it's okay for a child to have a day when he can relax and just look at books, if he does not disturb the rest of the children in the class library. If an upset or preoccupied child has not brought a note from home or talked to me before school, and if I will not have a chance during the day to talk to this child easily on a one-to-one basis, then I make certain her name is on the board for a reading conference. Sometimes nothing is particularly wrong, and children will simply go in spurts of reading intently for two or three weeks and then take a day or two to just look casually at books. I do the same. I have times when I just read intently and times when I just sit back and think about what I have read or not think but just gaze and dream. There is a rhythm to reading and learning.

AFTER THE FIRST FEW CONFERENCES

As you have more conferences with the child and he becomes relaxed, it's time to question the child about his comprehension of the story. After you ask a question give the child time to think over his answer. Do not intimidate a child with a rapid fire of questions. You can talk about the book by asking open-ended questions such as:

- Who did you like the most in the story?
- How do you think the story should have ended?
- How did you know that it was a good book for you?
- What was the funniest paragraph?

Try to stay away from convergent questions like:

- Where did Dick go?
- How did Dick run?
- What did his mother do?

After children can read well you can ask:

- Can you write another ending?
- Can you write another title?
- Can you find the table of contents?

Questions should be asked that:

- Encourage answers that are new and original.
- Drive behind the facts to the meaning.

- Begin with "Why," "What," "When,""Who," and "How."
- Are short and can produce long, thoughtful answers.
- Have no right "yes" or "no" answer.
- Show the child she has a right to her own opinions.

Until you are comfortable thinking of questions that check for the different areas of reading skills, you can use the list of questions from Jeannette Veatch's book, *Reading in the Elementary School,* as a guide.

When the conference ends with encouragement, students will feel better about themselves and become excited about reading, so find something to praise and end on a high point. Give them a pat on the back. You might say, "Thanks for reading to me. Your reading was fantastic. You are sounding out your words very well," or "This is a perfect book for you. I enjoyed that story. Thank you for reading it to me." "I have written in your folder that you knew all your words except 'bye,' and that you read with expression."

When that child has left the conference, glance over to the children in the Reading Area. Softly give them encouraging words such as, "You people started reading immediately." Notice how quietly they are reading. "Now I will have time to hear more people read without interruptions."

Things to Remember About Reading Conferences

- The child should always read to you from a story he has read first silently. No material should be read cold. If a child reads a selection cold he will not read fluently, and he may lose confidence in his oral reading ability.
- A favorable learning climate is developed in the Reading Area when children handle books to look at or read.
- A child is motivated when he has power over his learning, and he will perform at a higher level when he is reading from a book he has chosen. Thus, the child will accept responsibility for his own learning.
- Ask different questions about the story following the conference.
- Check only the best reading of which a child is capable. Children should read to you at their instructional level. When a child does less than his best, problems appear that have little to do with his reading ability.

◆ The reading conference should be relaxed and non-threatening without constant checking to learn what the child doesn't know.

Box 8.2

REVIEW OF STEPS DURING A READING CONFERENCE

1. Check the child's name off your class list.

2. Take out the child's reading folder. Fill in the date, name of the book she is reading, and page number.

3. Explain to the child what you are doing.

4. Ask about the story or whatever question is appropriate, to help the child be comfortable and relaxed.

5. Remark about the story to be read. ("This is one of my favorites," or "I would like to hear this story.")

6. While the child is reading:

   a) Follow the words in the book.

   b) If the child does not know a word tell her the word.

   c) Listen for clues

   What words does he miss?

   What mistakes does he repeatedly make?

   How does he read, haltingly or fluently?

   Does he ignore punctuation marks?

7. Be aware of the child's feelings. If she's nervous, put your arm around her shoulder.

8. If the child is emotionally upset she will not gain anything from reading to you. Do not have a reading conference at this time, listen instead to what she has to say.

9. Ask her questions about the story.

10. Read to her what you have written in her folder about her reading. Include something positive.

11. Tell her you will look forward to hearing her read next week, and let her know what book you hope to hear.

ALTERNATE WAYS TO HAVE CHILDREN READ

There is no one best method for children to learn to read. To teach reading you need a full bag of tricks. If one idea does not work for a child, look for other ways to develop an interest in reading.

Special Interests

I have not only had children read their own books to me, but have used other source material as well. One boy was trying hard to read but could not find anything he liked from my suggestions until I remembered he had brought a stack of baseball trading cards to school. I asked him if he would like to read those. His eyes lit up. He read every word on those cards, and I had a hard time ending the conference. He didn't want to stop.

Another child could care less about the letters on the page. She loved to draw beautiful art, great three-dimensional forms with fine detail. She didn't want to make up a story or a sentence about these pictures during her writing period. I suggested that she label the pictures, and I showed her a book in our class library that had the pictures labeled. She liked this and she let me label the pictures. She could immediately read what each label said.

Another boy who was not reading well wanted to read *Dr. Doolittle*. He brought it to me twice to read. My gentle persuasion in trying to direct him to find books at an easier level did not work at all. He was determined it had to be *Dr. Doolittle*. So I taped the book after school and gave it to him to read with a recorder and earphones the next day. The extra time I put in was worth twenty reading conferences. He was thrilled, he soon learned the words in the *Dr. Doolittle* book, and his reading improved rapidly.

Partner Reading

After they have spent three or four weeks reading in the class library, children may become interested in a book another child is reading at their reading level. You can develop partner reading, where two children read the same story. Each taking turns, one child listens and follows the words while the other reads the same book aloud. They can read to each other in soft voices while in the Reading Area and away from the other children, in order to keep this area quiet.

The Listening Area

The Listening Area is an aid in the early reading process. This area is set up with a record player or tape recorder, and enough headphones for a group of children. They listen to a story being read, and read along with it in books of their own.

One of my classes received a record, two posters with the words to the records, and six copies of *Chicken Soup with Rice* as a bonus from the Scholastic Book Club. They listened to this at the Listening Area, singing softly along with the record and they soon learned all of the words. The children were so delighted with their accomplishment that, after a class discussion, we decided to serve chicken soup with rice to their parents for Open House while the children sang along with the record.

Children from Other Cultures

How do you teach a non-English-speaking child to read?

A teacher needs to focus on creative lessons, viewing the child as if he were beginning to speak and understand language, rather than thinking about learning the child's native tongue. Pictures, actual objects, and field trip experiences are needed to develop oral language before this child is asked to read a printed word. During the individual reading conference the use of pictures—gathered from magazines, ordered from educational catalogs, the Peabody kit, and those pictures the child has drawn—develops his knowledge of the spoken language. Label the objects the child has drawn, as he learns to pronounce the words. A sentence can be written below the picture, such as, "This is a green tree." The child can repeat after the teacher, "This is a green tree."

Ruth French's kit, containing over two hundred objects, is a rich resource for teaching a language. (This kit is available from Multisensory Reading, Frank Adair Products, 2748 13th Street, Sacramento, California 95818.) The child can see and hold an object during a reading skills group. The child takes a drawer containing all objects beginning with the letter B. As he removes the objects from the drawer to the table he repeats after the teacher, "This is a ball." He must always use a complete sentence. He traces the ball on a paper and the drawing is labeled by the teacher, "This is a ball."

Non-English-speaking children, as all children, become motivated by something in which they can excel. One way to help these children is to be aware of their various cultures.

During a small group, paper-folding art session, Ti, a new girl from Vietnam, became very excited. She told me in her limited English that she knew how to fold many more objects. I told her she could show the other children how to fold the objects only if she talked as she folded. During our reading conference the following day I demonstrated what I meant. Ti folded the paper and I explained in simple sentences what she was doing. Ti repeated what I said. We practiced until her directions were understandable. The following day Ti was the teacher at the art area. Ti became highly motivated to learn English. Now she wanted to learn to write. I found many notes on my desk from her. Two page letters appeared by June (although she still did not know if I was a he or a she).

In Their Own Words

For children who are just learning to read, cut up sentences that they have dictated to you into individual words, and have them put the words into sentences again. This is their reading activity. The children like this because they have written about what they are interested in, and they can identify with their own words. The children can also dictate stories to you, which you can make into books. They will enjoy reading these to the class or to you during reading conferences.

Have a certain time each week when the children can volunteer to read their completed journals. Since these journals contain their own words, they all read their journals with ease because they remember the words they wrote. This develops a desire by many children to read aloud to the class.

Reading Aloud to the Class

When I first returned to teaching, I did not want to embarrass the children by forcing them to read out loud in front of the class. Yet when they have gained confidence, most children are so proud of their newfound skill that they want to read to the whole class.

They want to read their journals, books, and poems out loud. This is when all of the teaching for independence, self confidence, and sheer enjoyment of reading comes together. After groping to find enough time to accommodate the many requests to read, I devised a system. When a child would ask if he could read something to the class, I scheduled it according to two criteria:

1. The story or poem must not be too long.

2. The child must read the story to me first and together we would decide if it was too long or too difficult.

Keep your lesson-plan book nearby, letting the child see you write his name in it to read to the class on a certain time and day.

The child must be able to read the story fluently. The listening rules for the class were, "Be polite. If you do not want to hear the story, you are not to let us know by making a noise. Just as in the auditorium, you must sit quietly and politely without making faces. These people have taken time to prepare their story. If you can't say something nice or positive, then don't say anything at all. Only warm fuzzies!"

I made one exception to my criteria when a girl who was having a great deal of difficulty learning to read wanted to read to the class. She had repeated the same grade with her former teacher. She wanted to read the book, *More Spaghetti, I Say*, by Rita Golden Gilman. She diligently read the book over and over to me with much difficulty at first, until we both felt she was ready to read to the class with ease. On that day, I built up the girl's image by saying I admired the persistence she used in learning the story. I reminded the class of our rules in a firm manner. They knew I would not tolerate ridicule. Then I sat back and held my breath. When she finished the story, the class had a look of admiration and disbelief. They gave her compliments such as, "You read every word!" or "I didn't know you could read those words." She had such a wide grin. With her shoulders back she glowed with a sense of accomplishment and self-assurance.

Another child wrote a book and read it to my class. She asked if she could glue a library pocket on the inside of the book and put it in the school library. I thought that was an excellent idea and said I would talk to the librarian. The book went to the library and was put on a table. The author happened to be in the library when a sixth grader checked it out. The girl was ecstatic. Her news for the class was: "A sixth grader checked out my book!"

SUMMARY

The keys to children wanting to read include encouragement, positive remarks, and individual attention in a noncompetitive environment. Children feel good about reading when they are at their power level and are confident of their phonetic skills. Teaching reading should not involve only one system, one set of books, or one reading program. To me, the best approach for any individual depends on that child's particular level of emotional and intellectual development. A child reads best when he is reading books he has chosen on subjects that interest him, and when he is comfortable with his rate of progress.

Reading is where individual or personalized learning begins. When you are comfortable with this approach, then you can concentrate on the other areas and subjects for personalization.

SOURCES

Durkin, Dolores. 1980. *Teaching Young Children To Read.* Allyn and Bacon: Boston.

Veatch, Jeannette. 1966. *Reading in the Elementary School.* The Ronald Press Company: New York.

BOOKS FOR PRE-READING

Books without words and books with pictures labeled are:

Alexander, Martha G. 1970. *Bobo's Dream.* Dial Press: New York. A grateful dachshund dreams of returning his master's favor.

Anno, Mitsumasa. 1983. *Anno's U.S.A.* Philomel Books: New York.

Briggs, Raymond. 1978. *The Snowman.* Random House: New York. This is also a movie.

Goodall, John S. 1973. *Paddy's Evening Out.* A Margaret K. McEldeny Book: Hong Kong. This contains half pages that illustrate what is on the stage.

Hutchins, Pat. 1971. *Changes, Changes.* MacMillan: New York.

Krahn, Fernando. 1982. *Sleep Tight Alex Pumpernickel.* Little Brown: Boston.

Krahn, Fernando. 1981. *Here Comes Alex Pumpernickel.* Little Brown: Boston.

Mayer, Mercer. 1969. *Frog Where Are You?* The Dial Press: New York. A story in pictures without text about a boy and a dog who are dismayed when they awaken one morning to discover their favorite frog friend "gone!" They search all over, until finally, down by the pond, behind a log, their favorite frog is "found."

Ringi, Kjell. 1969. *The Winner.* Harper Collins: New York. The attempts of two neighbors to outdo each other ends in disaster for both.

Scary, Richard. 1971. *Fun with Words.* Golden Press: New York.

Spier, Peter. 1982. *Peter Spier's Rain.* Doubleday: Garden City, New York. Beautifully illustrated.

Holt, Rinehart, and Winston publishes a series, Little Owl Books, that is good, including:

Allen, Laura Jean. 1963. *Mr. Jolly's Sidewalk Market.*

Curro, Evelyn M. 1963. *The Great Circus Parade.*

Eitzen, Allen. 1963. *Birds in Wintertime.*

Gilbert, Elliott. 1963. *A Cat Story.*

Heller, Aaron and Robert Deschamps. 1963. *Let's Take A Walk.*

Mill, Eleanor. 1963. *My School Book of Picture Stories.*

Nicholson and Martin. 1967. *Let's Eat.*

Oechsli, Kelly. 1967. *It's Schooltime.*

Peterson, John. 1963. *Tulips.*

Watson, Aldren A. 1963. *The River.*

Webber, Helen. 1967. *Working Wheels.*

BOOKS FOR BEGINNING READERS

Children who are just learning to read find these books fun for recreational reading.

Eastman, P.D. 1961. *Go Dog Go.* Random House: New York.

Eastman, P.D. 1974. *The Alphabet Book.* Random House: New York.

Hewetson, Emily and Victoria Shima. 1975. *Stories From Sounds Books A, B, C, D and E.* Educators Publishing Service: Cambridge, Massachusetts.

Martin, Bill Jr. 1967. *Brown Bear, Brown Bear, What Do You See?* Holt: Erie, Illinois.

Patrick, Gloria. 1970. *A Bug in a Jug and Other Funny Rhymes.* Scholastic Book Services: New York.

Perkins, Al. 1969. *Hand, Hand, Fingers, Thumb.* Random House: New York.

Rasmussen, Donald and Lynn Goldberg. 1985. *A Pig Can Jig.* Science Research Associates: Chicago.

Seuss, Dr. 1963. *Hop on Pop.* Random House: New York.

Chapter

9

The Way to Write

From a class book titled, *If I Were*

If I were a cat I would cuddle up in someone's lap.
—Sara, age 6.

If I were a he-man I would fight skeletons.
—Fletcher, age 6.

If I were a cheetah, I would run very fast.
—Brandon, age 7.

here's my mother's name, joyfully exclaims the first grade child as she points to her creative writing paper. Primary school children must experience some form of creative writing at least three or four times a week. Through this process the child will see the language she speaks on the written page and hear the connections among speaking, writing, and, reading. Children learn to read by reading; what better way to learn writing than through their own thoughts in written expression?

I believe, as does Jeannette Veatch, that the child should enjoy writing, that the purpose of creative writing is to teach love of writing. No pressure should be applied to write long stories at first. Short sentences are fine until the child has had experience. Remember too that any criticism of the child's creative writing is to criticize the child.

The atmosphere at the Writing Area should be enjoyable, free from tension, where any idea, if not offensive, is valid. Most children are delighted to have their creative work read to the class or be asked to read it. Be certain to have the child who is reading next to you; this enables you to follow the words along with him. If he cannot read a word offer the answer immediately. If the child is shy, you could say; "Would you like to have me read your journal?"

At the core of the language arts structure is firm practice of reading and writing. All other knowledge uses and builds on language skills. Teaching language arts must be a creative practice, using many different methods, exercises, and resources.

Staff the Writing Area with an aide or adult helper who can assist the children in a quiet, warm, and helpful manner. During the twenty-minute writing session, anything can happen in a child's imagination. The aide helps to get these things on paper.

ORGANIZATION

Have a writing folder for each student in the class. In each folder keep the child's dated papers filed chronologically to show his progress over the course of the year. Keep both rough and final drafts of papers. Also include any records of observations you have made about the child's writing skills. These files will show each child's development and allow you to see at a glance the results of her progress. They are an excellent tool for parent/teacher conferences. The files can also be used to pass on from grade level to grade level as a record of student development if this method is appropriate for your school.

Be sure to provide various sizes of lined and unlined paper for the children to use for writing. Supply plenty of sharpened pencils, pens, crayons, and erasers. You can also cut an old blackboard into pieces. It is important for the aide or child to stamp the date on each journal, so supply them with a date stamp. Prepare alphabet books and journals ahead of time. (See Chapter 2 for more information on organizing the Writing Area.)

WRITING PROJECTS AND TOOLS

Alphabet Books

Alphabet books are a good way for beginning writers to develop letter recognition. The teacher's aide can make the alphabet book. Each letter of the alphabet is printed in capital and lowercase letters every second or third page. If the child needs to know how to spell a word, she raises her hand or puts out a colored card to indicate that she needs help. The child is asked to open the book to the page showing the letter that the word he needs begins with. (This is good practice for beginning sounds and alphabetizing.) When the child locates the page, the aide prints the word in his alphabet book. Often when opening the page to write something down the child will exclaim, "Oh! I already have the word," or while hunting for the correct page, he may say, "There's my sister's name." Each child can make up a title for her own alphabet book, calling it "Words I Use," "My Own Words," or "Jenny's Words."

At some point you can begin to call this a personal dictionary, so children can begin to see the connection. As they become better readers, you can encourage them to use standard dictionaries, and can phase the the alphabet books out.

Journals

Journals are open-ended and fun; the children can fill them up with whatever they want. Journals can be started the second day of school. Make each child a stapled booklet of about five pages of 9" × 18" paper folded in half (or you can use several stapled single sheets of 8 1/2" × 11") with a bright, construction-paper cover. The children can decorate the covers of their journals and create their own stories. When the child first dictates a story, blank paper may be used. After the child starts his own writing, paper with a space at the top for a picture and two lines at the bottom of the page for writing may be used. Some children use journals for writing on themes; others make up short stories.

During the late fall months, whole journals may be written on one topic such as Halloween, Thanksgiving, or Christmas, which are exciting times for children. Suggest giving the journal a title. Some children get quickly caught up by this idea, and will write other journals with one idea. Examples of single theme journals are, *Spring*, *Fairy Stories*, *Space*, and *Dinosaurs*. Sometimes second and third graders become involved in research; one child wrote a journal on state flags. When a child does use a book for information, he should be encouraged to put the information in his own words rather than copying the information from the book verbatim.

Not all the words in a beginner's journal will be spelled correctly, nor will the grammar always be correct. If a child does not ask you to spell a word, do not correct these errors. By not correcting journals you can show parents their child's progress. This is a creative writing activity, and someone pointing out an error interrupts a creative thought. My children enjoyed the freedom of journal writing so much that I had a special stamp made that read, "uncensored." Thus they learned about censorship. Sometimes, when reading what she has written, the child discovers a grammatical error on her own.

By the time most children are writing three sentences for a story on their own with the use of a dictionary, the teacher can begin to emphasize the correct use of grammar. Although you correct any errors in notes, cards, and letters taken home, do not correct the journals.

Children who have had journal-writing in previous years know what to do. The new students learn quickly from the experienced ones.

Dictation for Journals

Children who are not yet writers may dictate a story about a picture they have drawn. The aide may need extra help taking dictation and enlist the help of a sixth grader or the student teacher to write the dictated words into the children's journals.

In a mixed-grade class, the younger children soon want to be like the older students and write the words themselves. The aide can use a small blackboard or a piece of paper for this dictation. After the story is read to them, the children copy the story into their journals. Some children like to use these blackboards to write their story or sentence on. After they read what they have written to an aide they can erase any errors they notice.

Saving their dated journals till the end of April is a dramatic way to show each child his progress.

The Value of Dictation

The following is printed with the permission of Bart Schneider from a 1979 paper titled, "A Practical Guide for Taking Dictation in Kindergarten and First Grade."

One of the really difficult aspects of childhood is that children are so often left alone to make sense out of a staggering number of impressions. The process of dictation—telling a story to an attentive adult, and having it read back—gives children an opportunity to explore some of the things which are difficult for them to understand. It is important for children to be able to express themselves openly and to be taken seriously. Dictation helps children value what they think and feel and how they choose to say it.

A child may have a long, winding story to weave, or may have only a few words to tell. Either way it is a first step for children toward writing for themselves. Dictation is a bridge to writing. As children see their words being transcribed, they begin to sense the relationship of thought and speech to written words. It is a revelation to children to find that what they say, often casually, can be recorded and read back just as they have said it.

Dictation can help children understand new information. As they write about the contents of lessons, they recall and apply what they have learned. It is fresh in their minds. They are engaged by the subject and proud of all they know about it.

The Small Group: Working One-to-One with Dictation

An ideal situation for dictation is a group of four or five children sitting comfortably around a table. I usually have crayons or markers available and invite the children to make pictures. While they're drawing I ask them to think of what they have to say. I let them know that when they're ready to tell me their words, I'll write them down. The expectations are flexible and the situation is quite open. I try to give the children a sense that everyone can be successful. Developing a supportive atmosphere is crucial, and by keeping a low profile I feel I have a better chance of gaining the children's trust.

Most children become absorbed with their drawings. Generally, the older they are the longer the time they spend working on their pictures. Kindergarten children tend to do their work in a flurry and are usually pleased with their products. When a child comes over to me with a completed picture, I respond to something in it that I like or that I feel is important to the child. Most children are eager to say something about their pictures if an adult shows any genuine interest.

Some children are not fluent at the beginning. At her first time with dictation, a four-year-old girl brought me a picture of a house, a cat, and a little girl. When I asked her to tell me about her picture she said: "A house, a girl, and a kitty." I wrote it out just like that and read it: "A house, a girl, and a kitty, by Heather Ferris, age four." As the child feels less threatened by the process and sees other children weaving long tales, words and ideas begin to flow naturally. It dawns on children quickly that whatever they tell me becomes their story. Caption writing, like the above, generally disappears after the first couple of weeks.

After I've worked with the same children for a few weeks, and sense that they're comfortable with me and the process, I encourage them to tell me more and more. Children often have no idea how much they actually know. If a boy says, "I like camping because it's nice," I may ask him to tell me what it is that makes camping nice. He may answer, "It's just nice," in which case I would ask him to think a little bit about how camping is different from staying at home. Usually there will be some kind of breakthrough. The boy might say, "Well, you get to sleep outside. You can get dirtier than you can at home. You get to take a walk with your dad."

When a boy says, "Camping is nice," he already knows the particular things about camping that have helped him form his impression. Specific questions can open the experience for him again so that he can see and express the "niceness" of camping in detail.

Should you or shouldn't you accept the child's own language when it doesn't conform to standard usage? This can be a touchy question. Are we disregarding a good opportunity for teaching if we ignore a child's obvious grammatical errors? Or will we undermine a child's trust in us and inhibit fluency by saying, in the middle of a story, that "ain't" isn't a real word? The question here is really one of aim. What are we trying to accomplish with the dictation?

Do what feels constructive and natural. Your response will depend on what is being written, who the child is, how he or she is feeling that day, how fast the words are coming, and so on. Occasionally, it feels natural during the dictation to offer an alternative word or phrase. For example, if the child says "brang," I may pause and ask, "Should I write 'brang' or 'brought'?" Or I might read back the previous phrase, in a very casual way, as if to verify for myself that I heard correctly. This gives the child an unspoken option to rephrase, and occasionally the language changes the second time.

In first grade, where students are beginning to write, they can copy their words after adults transcribe them on scratch paper. Writing with first graders can be as simple as having them copy a caption or title from the board, such as "The Shadow on the Stairs," and then draw a picture. While children copy the phrase and draw, adults are free to take additional dictation.

Whatever methods are used for writing through dictation, it is important to read orally what children write. This is the real follow through, and without it a great deal of the value of dictation is lost. Children who can't write usually can't read. Hearing their piece is an inspiration to them to do both. Also, as they hear each other's work, they are exposed to new ideas and approaches. A kind of quiet instruction takes place. Each child is exposed to a range of possibilities—different styles, longer and shorter pieces, drawings—and it is a pleasure to see how much they enjoy each other's work.

The possibilities for dictation ideas are unlimited, and a good way to begin the program is to allow the children to write about any idea they choose rather than an assigned topic. A lively dictation program will go back and forth throughout the year between working with a fixed topic and this more open approach. If open writing is going to be effective, it's important to establish with the children the expectation that they learn to discover what they feel like writing about. In other words, choosing a subject is part of the assignment.

When I found myself in classes where I felt like monsters and rockets were coming out of my ears, my self-protective instincts went to work. As an alternative to assigning a definite theme, I began eliminating the students' possibilities. "All right, today you can write about anything you want except Ninja Turtles and Hulk Hogan." I wanted students to talk about more than just their favorite movies and television shows.

Class Collaborations

Writing together is adventurous and fun, whether on large tagboard or chart paper, typing paper, the blackboard, or a xerox with a square for individual illustrations of the group's writing. Any writing idea can be done by a group.

Writing Letters

Before students begin writing letters, it might be helpful to go through the forms for various kinds of letters and discuss such things as date, heading, salutation, the body, and the closing—as found in composition and language arts texts.

Talk with the class about what makes letters interesting to write and receive. How can students make sure their letters will say more than "How are you? I'm fine." Include in this discussion how letters look, what kind of paper they're written on, whether they include pictures or other enclosures, how they're addressed, even where the stamp gets stuck. Read some letters aloud in class. Ask students if they find them interesting, funny, or sad, if they think they have a personal style, remind them of the person writing, or make them want to write a letter back? Do they have the feeling of a conversation, the voice of someone talking? It might be helpful to remind students that when they write a letter they are in fact speaking to someone.

Students can write letters to friends, parents, relatives, teachers, or classmates. They may write to someone in their family, to an imagined (or real) ancestor, to an imagined future child or grandchild, to someone famous, or to someone in history. They can write letters to politicians or presidents of corporations about issues they are concerned about. I've also asked students to write letters to people that they will never send: an angry letter to a friend, sister, or brother after a fight; a love letter, particularly as the admission of a love which might otherwise go unconfessed.

Postcards are fun, especially when students make the pictures on the front and then write messages on the back, or children can make letterheads. Have each child include his or her address and a drawing. Copy masters and pass them out, to encourage note passing and letter writing.

Devoting the writing period to letter writing can be a relaxing break after working on some more intense and difficult writing forms, because personal letters are often so informal. Letters share things, news and information, but they are also simple friendly gestures. When children want to communicate, and have something important to say, the actual labor of writing becomes a secondary task.

Writing on a Theme

Writing on a theme helps children explore many aspects of a single subject. Take some universal theme and plant it in the classroom for a week or so. The theme may be explored in literature, art, class meetings, or sharing time.

Here are some examples of experiences the theme of "Night" may evoke:

babysitters, being left alone, sounds, walking, flashlights, coming home late in the car with the family, watching t.v. with the family, watching t.v. alone, listening to the radio, being sad, waiting for a phone call, being bored, staying up late, being punished and sent to bed early, going to bed hungry, going to bed worried, being sick and having already slept all day, fires in the fireplace, fights in the family, being out of toothpaste, having to take a bath, washing your hair, noticing the moon night after night, going out for an ice cream, going to slumber parties, getting in your mom/dad's bed, being kissed goodnight, getting a story read when you're in bed.

Consider other themes; the list is endless—Playing, Journeys, Sun and Moon and Stars, Rain, Wind, and Fog...

Writing the Whole Story

Fiction can be written by students as a whole, fluent experience, apart from the context of exercises and discussions. The reason is straightforward: children often do their best writing when it truly and spontaneously comes from themselves. A good writing program provides for both work on craft and story writing in a more open framework.

There are countless ways to help students find the stories they have to tell. For most children, some outside stimulus or structure is enough. The following list provides some concrete examples.

Begin with a drawing period. Students draw the picture that will become an illustration of their story. The drawing time works as an incubation period for the writing that follows.

Use a magazine picture in a similar way. Students select their picture and spend time carefully observing its detail before beginning to write.

Give students a list of ten to twenty words. Briefly discuss each word, emphasizing how each word might spark an idea for their stories. Think of the discussion time as an incubation period where students more or less plan their writing. The words themselves may or may not actually turn up in their finished stories.

Offer students several titles for stories. Emphasize that these titles are only to give them ideas. Be sure to include titles that will touch a broad range of interests. Choose good titles and avoid overused titles and titles that suggest predictable results, like "What I Would Do with a Million Dollars," or "What Love Is." In second grade, titles like "Black Holes in Space," "The Shadow on the Stairs," "Painting My Face," and "A Story My Father Told Me" should suggest ideas to most children, and yet leave open the specific possibilities of their stories.

Use one or two very open beginnings and discuss many possibilities for development. For example, "I had been wandering for several hours and didn't recognize the place..."

Suggest they write a dream, a dreamlike story, a story with a dream in it, or use a real dream or part of one to elaborate into a larger story. Talk about dreams and share dreams before writing over several days if that's possible.

Have them retell a familiar tale. This provides a fine opportunity for fluency, and there is room for personal style and modification of the story line. Try "Red Riding Hood," "Hansel and Gretel," and so on.

Have them retell a well-known family story that they have heard many times: the story of how their parents met, the time a little sister swallowed money, or how Grandpa got into the watch repair business.

Ask them to write a particular "genre" story, such as a mystery, adventure, romance, comedy, or horror story. This works for even the youngest children as long as they understand that a horror story has to scare people, a funny story should make them laugh, and so on.

Ask them to write a story as a "gift" for a particular audience—a comedy for the senior citizens who meet nearby, a fairy tale for a little brother on his birthday, or a story for a mother who loves mysteries.

IDEAS FOR TOPICS

Personal Writing

Personal writing is writing from experience, in our own voice, what each one of us uniquely knows. Personal writing in the classroom is a process of helping a child discover, recognize, and express his own voice. As a teacher you can encourage a child to know what he knows, to appreciate who he is, to value his experience, and to put these things into language. There are as many possible subjects for this topic as there are moments in a day. The following ideas are excerpted from a 1979 booklet by Phillip Holtzman (reprinted with permission).

Memories: What do you remember? Write your first memory, or your first memory of a kitchen/a day school/your own room. Write your memory of a time you stayed up past midnight/ someone hit you/you got lost. Write details of something you did yesterday/last week/last year.

Journals: Write in a journal daily, weekly, or monthly. Write what you feel or wish or hate or think, whatever comes to your head.

Dreams: Write down a dream as if it really happened. Write down a dream that you made up. Write down a nightmare. Tell why you dreamt a particular nightmare or what a nightmare means or why it was scary. Write a dream as if you are a particular person or object in the dream.

Physical Features, the Body: Write a description of yourself. Write a description of what you think you looked like when you were two years old. Write a conversation with some part of your body — hair, stomach, feet.

Portraits: Write a description of someone sitting beside you, or of the oldest person you know, or of a stranger you passed on the street, or of a room/home/town you've lived in.

Families

Families, beginning with mother, father, sisters, and brothers and extending to grandparents, aunts, uncles, and even family friends are excellent topics. Our family is the people we live with, the ones who care for us, love us, hurt us. For better or worse, family life is the one students know best, and families are a rich and complex subject for writing.

I had my third graders write descriptions of their mothers and fathers. From such an assignment, students could compose an entire family portrait, descriptions of all family members and the houses they lived in. Such a portrait might become a longer writing project for students to work on over a period of time and eventually work into a book.

Specific writing assignments can be devoted to describing particular rooms in the house—the front porch, the bathroom on Monday mornings, the kitchen after midnight, somebody's bedroom in late afternoon—and to descriptions of family routines and rituals, such as driving with the whole family in the car, family vacations, arguments, grocery shopping together.

Another possibility is to write a family conversation. This gives students a chance to practice writing dialogue and to begin contemplating "character" as they write in the "persona" of another person. Assign an entire writing piece in the persona of one family member: a mother talking on the phone to a friend, a sister's thoughts as she's bicycling to school, a father's part in a business conversation.

WHAT I CALL MY GRANDPARENTS
by first and second graders, Wade Thomas School, San Anselmo, Calif.
My grandma Diddlie and my grandpa Uncle Fritz.
I call my grandpa and grandma the regular old grandpa
and grandma.
I call my grandma Lenore cause it's her middle name and my
grandpa—grandpa.
I call my grandpa Paul cause that's his name and my grandma
Sophie cause that's her name.
I never saw my grandpas cause they got sick and died.
Well, I have a grandma. I call her grammy. And my grandpa I
called Pop Pop.
I call my first grandma Flo
my second grandma Nana
my third grandma Nanni.
I call my grandma Ester.

Holidays and Special Occasions

Christmas Eve at your house, or the night after Christmas day, or things you have on the Christmas tree every year, or what foods you always have on Thanksgiving or things you can do to celebrate Chanukah.

How you celebrate birthdays, the 4th of July, Halloween.

Making a long distance phone call to someone in the family.

The day a brother or sister went off to college, or a new baby came home from the hospital.

Visits from relatives.

Give somebody one wish. (I wish for my dad to be able to work with wood and move to the country like he wants.)

Describe the weather for Christmas day or the first day of vacation.

What you feel like on Christmas Eve or when Christmas/Chanukah is all over.

Write the Christmas or Chanukah story as you understand it.

How Santa looks, how a Christmas tree looks, how a menorah looks on the eighth night.

MY TRAIN

My train's still
Broken is the power pack.
When I fix it up
It will go choo-chooing down the track.

—Orpheus, age 7.

THE HOUSE

The House is haunted.
It sits silently
All dark and still.
I will never climb the hill.

—Briana, age 6.

One-Word Topics

The following are mostly simple topics and concepts. They can be used for individual writing, or for building a group piece, and they can inspire lovely poems.

Sky
Calm/Wild
Far/Close
Getting There
Growing/Dying
Obstacles
Rising/Falling
Open/Closed
Dark/Light
Rhythms
Things to Put Things In
Young/Old
Green
Faces
Three
Together/Alone
Wet/Dry
Night/Day

Up/Down
Deaths
Births
Earth/Sky/Sun/Moon/Stars
This Morning
Out the Window
Now
Love
Above/Below
When I'm Dreaming
Changes
New Things
Small Things
Rotting
Making/Breaking
Flat
Ground/Air

From a class book titled *If I Were In Charge of the World*

All of the vegetables would be fruit.

—*Courtney, age 6.*

Nothing would cost money. Everybody would be nicer
and guns wouldn't be made.

—*Daniel, age 6.*

Kids would be in charge of their family and I could have
a chocolate sundae every Sunday.

—*Leah, age 6.*

I'd make it so moms and dads cannot tell you what to do.

—*Allegra, age 7.*

Questions About Values and Feelings

This is a brief list of topics related to values and feelings. Chapter 5 also lists discussion questions that can be adapted to writing topics, perhaps to be used in conjunction with discussion times.

How do you get your way?
What is it like to die?
What is boring/lonely/exciting/sad/scary/old-fashioned/
   selfish to you?
Should people kill in war?
Should children be spanked?
Should there be billboards?
What you do when you're alone.

Things to Remember

- ◆ The writing is part of the child.
- ◆ No markings or grading of creative papers. The idea of writing is more important. Spelling, grammar, and sentence structure should be taught at another time.
- ◆ The child has a vested interest in his personal writing.

Writing is another area where children learn by doing. With the youngest and least fluent children, dictating their ideas to a teacher who writes them down gives them an introduction to the concept of writing in a way they can understand. It also makes children feel that their own ideas are important. As they gain in confidence, trust, and ability, children can transcribe the dictation into their journals. The more accomplished students can write on their own, using suggested topics as launching pads for their imagination. Thus writing becomes something for the class to look forward to. Children who learn to write in a flexible, creative atmosphere have a good foundation for the future.

SOURCE

Veatch, Jeannette. 1966. *Reading in the Elementary School.* The Ronald Press: New York.

Chapter
10

Teaching the Other Subjects

My favorite subject is math.
I do it every day in school.
I even take papers home to do.
Yesterday I finished my first book.
Now I have another.

— Jeromiah

ther topics can accommodate the individual child just as successfully as reading and writing, with the help of learning areas, conferences, and heterogeneous groups of children within the class. A word of caution, do not individualize every subject your first year. Begin with reading, then, when you and the children are comfortable with the way the reading program is functioning and when you are confident with your teaching style, you can begin to reorganize your math and spelling programs.

By choosing open-ended tasks—pattern blocks, dot-to-dot papers, puzzles, and geo boards—you can give children non-threatening tasks until you know where they are academically. Find open-ended materials that will be effective and challenging to learners at all levels.

You cannot give the same assignments to all of the children throughout the year. Children who are academically beyond their grade level will soon be bored and likely to get into trouble. Children who are not up to grade level will become frustrated, tense, and may cry while performing a task or act out in class. Constantly think about how you can change the program in order to meet each child's needs.

INDIVIDUALIZING MATH

In my schedule, a math, science, social studies, art, and health period followed the language arts and reading hour. This time is more active but is still a time for involvement and not play. Since we are focused on five-to eight-year-olds, we need to provide many manipulatives. Children at this age are in the preoperational stage, moving from concrete to abstract functions. Be sensitive to this transition.

It can be assumed that young children need concrete materials to work with before abstract pages, and they cannot be pushed from one stage to the next until they are ready. Some experiences children can perform before they are given abstract pages are explained below.

Sorting

The first classification experiences for school children are of a sorting type. Children should learn to put objects back where they belong after they have finished playing with them.

The idea of sorting or classification is based on the idea of relation: belongs to, heavier than, lighter than, larger than, smaller than, the same color, darker, larger than, shorter than, the same as.

One-to-One Correspondence

Young children can learn how objects relate to each other functionally. Having students match corresponding objects or objects to specific purposes helps them understand this concept. Experiences for developing one-to-one correspondence include: straws to milk bottles, coins to buy objects, paintbrushes to paint containers, cups to saucers, pieces of paper to children.

Ordering

Young children can learn to order such materials as sticks, doweling rods, colors by shade, containers by size, round objects, paper of different sizes, objects in patterns.

From the age of seven on a child can usually take the shortest rod, then the next in length, and so on, knowing in advance that he can build the series. Cuisinaire Rods are one source for the children to practice ordering.

Math at the Child's Level of Development

A new third grade student in my class shivered every time we had math. She said she hated math and she couldn't do math problems, couldn't even add. She would freeze whenever she looked at an abstract math page. I let her parents know what I planned to do. I talked to the girl before school and told her that she needn't worry about completing the assigned math book. She would have a supplementary book instead. I gave her a math workbook that was much easier than the adopted textbook and contained actual pictures of objects to count, making it more visual than the more abstract adopted text. To help eliminate any more feeling of failure, I let her keep the adopted textbook. I explained to her that the workbook was something extra for her to do. I tore many of the repetitive pages out of the workbook to make it less overwhelming. I let her use red plastic disks as silent counters. I told her to work the math problems in the workbook in whatever manner she wished and assured her she would not fail math. About halfway through the book she seemed to suddenly understand. She was feeling relaxed and not as concerned. This girl improved in her math skills from below the 50th percentile to her grade level in one year—the equivalent of a full grade level and a half! She was ecstatic. Needless to say, so were her parents.

PREPARING YOUR MATH PROGRAM

In order to prepare an individual math program use the same steps as when you developed your individual reading program.

Before school starts, review and study books about how to teach math. Next, read the course of study for your school district at the grade level or levels you will teach. After you have done this, begin to gather books, ideas, and materials for math skills. Next, read the teacher's manuals that accompany the math books for ideas as to how to make the best use of the books and materials. Become familiar with the text or workbook adopted by your district.

When all of the materials you can find are gathered together, sort master copies, ideas, and games according to the math concepts they teach. For example, master copies for addition from 1 to 10 and games for adding to 10 go together. You will quickly see the areas in which you are lacking materials.

Where to Find Materials

School supply catalogs are an excellent resource and the larger teachers' stores also have a wide assortment. Shop keeping in mind that you want products that help children to think and discover, not those that are mostly drill and repetition. The children are eager to work a math problem at their level when given math worksheets that contain a hidden message or code such as that used in the Frank Schaffer publications. At the end of the chapter you'll find a list of publishers that I found supply good workbooks.

For the first two weeks of your program you will need open-ended worksheets. This is the period before the children are tested, and you do not know what concepts each child knows. Therefore, everyone will have the same page, preferably an enjoyable one such as a dot-to-dot or a color-in-the-numbers project.

Preparing these worksheet pages before school starts will ensure a smoother running classroom. Prepare several sheets and staple them in a packet for each child. When a child completes his work faster than the others, he can proceed to the next pages. Eight pages per packet seems to work well. Number each packet in sequence and write this number next to the child's name on the class list. Check the worksheets and eliminate any that would be too difficult for the children to do on their own. Since you know you will be giving the entry-level math test for the adopted math book for your grade or grades, now is the time to prepare these tests.

Classroom Arrangement

When you are arranging your classroom (as described in Chapter 2) give some thought to the kinds of math activities that will take place.

If you have three areas that contain groups of tables similar to the floor plan described previously, you will not need to use the rug for math activities. The rug area is conducive to quiet reading and for meetings but using this area for math manipulatives tends to be unmanageable.

Personalization is an important part of learning math concepts. The children who learn a concept quickly and work faster will move ahead of the children who need more help and progress more slowly. The slow learners cannot afford to become frustrated by being pushed to keep up with the others in order to have everyone on the same page.

Small groups at an area or circular table make it very easy for a teacher to observe and help the children as they work. The teacher can ask questions to determine how the child is thinking.

Lesson Plans

Your goal is to develop an involved, progressive learning environment to challenge and motivate each child at his or her own individual level of development. Math skills are not introduced until the third week of school.

Plan how you are going to introduce the papers and materials. When manipulative materials are presented for the first time, demonstrate and take time to explain how to remove the pieces carefully. "In order not to chip the pieces of pattern blocks, they cannot be dumped out on the table." Show the class the proper way to remove the blocks and how to clean up slowly and carefully. Be certain that enough materials are available for each group. Three sets of pattern blocks are needed for one area of six children, one set for each two people to share. Borrow extra sets from another teacher or from your school library. The children need to know that the borrowed sets must be kept separately.

Another learning area could be for dot-to-dot and color-by-number sheets and the third area could contain an easy math game such as Bingo or Veri Tech. Remember, this is a learning program, so two independent activities and one activity with a helper or sixth grade student will leave you free to float around the room and help the children.

Because the math activities come after recess, be certain that these three areas are supplied before recess is over. For example:

1. Bingo games at one area.
2. Fun worksheet papers ready at the next area.
3. Pattern blocks on the shelves.

Testing

Most district/state-adopted math workbooks are accompanied by an entry-level test. When administering the tests, sit in the U-shaped arrangement of desks, noticing the speed and accuracy of each child as they work at the different levels. If you do not know each child's ability, you can conduct this test by having everyone start at the same level. As some children whiz through the test with correct answers, have them complete the next level by performing only half of each test until they come to a level that challenges them. Explain that these tests are to teach you what you will need to teach them. As soon as the tests become too difficult, they are to stop. Maintain a supply of entry-level tests for all children at each grade level. Keep a confidential class list in a file and mark next to each name which tests are given and passed.

Often the testing will take more than one day. Those who have completed their tests up to the point where the next level is too difficult will enjoy a dot-to-dot or an easy worksheet while waiting for others to finish their tests.

When all of the children are tested, you can chart each child's level as shown in Figure 10.1. Keep the chart confidential, for only you and your aide's information to use in providing appropriate workbooks.

Figure 10.1

RESULTS OF ENTRY-LEVEL TESTS FOR MATH WORKBOOKS

	LEVEL	CONCEPT
Abner Park	7.1	add to 20
Abigail Lock	7.1	add to 20
Bret Hayes	8.4	2 digits + 2 digits
Brice Lee	2.2	add to 10
Calvin Brown	7.3	add to 30
Cara Smith	1.3	before addition
Candace Miller	1.2	before addition
Casey Watts	1.3	before addition
Dale Hall	8.2	3 digit addition
Dan Gans	2.3	add to 10

Preparing Math Workbooks

If a child can complete all of the tests up to level 7, for example, remove all of the pages up to level 6 from his math workbook, allowing him to review the material just before the level he completed successfully. It is essential to review at the first of the year, when school is so new to children, and they are returning from a long summer recess. Beginning in an area that is familiar to them gives them self-confidence.

Children grouped around a U-shaped table with the teacher in the middle can work well when they are computing a page in their math book. As problems arise, the teacher is there immediately to explain or, if needed, to teach the concept the child doesn't understand. You will find that the best teachable moment is when they are confused or need help. However, you must be ready to teach how to tell time, linear measurement, regrouping, and many other concepts each day because they are all at different levels. Even within one grade, abilities vary as widely as they do in reading. The blackboard, plenty of paper, a clock, counters, rulers, and other materials should all be easily accessible to assist you in teaching. As students move to the next group they put their math books in their cubbies and completed papers in the basket.

Post-test the children after they complete a level in their math book. For those who do not know the concept they have just completed, additional worksheets and instructions at the same level are needed.

Skill Groups

Use the results of the district test given in the fall to help determine the math skills you need to teach the children. Put these results in the same type of stamp collector's book chart described previously for reading in Chapter 8.

Now you can form math skill groups. Still using three groups of math activities, you can list on the board the names of the children who will come to the homogeneous math skills group from the various groups. They will know by your explanation and seeing their name on the board, that they are to leave their activity at the appointed time when you gather them at a table to learn a skill.

So that the children in the skill groups will not miss other subjects or a new lesson, conduct the math skill group once every other week.

Individual Math Worksheets and/or Copy Masters

Buy booklets containing open-ended, fun, and interesting work pages, and arrange them in levels from easy to hard. Look for interesting, creative books that make children think, not just fill in the blanks. Arrange the workbook/copy master books at the different levels—easy, middle, hard—during the summer when you have more time.

To save you from duplicating the pages already printed, a good tracking system is to staple a paper in the front of the copy master book. On this paper note the number of pages reproduced, the page numbers, and the date. This helps keep track of which page was given to the class when. The page numbers tell which group it was run off for. Pages at the beginning of the book would be for easy work; middle and harder work at the end.

Number of Pages Printed	Pages	Date
20	1-20	9/6
19	21-40	11/20
12	45-57	11/30

Put seven or more pages into packets and number them. Keep the numbered packets in a file box that fits on a shelf labeled Math Papers. Make a class list with the children's names on it to indicate who has each packet. For example, Conrad has #1 pages 1 to 7 and Barry, #5 pages 32 to 39. When they complete their packet, put the number of the next packet given to them on the class list (see Figure 10.2).

Figure 10.2 Math Packets

NAME	10/3	10/10	10/17	10/25
Abel Perry	3	–	–	5
Agnes Laurence				
Barry Howe	5	6	7	
Bernice Lee	5	6	7	
Calvin Bain	1			2
Charlotte Smith	3	4		5
Clara Myer	3	4	5	6
Conrad Webb	1			2
Dale Hass	1			2
Daryl Gans	5	6	7	9
Floyd Caine	1			2

If a child moves rapidly ahead, it is easy to note that he has received many numbers of packets with a quick glance at the class list. You can quickly observe that the work might be too easy. The children with many numbers by their name are sprinting way ahead and may need more challenging work.

The children need instructions before they receive the worksheet packets. Have a basket, folders, papers, and whatever else you need in the rug area to illustrate and explain before they are dismissed to their areas.

Check for understanding by asking "What do you do if you need help? Right. Raise your hand and the helper at the area will help you." "What do you do when the bell rings for the next area? Right. Put your packet in your cubby."

Give the teacher's aide the packets selected for each child. The aide will explain how to complete their packets again. Before the children start, each child should write his name on each page in the packet. When he finishes a page, he should tear off the completed page and place the paper in the finished-paper basket. If a child still has papers to complete in his packet when the bell rings, the packet is put in his cubby.

If you do not have an aide, enlist a sixth-grade helper or volunteer to quietly answer questions, but stress that the child's work should not be done for them. If a child does not understand what to do, the sixth-grade helper or volunteer explains, being careful not to give the answers. Make sure they understand that the child they are helping is there to learn and that the child will not learn for himself if someone else gives all the answers to him. You might say, "We are all thinkers, and it is more fun to discover that you can think than it is to have someone else do your work."

All the children who need practice learning to compute addition to 10 are given a packet of seven worksheets. Start with very simple fun sheets (such as the Frank Schaffer worksheets containing secret messages) and progress to more difficult tasks. Move the child to the next packet of skills when she has successfully learned and performed the skill. If she needs further practice, give her a packet from another workbook.

To be prepared, put new packets in colored folders for that group before the math period. Keep these colored folders and the math packet class list in a file. Have the file ready near the table before school starts.

If possible, try to correct papers and explain the correction before the children move to the next area. This makes for more immediate help and understanding for the children. If this is not possible, file the papers that need corrections in the colored folder for that group for correction on Friday or the next day. The children may be given the papers to correct with the help of the aide next time they are in the Math Area and before going on to the next page in their packets.

Some of the pages require more time to complete. Some of the children will take longer to think and will work more slowly. Completing packets and getting new ones seems to create enthusiasm and strengthen self-motivation. The children will soon be working on their different pages for their own interests and not to compete.

When you are confident that the math groups are functioning smoothly, you can introduce science, art, health, and social studies two days a week, as one or two groups.

INDIVIDUAL SPELLING WORDS

Spelling words should be given only to children who are reading; this could be a few first graders and almost all second graders. If you have a combination first/second grade class, take time during the small afternoon reading skill group from 2:10 to 3:10 p.m. to have fifteen or twenty minutes for spelling. The children in that group are usually all on the same level in their reading skills.

Most spelling workbooks are too difficult for young children. If the workbooks are not self-directed, the children have difficulty trying to figure out what is wanted. Often the pages are mostly fill-in-the-blank.

Here are two methods to teach spelling that work well. One is to use the words in their alphabet book. These are the words they have used for their written stories—their own personal words. Many children, when told to choose five words from their alphabet book, will become excited and exclaim, "I know this word, I used it in the story I wrote last week." When they choose these words, they are instructed to stamp the date next to the word. Have enough date stamps handy for each child. (Date stamps can be purchased in a stationery store.) Thus the children keep track of the words they have chosen.

The children are given lined spelling paper. As they choose each word, they write that word on the paper.

With the second method, the children learn to spell words they are reading and this proved to be the most successful method for me. Give the children a booklet of words they are learning in their skill groups. (See Figure 10.3.) If they are reading at the short-vowel pre-primer level, they are given a list of words containing short vowels for their spelling words. The list changes as the child progresses to the next skill. Prepare booklets containing lists of words for each skill at the beginning of the school year.

Figure 10.3

	Date Chosen	Date Spelled Correctly
mat		
bat		
fat		
pat		
rat		
cat		
sat		
hat		
Nat		
mad		
bad		
fad		
pad		
sad		
had		

If they are in the skill group that is learning irregular words, they are given a list of irregular words. (See Box 10.1.)

When introducing spelling, explain the process step by step and check for understanding.

Step One: When you receive your Spelling Booklet you can glance through the booklet and choose five words you wish to spell.

Step Two: As you choose your words date stamp in the column Date Chosen next to the word you choose, until you have date stamped five words.

Step Three: Now take the paper titled Spelling and follow the instructions which are:

    1. Write each word five times on scrap paper.

    2. Say the word as you write it.

    3. Spell the word as you write it.

Step Four: Next take the paper titled Words I Need to Study and copy the five words onto the Words I Need to Study paper.

Step Five: After you have studied your words, give the spelling paper to the aide. The aide will put your paper into a colored folder for your group.

Step Six: Put your Spelling Booklet in your cubby along with your list of words on the Words I Need to Study paper. Take the Words I Need to Study paper home for homework.

On the following day, the day of the spelling test, the children can write their name on a blank paper and number it from 1 to 5. Have the spelling paper with the words they have chosen from the previous day written on it. Sort the papers according to how the children are seated at the table for that group. Then proceed around the table, giving each of the seven children his own word from each spelling paper.

First, pronounce the word, then say the word in a sentence. Then pronounce the word again. When all of the individual words have been given to each child, gather the papers and check for correct spelling.

While you are correcting the papers, tell the children to select five more new words and date stamp in the column Date Chosen next to each word. They then copy the word from their booklet onto their spelling paper.

As you correct each paper explain it to the child. If she misspelled a word, the word is entered into the teacher's notebook for that group, and she does not date stamp this word in her book under Date Spelled Correctly. The word is put onto her new spelling paper by the aide along with the five new words she has chosen. Thus, the child's next spelling paper will have five new words, plus her misspelled words.

Compare the correct spelling with the way the child spelled the word. This could be a teachable moment to focus on reversals, word families, or a new skill.

Box 10.1

WORDS WITH IRREGULAR SPELLING AND PRONUNCIATION

Above across again against aisle already another answer anxious any, Bear beautiful beauty because been behind believe bind both bough bread break bright brought build bury busy buy, Calf captain caught chief child clothes colt coming cough could couple cousin cruel curve, Dead deaf debt desire do does done don't double doubt dove dozen, Early earn eight enough eye eyes, Father fence field fight find folks four freight friend frown, Garage get ghost give gives gloves gone great guard guess guest guide, Have head heart heaven heavy here high , Idea Indian instead isle, Key kind knee knew knife know, Language laugh laughed leather library light lion live lived love, Machine many might mild million mind minute mischief mother move Mr. Mrs. Ms., Neighbor neither night none, Ocean of office often oh once onion only other ought, Patient piece pretty pull purpose push put quiet, Ranger ready really right rough, Said says school science scissors shoe should sign snow soften solder soldier some someone something sometime son soul special spread square steak straight sure sword, Their there they though thought to together ton tongue too two touch, Use usual, Vein very view, Was wash weather weight were where who whom wild wind wolf woman women won would wrong, You young your

---

SCIENCE, SOCIAL STUDIES, HEALTH, ART, PHYSICAL EDUCATION, MUSIC

When you are confident that the math groups are functioning smoothly you can introduce social studies, science, health, and art. I found the children became too scattered if all of these subjects were given at the beginning of the school year. The preparation for other subjects in your curriculum should also be started before school begins. Become familiar with the course of study for your district, the adopted textbooks, and teacher's manuals. You will find that quite often these subjects overlap. Sort the materials you have gathered for each subject, supplementing your materials when necessary.

By categorizing materials by subject, you will have worksheets, copy masters, and related materials all in one section, eliminating the time-consuming task of having to search through all your materials for each subject. This will save time on your part and possible boredom for the children, because you will not be teaching the same concept more than once.

This, of course, means that each textbook cannot always be followed in sequence. Most books are written in units, however, and you can take the third unit of one subject, for example, and teach it with the first unit of another, putting all of the same ideas together.

Teaching Thematic Units

The thematic approach to teaching uses a central theme such as the study of the family. The other subjects in the curriculum are incorporated into this one theme. The many subjects used can be cooking, writing, poetry, science, art, drama, social studies, math, circle meetings, health, and physical education.

This approach is an excellent way to develop the expansion of the subject. It gives the children an in-depth study of the subject and knowledge that it applies to all areas of their learning. When the unit is complete the children have a fuller understanding and knowledge of many subjects.

For example, a student teacher of mine presented a thematic unit in science, writing, art, physical education, health, and social studies about the body. He labeled each bone on a human skeleton. Each child was given a label from the skeleton to learn. He had a physical therapist visit the class to talk about exercising their muscles. He taught them aerobic exercises during physical education. The children discussed healthy ways of caring for their bodies and wrote down what they do to take care of themselves for writing. They studied the cells of a lung damaged from cigarette smoke under a microscope for science. They drew healthy lung cells for science and art. The children studied and then drew an actual cow's heart.

For such projects, you must be flexible. We found it necessary to use all three areas during the math time for the unit about the body and forgo math until the next day. One group studied the heart and drew it, one group looked at the cells under the microscope and drew them, another group drew what they do to exercise their muscles.

If a discussion is needed before the children go to their groups, the fifteen to twenty minutes after recess is the best time for this to take place.

Another student teacher of mine thematically integrated the study of Native Americans in the following manner:

Art: The children drew Native American designs.

Social Studies: We studied how Native Americans lived and made a field trip to visit a Native American smokehouse. While in the smokehouse, the children listened to a Native American story.

Reading: We read a story written in Native American sign language.

Writing: The children wrote an imaginary story about what it would be like if they were Native Americans.

Music: We learned a Native American chant.

Math: We played a Native American game using pebbles.

Physical Education: We learned Native American dances.

SUMMARY

Time, preparation, and organization are necessary in order to form individual programs for other subjects, after the reading program is functioning smoothly. Only individualize one subject per year, and don't proceed to another until you are comfortable with the process. Have a variety of manipulative materials available so that the children can begin to learn without feeling threatened. When individual children are ready for more abstract challenges, have packets of worksheets ready for them to work on. The math program, like reading, can offer skills groups for children who need to learn specific skills. Be on the lookout for new and interesting ideas to teach children about social science, science, health, art, and music. Listen to the children's ideas and let them follow their interests; consider individual or group projects on a subject encompassing several subject areas. Some of the workbooks I used came from the following publishers: Creative Teaching Press, Education Insights, Frank Schaffer, Good Apple, Incentive Publications.

INDEPENDENT ACTIVITIES FOR MATH, SCIENCE, AND ART

The independent activities listed below are best used during the math, science, and art periods, because they relate to math and tend to be noisy.

- Pattern blocks (one half of a set for each child and worksheets)
- Discovery blocks and task cards
- Cuisenaire blocks and task cards
- Geo Boards and task cards
- Tangrams and task cards
- Balances and task cards
- Mirror cards and task cards
- Completing designs and patterns to answer problems for Veri Tech
- Observing a science project, model or experiment and drawing their observation
- Practicing origami by following the diagrams in a book
- Unifix mathematic activities
- Geo blocks
- Base ten blocks
- Attribute logic blocks, tiles, and job cards
- Chip trading, for learning place value

SOURCES OF MATERIAL FOR INDEPENDENT ACTIVITIES

The following catalogs carry useful supplies for independent activities in math, science, and art.

Cuisenaire *Materials for Learning Mathematics and Science*
Cuisenaire Company of America
P.O. Box 5026
White Plains, New York 10602-5020

Delta Education *Hands-On Math Catalog*
P.O. Box 950
Hudson, New Hampshire 03051

Creative Publications
Order Department
5040 West 111th Street
Oak Lawn, Illinois 60453

Mathematical Manipulatives
Nienhuis Montessori U.S.A.
320 Pioneer Way
Mountain View, California 94041

The following catalog contains material for teaching with themes and grade level paperback books:

Scholastic Inc.
Instructor
P.O. Box 53896
Boulder, Colorado 80322-3896

Catalogs containing software are:

Videodiscs and C.D. Rom
Z teck Co.
P.O. Box 1055
Louisville, Kentucky 40201-1055

Computer Software for Apple II & IIe, IIc, IIgs and Macintosh
National School Products
101 East Broadway
Maryville, Tennessee 37801-2498

Midwest Products *Critical Thinking Press and Software*
P.O. Box 448
Pacific Grove, California 93950

Softwarehouse
P.O. Box 9204
Fargo, North Dakota 58106

The company below carries individual independent language development tasks:

Developmental Learning Materials
D.L.M.
P.O. Box 4000
One D.L.M. Park
Allen, Texas 75002

Veri Tech can be ordered at:

E.T.A.
Educational Teaching Aids
657 Oak Grove
Menlo Park, California 94025

Chapter
11

Working with Parents

Parents who wish to train up their children in the way they should go, must go in the way in which they would have their children go.

—Thomas C. Haliburton,
Nova Scotian humorist (1796–1865)

Parents are an important part of their children's education, and from the first day when they bring their children into class, you enter into a relationship with them. Parent/teacher conferences are regularly scheduled events, but sometimes you need to seek out a parent when there are issues that need to be discussed between conferences. Other times, parents may come to you seeking advice on how to supplement their child's education at home, or on dealing with certain problems their child is having. This chapter addresses some of the situations you might experience with the parents of your students, and offers some insights on handling them. Since I am a parent as well as a teacher, I've tried to present a well-rounded picture.

PARENT/TEACHER CONFERENCES

The First Conference

To listen well is as powerful a means of influence
as to talk well, and is as essential to all true conversation.

—Chinese proverb

Most teachers wait until November before they begin holding parent/ teacher conferences, but I always preferred to meet with each parent as soon as possible. At this time test results are not complete and the conference is more of a receiving, listening time for you, with a few questions directed toward learning more about the child. Ask about the child's likes and dislikes, friends and siblings. Ask, "What is your child's favorite activity?" "Does he have a room of his own?" "What do you expect for your child in school?" Ask questions only to keep the conference moving, and listen carefully to the answers. You will learn much about the child—her interests, background, potential problems—that you'll find helpful in the classroom.

The Second Conference in October/November

Parents need to know their child's progress in school as well as his relation to his grade level, within the school and nationwide. At least three conferences a year are necessary to keep parents informed and to develop the relationship between home and school. Some school districts designate more than three conference periods for the school year. Before a conference with parents, the teacher needs to prepare a folder for each child that contains:

- the results of the tests given in September
- the book the child is reading (be ready to explain the grade level of the book)
- the child's math book
- the child's social studies book
- the child's English book
- notes on the child's interests in reading
- a self-evaluation sheet from the child stating how he thinks he is performing in school
- the child's spelling level in the O.A.T. test or spelling book

- records of your weekly reading conferences with the child (help explain the progression from the first book read to the current one)
- samples of the child's various assignments (the most dramatic change occurs between the task given on the first day of school and the current task)
- the child's ongoing test results of reading and math skills
- any other books used by your district at the child's grade level

Parents have a right to know all of their child's test results, including their child's Intelligence Quotient, and the grade placement in math and reading that the test results suggest. Parents also need to be informed that standardized tests are not necessarily accurate. Other factors must be taken into consideration, including how the child was feeling the day of the test, the child's attitude towards tests, and the child's history with tests. If the teacher presents a balanced picture of test results tempered by a knowledge of the child as an individual, parents will leave the conference with a satisfied feeling that they know something about their child's capabilities.

Keep in mind that it is impossible to discuss every aspect of the child's school day and academic work within the time allotted for a parent conference. You must decide what is most important to discuss during each conference. If the test results were received recently, then parents will want to know the meaning of these results. Some school districts provide a duplicate of the child's test results for the parent to take home. You can explain the results and their meaning during the conference. You might find it necessary to delay the details of their child's work until the next conference in January or March, and settle for a summary at this time.

Steps Toward a Parent Conference

- Send a conference calendar home with each child to enable scheduling of your conferences (see Figure 11.1).
- Answer the parents' response promptly with a note telling them of their assigned time accompanied by an information sheet for them to complete and bring to the conference (see Figure 11.2).
- Decide if you wish to have the child attend the conference.
- If the child is not attending the conference, talk to the child before the conference and tell him you are going to meet with his parents. Ask, "What shall I say?"

Figure 11.1

THE PARENT CONFERENCE NOTE

Dear Parents,

I will be starting my conferences on Tuesday, September 15th. Please mark on the calendar below the best dates and times for you to conference with me and return the calendar tomorrow. This is only tentative, and I will confirm your appointment by another note.

	Tues. 15	Wed. 16	Thurs. 17	Fri. 18	Tues. 22	Wed. 23	Thurs. 24	Fri. 25
September								
2:20 2:40								
2:40 3:00								
3:00 3:20								
3:20 3:40								

☐ I do not wish a conference.

☐ I am able to come at any time.

☐ I would like a phone conference.

Signed _____

Parent of _____

Phone _____

Figure 11.2

CONFERENCE INFORMATION

1. Student's name: _____
   Address: _____
   Birthdate: _____
   Phone: _____
2. Names and ages of siblings: _____
3. Names of any other people living in your home: _____
4. Do you speak another language than English at home? (Circle: YES NO)
   If yes, which language? _____
5. Is there anything I should know about your child? _____
   _____
6. What does your child really like to do at home? _____
   _____
7. What pleases you most about your child' development? _____
   _____
8. What concerns you most about your child's development? _____
   _____
9. Does your child have any health needs or problems (allergies, etc.)?
   _____
10. How do you see your child in relation to others? _____
    _____
11. What are your expectations for your child in school this year?
    _____
12. What responsibilities does your child have at home? _____

For parents of kindergartners, add the following questions:
13. Did your child attend pre-school? (Circle: YES NO)
    If yes, which school? _____
14. Does your child have a dominant hand preference? (Circle: YES NO)
    If yes, which? _____

◆ Know and understand everything you can about the child. Samples of work, test results, absences, social adjustment, health, work habits, books the child is reading, and interests are all relevant. Read the child's cumulative record to learn previous test scores, special problems with vision, illness, or psychological issues.

I usually read only the health record and not the accumulated record before the first conference in September when parents would tell me about their child's special needs. If necessary, consult the nurse, social worker, principal, or counselor when the situation on the records needs clarifying.

Keep the classroom neat and attractive, displaying on the bulletin board examples of what the class is learning. Show the children's work in plentiful supply.

The Day of the Conference

Put a sign on your door that says, "Please Do Not Disturb—Conference in Session." Tidy up the room. Have the room well ventilated. Have the child's folder and books next to the chair where you will sit. Have paper and pencil for notes. Allow time to sit down, take a deep breath, and see yourself relaxed during the conference.

Starting the Conference

Greet the parent in a relaxed, friendly manner. Sit next to or opposite the parent in the same size chair; do not meet the parents from behind a desk. Be accessible. Take notes during the conference to help you follow through on an agreement or plan and to show you are listening. Clarify what their understanding of the purpose of the conference is. Outline your goals for the conference.

During the Conference Be Prepared To

◆ Discuss the curriculum and the school district's course of study.

◆ Discuss your goals and philosophy of teaching.

◆ Discuss how their child will be graded on the next report card.

◆ Avoid excessive use of educational jargon. If parents do not understand these terms this will close the communication. Keep the discussion meaningful to the parent and listen carefully.

Conferring with Parents about Report Cards

Report cards should allow for the success of the child. A card with all failures not only signals to the child that he is a failure but also reflects poorly upon the teacher. It says the teacher has not been able to develop a situation for this child to experience some success.

Jeannette Veatch discusses a study by Norman Chansky of teacher's personalities connected with the type of reporting systems they prefer.[1] If a teacher had high self-esteem, was not anxious or apprehensive, was mentally alert, and had a wide range of interests, she chose report cards that measured the "complete child" rather than narrow single-symbol reports. Think about this as you decide upon the grading of the children in your class and your explanation to the parent.

Topics to Discuss

If you are reporting on:

Comprehension Skills. Discuss the types of books the child chooses, such as sports, the basal readers, animals, etc. Be specific about the child's skills. From these books he is able to read and get the moral of the story. He can read between the lines and understand the main idea.

Other points to touch upon:

Personal Adjustment. Let the parents know how the child interacts with his classmates and handles difficult situations; this points to his level of adjustment to the class and himself.

Mechanical Skills. Discuss the reading skill the child is learning and show the parent the child's progress on tests. Indicate specific skills the child has mastered and ones he needs to work on. Then you can ask the parent to help the child with skills such as the use of a dictionary or index. Mechanical skills tests might indicate whether the child needs to broaden his vocabulary, whether he can read carefully for details without losing sight of the story, whether he has learned how to compute two-column addition or needs to learn how to carry a number to the next column when the answer is more than nine.

Class Participation. Talk about the child's performance during class discussions. Note the number of times each week he has volunteered to speak in the Meeting Area. If the child needs help in this area, suggest that the child read to younger siblings or join a theater group. Refer parents to a good book on this subject (see the list at the end of the chapter).

Child Participation

Consider including the child in the parent conference because:

- She will a gain a sense of personal power.
- She can help develop plans for her educational and personal progress.
- The child can hear first hand what is said about her strengths, and parent or teacher concerns.
- You can observe how the child relates to her parent.
- You can ask for the child's opinion.

Gordon's list of advantages of a child attending the parent conference[2] are summarized below.

- Gives the child the power of participating in the decisions that involve him.
- Increases the child's motivation to cooperate.
- Decreases the chances of later misunderstanding by letting the child hear firsthand.
- Allows the child to feel less anxious and more secure.
- Gives all participants a feeling of education as a cooperative process.

Elenya Stephan has the following excellent advice regarding the presence of children at the conference.

> Other arrangements should be made for children in the family who are not the focus of the conference. Having a sibling at a parent/teacher conference makes information too readily available for youngsters to use in the process of normal sibling competition. Information so gathered may function to reduce the self-esteem of the one who doesn't quite compete on the level of the other, and be just as damaging on the other side of the coin, most commonly manifested in the practice of bragging!…
>
> Should you desire the child's presence, don't feel burdened with feeling you must constantly gear your conversation to fit the child's vocabulary or level of sophistication. A good part of your conversation should be understood by the child, of course, but the youngster will be experiencing your tone of voice along with other non-verbal clues, and when he experiences your goodwill, actual comprehension of all the words you choose will become less important.

In some cases, a conference has begun and parent or classroom teacher find they would like to discuss an area without the youngster's presence. Some feel quite comfortable openly asking the child to leave to play while they discuss some things they'd feel more comfortable discussing alone. However, let me offer some food for thought on this.

The child's fantasies about what you might be talking about may be more threatening than his experience of actually being there to hear it....

Children are more often than not, if not always, aware of the major issues in their lives from which the adults around them, often with good intentions, want to protect them. There is valuable potential release for the child in openly acknowledging these areas of difficulty—areas of which they have long been aware. This includes family relationship patterns, peer relationship patterns, difficult-to-discuss areas of ability level, as well as the less-difficult-to-discuss areas of ability and achievement discrepancies. Youngsters are sometimes surprised to find we know as much.[3]

During the Body of the Conference

- ◆ Allow the parents to feel nervous; think about how you would feel in their place.

- ◆ Be empathetic with their feelings.

- ◆ Discuss the positive traits of their child.

- ◆ Question in a relaxed, nonlinear fashion to make the conference less tense.

- ◆ Tune into concerns the parents have about their child in school.

- ◆ Find out what the child does and how he behaves at home.

- ◆ Ask about the child's interests and hobbies.

- ◆ Find out how discipline and love are carried out by each parent.

- ◆ Ask about the child's responsibilities at home.

- ◆ Give the parents time to ask questions.

Upon Concluding the Conference

- ◆ Define areas where you can be supportive or complementary to the parent and child.

- ◆ Decide if future contact is necessary and when will it be.

- ◆ If necessary, agree with the parent on a plan of action that can be carried out both at school and at home.

 ◆ End the conference with a statement of encouragement and reassurance.

Things to Avoid

 ◆ Dwelling on child's inadequacies.

 ◆ Comparing the child to his classmates or to the class as a whole.

 ◆ Discussing other teachers, parents, or students.

 ◆ Answering questions that involve administrative decisions.

 ◆ Arguing with a parent.

 ◆ Being defensive.

 ◆ Assuming a parent wants advice.

You can learn a great deal from your conferences with parents, but they can also be uncomfortable, especially for new teachers. To help ensure that your conferences go smoothly, I strongly recommend that you read the thought-provoking excerpt from Elenya Stephan's book, *Stir Until Clear*, at the end of this chapter.

OTHER WAYS TO MEET WITH PARENTS

Schools institute parent/teacher conferences as a matter of course, because it's important to have communication with parents. There are many other ways to meet with parents, though, and many ways to gather parents together.

Back-to-School Night

Back-to-School night occurs soon after school starts, either as a whole-school activity or in individual classrooms. This is your opportunity to speak to the parents about the class, the curriculum for the school year, the school district's course of study, your goals, your hopes for their children, and your expectations about homework. I found that having parents actually be in their child's color group and move quickly from area to area in simulation of, say, the language arts period gave them a good understanding of my program. You can use the class schedule for the next day thus giving the parents the opportunity to discuss the schedule with their children. Give the parents your phone number and let them know that you are available to talk with them one-to-one. I also invited parents to sign up to participate in class activities in whatever way they could, whether as an aide, a resource parent, or a driver for field trips. (See Parent Volunteers below.)

Parent Gatherings

Here are a few opportunities that a teacher, a school, or a P.T.A club can create for parents to come in contact with each other and the rest of the school community.

Family Picnic. The first weekend after school started I would hold a picnic at the local park, having each family bring their own supper so that there was no extra preparation involved. This is an opportunity for the parents to meet one another. This is also a chance for you to meet your students' sisters, brothers, and other family members. In your invitation to the parents encourage them to schedule a conference with you as soon as they can to set the tone of the picnic as a social event and not a place to discuss their concerns about their child.

P.T.A. Meetings/Parents Clubs. These are regularly scheduled meetings of the parents of children attending a school, at which the teachers are represented. Lectures and discussions may be given on a variety of topics, from "Family Math" to "Self-Esteem."

Class Lunch. Invite the parents to a luncheon the children have prepared for them.

Parent Education/Teachers' Display Night. Each teacher can bring a few good skill-builders and other materials to the cafeteria area for the parents to view. Each teacher has a special display table and is there to explain the exhibit and answer questions. Coffee or snacks might be served.

Potluck Dinner. Gatherings can be held for parents of one or two classrooms. Use two rooms in either case, one to baby-sit children and one for parents to converse. Encourage parents to bring ethnic dishes.

Discovery Day. The whole school participates in a fair. Parents set up activity areas (kite-making, baker's dough, pottery, art) and children sign up to go to the various activities.

Coffee Klatsch. The principal meets informally with parents one morning each month to communicate about school-related concerns. A sitter is available for pre-school children.

Play Day. Competitive games for children at all levels. Parents bring a picnic lunch for this end-of-the-year activity.

Single Parents Club. Single parents can schedule one evening a month for meetings with lectures, workshops, or potluck dinners.

Color-Code Night. At a night meeting of parents, run a learning area in the fashion of your classroom. Parents are color-coded and move according to a schedule.

P.R. WITH PARENTS

Building a positive public relationship with parents will pay off, when you find parents becoming relaxed about seeing you because they know they are accepted. Weekly newsletters from teachers or children to parents help keep the parents informed. Tell them what's happening, what the class needs, and thank parents who have helped. Some other ideas to build this relationship are:

- Invite parents in to discuss their experiences with the class

- Use parents as classroom aides (be sure to train them!)

- Don't wait for a problem to communicate with parents—phone them with *positive* reports about their child

- Write informal notes about what the class is doing and their child's progress

- Enlist their help with parties, projects, fairs (see following section on volunteers)

- Invite a few parents and their children to have lunch with you

- Set up a workshop to have parents use class materials

- Create a parents' library in the classroom with books on parenting and teaching

- Give out your home phone number and encourage parents to call

- Inform parents of community resources for parents and children

- Make use of the ethnic diversity of parents with special celebrations or talks given by parents

- Write positive notes on children's papers for parents' information

- Ask parents to build or make something for the class or playground

- Send children birthday cards in the mail

- Have birthday celebrations in school, and ask the parents to provide cupcakes

- Send a welcome card to each child before school starts

- Have a Mother's Day program

- Keep a children's recipe book

- Hold a pancake breakfast for parents and children

◆ Involve parents in fund-raising drives

◆ Host group picnics with family participation

PARENT VOLUNTEERS

Parents can help out in a myriad of ways. They can bring flowers for opening day, organize parties or special events; they can supply food for cooking class, snack time, or lunch; they can help during P.E. by teaching tennis or working on playground skills (throwing or catching a ball, for example). They can help paint, refinish, or make whatever is needed in the classroom. Parents—or other adult family members—can come speak to your class about interesting things they do or about a topic you are studying.

Solicit volunteers at Back–to–School night (see Figure 11.3) with a sign up sheet and encourage parents to participate by sending home a letter that invites them to get involved (see Figure 11.4).

Volunteer Handbook

Supply a handbook to the volunteers in your classroom. Include a plan of the school physical plant, and class and school rules. Provide a code of ethics such as the one that follows.

Box 11.1

VOLUNTEER CODE OF ETHICS

Volunteers agree that they have a responsibility to be present when promised or provide a knowledgeable substitute.

Volunteers agree that concerns they may have about what is taking place in the classroom should be discussed privately with the teacher.

Volunteers agree that the achievements of children are to be valued and their rights respected, and that any personal information about them is CONFIDENTIAL.

Volunteers agree that any authority they are given is at the discretion of the teacher or the staff member who is directly responsible for the instruction, safety, and discipline of the students.

Volunteers agree that the regulations and procedures of the school should be followed at all times.

Figure 11.3

VOLUNTEER SIGN-UP SHEET

Parent Coordinator

_____

Room Parent _____
P.T.A. Rep_____
Cooking Coordinator_____
Typist for Weekly Newsletter_____
Additional Typing_____
Office Assistant_____
Library Assistant _____
Art Docent_____
Projection Preparation   1._____   2._____
Badge Preparation   1._____   2._____
Sewing Projects   1._____   2._____
Art Preparation   1._____   2._____
Willing to Help Any Way   1._____   2._____
3._____   4._____   5._____

Playground Beautification Committee
1._____ 2._____ 3._____ 4._____
5._____ 6._____ 7._____ 8._____

Party Helpers

Halloween
1._____ 2._____ 3._____ 4._____

Christmas/Chanukah
1._____ 2._____ 3._____ 4._____

Valentine's Day
1._____ 2._____ 3._____ 4._____

Easter
1._____ 2._____ 3._____ 4._____

Drivers and Chaperones for Field Trips
1._____ 2._____ 3._____ 4._____

Figure 11.4

Dear Parents,

In the coming school year, we could use help from you particularly during field trips and for special events. If you can help with any of the following, please check the appropriate box and return this note.

Volunteers for field trips

1. Morning trips   ☐

2. All day trips   ☐

3. Afternoon trips   ☐

4. Can drive a car   ☐

5. I would be willing to pay for a chartered bus (cost about $5.00 each). ☐

6. I would be willing to visit the class to talk about science, nature, a special collection of mine, hobbies, health, ceramics, or_____

    _____

    _____.

7. Suggestions for an interesting place or activity for a field trip:

    _____.

8. Could the class visit your workplace? Where do you work? _____

    _____

    _____.

9. I would be willing to be called for miscellaneous help during the year.

    Name:_____.

    Phone:_____.

Thank you for your interest.

Classroom Aides

Parents can be most helpful as classroom aides. What kinds of things do you look for in a parent who would like to be an aide? First of all, you want your biggest supporters in the classroom, parents who really appreciate you and your methods. Second, look for a parent who has time to volunteer, who doesn't work during the day, who has a natural interest in school. Finally, look for a parent who is relaxed and patient with children, who the children like and relate to.

WORKING TOGETHER WITH PARENTS
When to Go to Parents

There are certain things you should contact parents about, and certain things you should go directly to the principal or counselor about. If a child has behavior problems that require the involvement of parents, contact them in a spirit of cooperation and with the attitude that a solution is possible. Also contact parents and the school nurse about physical problems you don't understand. For example, Terry, while reading aloud to me, seemed to suddenly go blank and stare. When he did it more than once, I became concerned and contacted the nurse and his parents. They discovered he had epilepsy, which they had not been aware of. If a child is frowning or squinting a great deal, you might consult the school nurse about having his eyes tested. A speech therapist will be responsible for contacting the parents about speech problems.

If a child suddenly lags behind, you may want to get in touch with the parents. Tell them what you notice, but do not pry, wait for the parent to volunteer information they think you should know.

Sometimes, when a child is lagging behind in schoolwork and you can't find a reason for this, a parent needs you as an advocate to obtain help for their child. You need to take the lead and advise the parent of the services available to test the child and render expert opinions. The teacher is responsible for following through and obtaining school services with the parent's permission. Get to know the school counselor who can help you build your awareness of the resources in the community available to parents and families.

Do not go directly to parents if you suspect a case of child abuse or drug or alcohol abuse. If a child comes to class with suspicious bruises or smelling of marijuana or alcohol, talk to the principal first. If you have any cause to suspect child abuse, you are required by law to report this.

Testing

If a child is not progressing at all in reading and other skills and shows a high level of frustration, the child must be referred for testing by the Special Education Committee, with the parent's permission. Follow the procedure established by your school district to have the child tested and keep on top of it. Parents have experienced bureaucratic nightmares in this area. You are their advocate, and they need your support.

These testers almost always find the reason for a child's slow progress. It can vary from coming to school thinking he can't read, to a more serious learning disability. Gather literature on learning disabilities for parents to borrow.

When Parents Come to You

> *When a man seeks your advice*
> *he generally wants your praise.*
>
> —Philip Dormer Stanhope Chesterfield
> 4th Earl of England (1694–1773)

When parents call for a meeting, this usually worries a new teacher, who assumes something is seriously wrong. This is rarely the case. Questions are usually as benign as "We didn't understand the homework assignment last night," or "The papers seem too hard for Samantha." These are issues that require attention; you will learn a lot from them. No teacher wants to make mistakes, but everyone does, and remember that it's okay. Avoid being defensive. Be understanding and helpful, take parental concerns seriously, and be available to meet with the parent immediately to handle any problem before it enlarges or explodes. Only a few parents are impossible to please.

The mother of one of my students once asked for a conference immediately, and from the urgent tone in her voice I felt I needed to put everything aside and see her. At the conference, she explained that she was to have an operation the next week that could be fatal. She wanted me to be aware of this, and she wanted to be reassured that I would make allowances for her son and help him if she did not survive. I told her that I knew a minister who was interested in giving his time to any of my students who needed him. I also told her that I would understand if her son's schoolwork lagged, that I would not pressure him. The mother did die. I carried out my promise and helped her son through this difficult time. The minister came twice a week to go for walks and talk with this boy. In this case, a timely conference with a parent made a big difference in a child's life.

Parent and teacher working together in the interests of a child is one of the most dynamic ways to solve many problems. It can also be one of the most volatile.

Parents don't always want advice. On some occasions, a parent will ask for an appointment, but the real reason they have come is to criticize. Do not get defensive! Use active listening to get to the bottom of the problem, and stay as impartial as possible. Let them talk about their concern from every aspect, and then put into words their expectations and doubts.

Viewing a parent as nonthreatening helps set the tone of the meeting as relaxed but this is easier said than done. It takes years of experience to build your self confidence and self esteem. A new teacher could experience a nervous, defensive meeting with an angry, dissatisfied parent. If you are concerned about a meeting, take some time to lock your door, sit in a rocker or comfortable chair, and relax. Take a deep breath, close your eyes, and see yourself relaxed with the parent. Say to yourself, "I am confident, with self-esteem I am not defensive or competitive." If you have reason to believe the parent may be abusive or difficult, ask your principal to participate in the conference.

Meeting with a parent who asks for help can be a wonderful give-and-take experience. You both are very interested in helping the child, so with such an open meeting you can both learn a lot just by inquiring as to how they handle situations and how their child reacts. It is essential, however, to keep family information as well as expert opinions confidential. Do not discuss them with anyone else, especially not other faculty members. Confidentiality goes a long way toward building trust with each parent.

Parents often become your advocates, and the longer you know them (which happens more often when you teach a combination classroom) the more trust, warmth, respect, and cooperation you build with them. You can learn how they feel with ease. Nonetheless, even when I feel capable of it, I have turned away from actually giving advice about family problems. I refer parents to the school counselor and have her attend our next conference, or help set up an appointment for parents to meet with her.

The best response when parents ask you for advice is to listen and ask their opinions. Through this questioning by the teacher, the parents put their thoughts into words and usually can answer their own questions and solve their own problems. Active listening is imperative.

How Parents Can Help Their Child Learn

When parents ask how they can help their child learn, the first thought that comes to my mind is always, "Read to him." Read stories and nursery rhymes or books in which a child can follow the words. Read books that challenge a child's imagination, and books that address issues relevant to his life. Include children in family discussions and decisions. Keep a dialog going about current events, morals, and values. Tell jokes. Television can be an asset. After a program a parent can discuss with their child what he saw and heard and his reaction.

I tell them to look at a magazine with their child and find all of the pictures with the same beginning sound. Say the name of the picture with the child. Find other words that begin with that letter. Have the child describe pictures in magazines.

I also suggest that they give their children firsthand experiences at the zoo, planetarium, park, lake, museum, aquarium, and science hall. During these excursions a parent can give a child their full attention and show their own interest in what they see by answering any questions. I tell parents to keep in mind that no question is a dumb question.

My Child Is a Late Bloomer

Parents may come in with specific questions, problems, or concerns. There are many possibilities for concern when raising a child, so your job is to reassure a parent that their child is developing normally if he is, or to seek help for that child if he is not. If there are two children in a family who learn to read at different speeds, parents may become concerned about the slower one. If the slower reader is not way behind in reading (such as a complete grade level), assure them there is no cause for worry. Tell them, "You simply have a late starter, and that's perfectly normal. Children learn at their own rate and should not be pressured to read above their own level. When they do read, they need to enjoy it, and not be compared with superior readers."

Occasionally parents have more specific questions about reading. For example, some children reverse letters and numbers up to the third grade. Then, when they are eight or nine years of age, they reverse less and less. If this reversal continues after the third grade, they need to be tested by a reading specialist.

Reversals can sometimes be indicative of a complete lack of interest, when a child is not even trying to make sense out of what he is reading. This can be related to the experience of reading itself. The newness of the concept of text often restricts children from paying critical attention to the subject of what they are reading.

Counseling

Some parents are concerned about a fear a child has or a sudden change in behavior in their child. If it seems severe, you can refer them to the school guidance counselor, who will know how to deal with severe emotional situations in strict confidence. Remember, the parent expects you to keep the child's problems in confidence. This is not something to discuss openly. The privacy of the principal's office is best when you need to help with such a problem.

Negative Attention

As a teacher, be aware of patterns in your parent/teacher conferences. You might want to suggest to the parents with whom you seem to be having too many conferences about behavior and learning problems that you will agree to have a conference with them only if the child is doing well. You can get caught up in scheduling a parent-teacher conference whenever a child is not doing well in school. This means the child is getting attention. Since all children want attention, those who are not getting much will often engineer circumstances to create a need for the parent/teacher conference, even if it means negative feedback. This is turned around if a child realizes the teacher will contact the parent only when he is doing well (by means of a note or other signal), and the child will learn to seek positive feedback.

When a parent asks how she can help at home when a child is getting negative attention, you might suggest letting bad behavior slide a bit and using positive reinforcement when noticing acceptable behavior, or lend them a book on discipline.

Positive Reinforcement

Suggest that parents try to keep their attitude with their children positive and consistent in what they expect.

"Start noticing when your child does what you would like him to do. For example, thank him for not interrupting you while you were on the telephone. You appreciate that, and to show your appreciation, suggest a game or a story."

"Have a time when your child knows that she will be the only one with you. They are so excited when they tell us in school, 'Saturday I am going fishing with Dad,' or 'Mom and I are going to lunch.'"

"Point out behaviors that impress you. Notice efforts your child makes even if it is not perfect behavior all the time."

Praise

Praise can help a child feel ten feet tall, loved, self-confident, and in control of herself. Strangely enough, praise can also cause a child to feel anxious, dependent, defensive, and manipulated.

How can you help a child feel good about herself? By being aware of your motives. Are you and her parents truly meaning what you say? Are you giving praise genuinely or as a reward? You can create a cycle of conditional praise so that the child will feel manipulated, anxious, and dependent on approval for self-worth. Praise can help a child continue his desired behavior or go out of control because of his anxiety. Watch out for statements like, "That's a good girl," when a job is done right. Try, "That's a good job!" instead. Acknowledge the child's efforts, help, work, or accomplishments. Praise good judgment and character traits. Ways to praise include a smile, hug, or pat on the shoulder when you see a child behave. The mere act of touching conveys the message of your love.

You and her parents can build trust with a child by being sincere and always telling the truth; this can help her feel more self-reliant. Don't, for example, say the doctor won't give her a shot, when he might. Keep your promises. See the end of the chapter for books to suggest to parents.

Handing a parent a book to read after the conclusion of the conference sometimes helps the parent leave with something concrete to refer to. Collect books about discipline, child development, parent-child relationships, families, shy children, and self-esteem.

What Can Parents Give Their Children?

You cannot teach a child to take care of himself unless you will let him try to take care of himself. He will make mistakes, and out of these mistakes will come his wisdom.

—Henry Ward Beechner
American clergyman (1813–1887)

Many parents ask, "What can I give my child?" The answer is interest and acceptance. If a child is listened to and if even his negative feelings are acknowledged and respected, he will feel good about himself. Recognize the child for the individual traits that make him special, not in relation to other children. Tell the child that he is recognized as a person with his own personality, feelings, and needs, and he will value himself. Parents can make a special time for each child, to get to know him, understand his interests, and get involved in them. This kind of positive attention develops a child's sense of self-worth.

Parents need to encourage independence in their child, even if this means letting the child fail. It may be easier for a parent to make the child's bed herself, but if she does this all the time, the child won't learn to make it himself. Although the child may be frustrated at first, if the parents reassure him that he can do it, he will learn.

Parents can support and encourage their child's interests and activities. If a child shows curiosity and determination about something, parents can help him realize his goals to help build self-confidence. Parents should actively support activities such as learning to ride a bike, building models, making roads in a sandbox, playing music or sports, or creating art. Praise the child as he gains skill.

Parents need to let their children know that they love them. Sometimes this may mean a warm hug, but physical affection is hard for some families. A child likes to hear, "I love you." The best show of love of all is the attention and respect that parents can show their children.

SUMMARY

You and the child's parents are allies working together to provide that child with the best possible education. It is important for parents and teachers to work together and to communicate. Be prepared for each parent/teacher conference. Let the parent know how and what their child is doing in school, show them any available test scores, discuss the curriculum, the books their child is using, and any other issues or problems. Most parents will be very cooperative, but special circumstances may arise. Try not to give unsolicited advice, but if a parent comes to you asking for help be ready to use active listening and have referrals for counseling available.

SOURCES

1.   Veatch, Jeannette. 1966. *Reading in the Elementary School.* The Ronald Press: New York.

2.   Gordon, Thomas. 1974. *T.E.T. Teacher Effectiveness Training.* Peter H. Wyden: New York.

3.   Stephan, Elenya. 1982. *Stir Until Clear: A Handbook on the Counseling Relationship in the Schools.* R. and E. Associates: Palo Alto, California.

READING LIST FOR PARENTS

Binkley, Marilyn R. 1988. *Becoming a Nation of Readers, What Parents Can Do.* Heath: Indianapolis.

Condit, Martha Olson. 1976. *Easy to Make, Good to Eat.* Scholastic Book Services: New York.

Gordon, Thomas. 1970. *Parent Effectiveness Training.* Peter H. Wyden: New York.

Ginott, Haim G. 1965. *Between Parent and Child.* Macmillan: New York.

Ginott, Haim G. 1972. *Between Teacher and Child.* Avon Books, New York.

Hart, Louise. 1990. *The Winning Family, Increasing Self-Esteem in Your Children and Yourself.* LifeSkills Press: Oakland, California.

Honig, Bill. 1986. *A Parent's Handbook on California Education.* California State Department of Education: Sacramento.

May, Marrian. 1968. *Sunset Crafts for Children.* Lane Books: Menlo Park, California.

Moore, Eva 1973. *The Cookie Book.* Scholastic Book Services: New York.

Moore, Eva. 1971. *The Lucky Cookbook For Boys and Girls.* Scholastic Book Services: New York.

Neuwirth, Sharlyn. April 3, 1979. "How T.V. Can Help Your Child's Reading." *Family Circle Magazine.*

Patterson, Gerald R. and M. Elizabeth Gullion. 1974. *Living with Children.* Research Press: Champaign, Illinois.

Wood, Paul and Bernard Schwartz. 1977. *How to Get Your Children to Do What You Want Them to Do.* Prentice-Hall: Englewood Cliffs, New Jersey.

Books of Card Games for Recognition of Numbers

Brown, Douglas. 1966. *150 Solitaire Games.* Harper and Row: New York.

Quinn, Vernon. 1933. *50 Card Games for Children.* Whitman Publishing: Racine, Wisconsin.

Morehead, Albert R. and Geoffrey Mott-Smith. 1980. *The Complete Book of Solitaire and Patience Games.* Bantam Books: New York.

ABOUT LEARNING DISABILITIES

What Every Parent Should Know About Learning Disabilities. 1979. A Scriptographic booklet. Channing L. Bete Co: Greenfield, Massachusetts.

For more information write to:

Closer Look
P.O. Box 1492
Washington, DC 20013

National Association for Children with Learning Disabilities
4156 Library Road
Pittsburgh, PA 15234
(Send $1.00)

The Council for Exceptional Children
1920 Association Dr.
Reston, VA 22091
(Send a self-addressed, stamped envelope)

Foundation for Children with Learning Disabilities
Box 2929
Grand Central Station
New York, NY 10163
(Send $4.00 for a copy of *Their World*)

Orton Dyslexia Society
Dept. U.S. AT
724 York Road
Baltimore, MD 21204
(Send $1.00)

MORE ABOUT CONFERENCES FROM *STIR UNTIL CLEAR*

The following, excerpted from *Stir Until Clear* by Elenya Stephan, discusses in detail strategies for dealing with difficulties that may emerge in a conference.

Evaluations and Comparisons During a Conference

These conferences are usually evaluation sessions. In this light, some specific areas for comparison and evaluation to include in conferencing may be the following:

- ◆ How does the child see himself in relation to others at school, socially and academically?
- ◆ How does the child's achievement level compare with his own ability level?
- ◆ How does your understanding of the child compare with the understanding and experience of the parent or teacher?

Evaluations should be limited to comparisons of the individual's ability and achievement, and, where appropriate, to achievement and grade level. Comparisons of one child's growth against another child's growth, particularly that of a sibling, are damaging. Further, I do not recommend that a child be compared with the class as a whole. I have not experienced information of this kind to be useful or constructive. Where such comparisons do seem appropriate, use of the more objective, literal grade level indicator accomplishes the same task and still leaves the classroom a safe place to be from the child's point of view.

Goals and Expectations

What are your expectations for the education of children? What expectations do you hold for the parents or teacher of the child? for the child himself? What are your own goals and expectations for yourself? Are you as a teacher trained or even interested in meeting the requirements of students' escalating emotional and socialization needs?

These are questions that can produce discomfort. Confusion in regard to them is the major source of stress and dissatisfaction in the parent/teacher conferencing experience. Assuming responsibilities that are not your own may make you feel resentful and produce barriers to clear communication as well as physical and emotional strain. For others to assume responsibilities that are yours may make you feel guilty, defensive, and lower your self-respect. It is vital that we be clear which responsibilities we are willing to take on.

For the most part, these issues can be worked with in relation to a class as a whole. In some cases, where you feel it to be appropriate, you may want to focus in on an individual youngster. Parents can answer these questions in relation to each of their children.

1. What do you expect of yourself as teacher or parent in relation to the child's (children's) education? What are the limits of responsibility beyond which you are unwilling to go?

2. What do the children expect of you? Is this speculation or have you asked?

3. What do the children expect of themselves in growth and responsibility?

4. What do the significant others who relate to the child or children (parent, teacher, principal) expect of you? of the child?

5. Of these expectations, which ones do you feel trained to meet? are you willing to meet? Have you handled this so that during a conference you would not feel defensive?

7. Where there is a discrepancy between your own goals and those others hold for you, have you come to some agreements with those involved?

8. How have you provided for the periodic redefinition of these relationships in accord with your changing needs, desires, and expectations?

9. Using your responses to these questions, self-evaluate from time to time.

Pre-Conference Preparation

Pre-conference preparations may include parents sitting with each of their school-age children, jotting down notes regarding their concerns and particular areas of interest to be covered during the conference. A simple form may be devised and sent home as a format for such parent/child pre-conference preparations, and classroom teachers may want to discuss with each youngster prior to conferencing those areas to be covered during the conference, asking the child for suggestions.

Note-taking and Establishing the Conference Context

We often recall only that which we want to hear. This frequently results in little or no follow-through on agreements which may have revolved around difficult conferencing areas. Note-taking during a conference can eliminate this problem. Note-taking is sometimes used manipulatively to gain an edge of power or control which then produces an adversary situation out of the conferencing experience. On the other hand, note-taking to clarify and assist in recall of agreements can be valuable. Explicitly stating the purpose of note-taking can reduce misunderstood intentions.

One teacher uses a simple form during parent conferencing to establish parent-child expectations. She jots down notes for each area as she asks the parent and child to respond regarding these areas at the beginning of the conference: parent's primary concerns, parent's primary goals for the child, child's primary concerns and self goals, expectations either holds for the teacher role.

Discussing these areas while jotting down notes provides for a context within which to hold the conference, establishes priorities for areas of importance to be covered during the limited amount of time available, and gives those involved the experience of feeling acknowledged.

Availability of Both Parents for Conferencing

Teachers occasionally find themselves caught in a tug between two parents who don't see eye to eye regarding their youngster's school life. This is uncomfortable to say the least, and definitely unproductive. Parents need to acknowledge the classroom teacher's position and not play off him or her in their efforts to resolve difficulties between themselves. In situations where parents are separated or divorced, non-custodial parents interested in their children's school experiences can ask the school office to make note and let the classroom teacher know of this welcomed interest. Arrangements may then be made to contact both parents about conferencing. If both parents are unable to attend a conference, the parent who won't be attending may want to discuss with his or her spouse which aspect of their child's school life they would particularly like clarified.

Reducing Threat and Defensiveness

Make contact. Notice body language. Are you sitting face to face or in such a way that you are comfortable? Notice how you sit in relation to others in the conference so that you can be comfortable. Are your choices of seating to avoid contact? Is there a table between you? If you take notes, notice whether it helps you avoid contact, or whether it genuinely serves the conference goals. Does eye contact feel comfortable or uncomfortable? I don't suggest you make changes here as much as that you simply notice.

Acknowledge feeling threatened from the beginning. You can ask, "How do you feel about being here?" or say how you feel. You can later back up if tension mounts and say at that time, "I was afraid we might get so upset that we wouldn't be able to hear each other," and then go from there.

Allow the feelings. As a messenger of information, can you allow the receiver to have sad or angry feelings?

Integrate strong feelings with workable solutions. Say what you feel. Oftentimes the intensity and tension are reduced: "It concerns me to give you unpleasant news," "I can see you are so very upset," "I believe in Y and you believe in X," and "I can imagine that you would feel disappointed to learn that I can't do what looks like the only solution to you." Tension and fear increases not usually as a result of communicating, but from incomplete communication. Overly harsh, offensive or defensive statements are incomplete. Look to see what you really have to say, fully.

Ask the parent what his or her hopes are for this child.

Ask the person with whom you are conferencing to help you understand the focus child, to give you a more complete picture of the child in those settings you don't share. If parent or teacher isn't having the problem you're having, be aware that people often behave differently in different settings, depending for example on pressure systems—siblings, an entire classroom, and so on—and ask what approaches that person finds work for them.

Let them know you appreciate the investment of time such conferencing involves.

Focus on the well-being of the child. For example, it isn't fair for children to act out, not only because of its effects on others, but because they develop maladaptive patterns, don't do well academically, and hurt their own self-esteem.

Reprinted with permission of the author. From *Stir Until Clear: A Handbook on the Counseling Relationship in the Schools*, by Elenya Stephan. R. and E. Associates: Palo Alto, California, pages 155–158.

Chapter
12

▼▼▼▼▼▼▼▼▼▼▼▼▼▼▼▼▼▼▼

Gold-Star Ideas

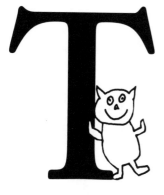

This chapter contains some ideas I've had over the years that have proven to be valuable over and over. The ideas are organized under Special Days, Learning Games, Special Touches, Special Events, and More About Classroom Management. Feel free to browse and use what you like.

SPECIAL DAYS

Rainy-Day Recess
On rainy days, when recess is spent inside, make a sign-up chart on the blackboard. Ask the children what quiet activity they would like to do in the room during recess. Remind them that even though it's recess, they may not run or shout in the room due to its small size. As the children give you suggestions, list them on the blackboard. If the suggestion is too noisy or requires too much movement around the room, do not accept it. When the chart is full of

suggestions, draw a colored paper from a box. If the paper is orange, for example, call the people in the orange group to write their initials in chalk under the activity they choose to do. The blackboard chart will begin to look like this:

Draw	Read	Books	Puzzles	Geo Boards	Weaving
A.M.		J.C.		1. P.K.	1. L.S.
B.H.				2.	2.
				3.	3.
				4.	4.

Explain that after they have done that activity and find that they would like to do something else, they are to erase their initials under the first activity and put them under the activity they want to do next.

They can only move to another activity when they erase their name and sign up for a new one. Once they have committed themselves to an activity, they must stay with it. They may not run around the room from one thing to another. This system has worked well for me. The children go to one area and do what they wish quietly. List numbers if there are limited numbers of spaces at one activity; for example, if there are only four geo boards, only four can sign up for geo boards.

When the recess bell rings, that is the signal to clean up. If an area is not neat, check the sign-up board, read the names under the area that needs attention, and send those children back to clean up.

Upside Down Day

One good idea leads to another. Rainy-Day Recess was a huge success. The children dreaded hearing the recess bell ring. We decided to have what we called Upside Down Day. Once a week an hour was devoted to the sign-up schedule used during Rainy-Day Recess. The children got to sign up for the activity they enjoyed the most.

Everyone Reads

Children learn by imitation and experience. If younger children see older children and adults interested in reading, many will want to imitate them. In one school where I taught, our principal set aside a certain time each week when everyone would read—not only children and teachers, but also the secretary, principal, nurse, and librarian. Every Thursday after lunch, the school would fall quiet. The children were told that when they came back from lunch, they were to have a book in their hands to read or look at. This was quiet time throughout the school, and no one talked. After lunch when the children came into the room, I would stand by the door and remind them, "Today everyone reads. Find your book, get comfortable, and read." One curious boy, after ten minutes, signed out to go to the bathroom. He reported to me on our way to recess that he saw even Val, our custodian, reading! After our principal retired, I continued that one afternoon a week when everyone in the class read—even me.

Fridays Are Cleanup Days

After the children understand the rhythm of the schedule and have been in school for about six weeks, schedule a certain time on Friday (following the afternoon story, for example) to clean the room. Explain that this is their classroom and if everyone helps, the job can be completed quickly. Each child's major responsibility is to clean and straighten his cubby. Those who have time and want to help, may then sign up to help with cleaning the rest of the room. Only those who want to help clean the room should do so. Those who do not want to clean the room are to sit on the rug and read after their cubbies have been inspected.

Put a sign-up chart on the blackboard similar to the one for the Rainy-Day Recess.

CLEANERS:			
Straighten books	**Papers or shelves**	**Puzzle shelf**	**Clean sink or table tops**
1. Maria	1.	1.	1. Bill
2.	2.	2.	2.
3.			
4.			

Then ask who would like to straighten the books, and write their names in that column. When all of the areas have been filled, state the ground rules.

1. None of the class rules should be broken.

2. Everyone is still to walk and talk softly, and not rush.

3. If anyone breaks a rule, they are telling the rest of the class that they do not want to help clean. They will be asked to sit in the middle of the rug and look at books, out of the cleaners' way.

Be sure you take time out to check each cubby after the children are finished and move on to their next activity, whether it is reading or cleaning. Use the class list to check off each name so you won't miss any cubby inspections. Time is well spent, after the room is neat and clean, to mention the improvement in each area. The children glow with pride when you report the custodian's appreciation of their efforts.

The Last Three Days of School

At the beginning of the year the children are too excited, scared, and new, to help you unpack boxes and organize the room. At the end of the year they know the routine, have learned to work together, and are accustomed to the regular organized Friday clean-ups. Packing books, games, and papers and cleaning chairs, desks, and shelves is a culmination of the school year. Use three signs for each of the three groups of children and rotate the children as you would if they were progressing from area to area. One sign could say "Pack Books," the second sign and area could say, "Pack Games," the sign over the third area could say "Pack Paper." The next round could be "Clean Desks," "Clean Chairs," and "Clean Cubbies." The tasks can be accomplished in one day with a picnic the next day as the reward. The last day of school is best spent at school, joining another class for movies and organizing teams for gunny sack races, water balloon throws, musical chairs, and races around the school yard. The last day at my school culminated in awards and a party. I always enjoyed these last three days. After we had packed all of the books, supplies, and skill builders, I and my students sat among the boxes and planned our excursion and party. The school year seemed complete.

LEARNING GAMES
When You Have Time to Kill

When you have only five or ten minutes left before recess or lunch or while you are waiting to be called to the auditorium for an assembly, it's not the proper time to start a lesson. What do you do?

While children are in line count by fives, tens, and so on. Stop at a number, say 25, and let a child volunteer to give the following number. Give addition and subtraction problems and ask for the answer. Recite the days of the week, the months, and the hours of the day. Recite the alphabet; give words and ask what letter the word begins with.

If you are in a circle on the rug always have the Peabody Kit nearby and a Sponge Activities book next to your chair. (The Peabody Kit is available from American Guidance Service, Inc., Minnesota. Two good sources for Sponge Activities books are: Dale Seymour Pub., P.O. Box 10888, Palo Alto, California 94303; and the Ventura County Superintendent of Schools, Ventura, California.) Both the Peabody Kit and Sponge Activities contain fun and stimulating group learning games. For example, from the Peabody Kit there's *Brainstorming Time*.

Say: "I'm going to say a part of a sentence. You will add as many ideas as possible to what I say."

A basket of _____	A room of _____
A bag of _____	A stable of _____
A bunch of _____	A row of _____

When you have five extra minutes with nothing planned, these sponge exercises are helpful.

Beginning Sponges

This was a list given to me by the Marin Teachers' Learning Cooperative and is reprinted with permission.

- Tell the children to be ready to tell one playground rule.
- Tell them to be ready to tell you the names of the children in class that begin with J or M, etc.
- Ask them to draw something that is drawn only with circles.
- Ask them to tell a good health habit.
- Write a color word on the board. Have children draw something that color.
- Flash your fingers—have children tell how many fingers.
- "I went to the sporting goods store and I bought…" Each child names an item.
- Ask them what number comes before/after 46, 52, 13?

◆ Write a word on the board. Have children make a list of words that rhyme or that have the same long or short vowel sound.

Finger Plays

Finger plays are another way to fill in the time when you have only a few minutes left. The children in the first grade resent doing some of the simple ones they think are babyish, but enjoy campfire songs.

A good finger play for kindergarten is:

The itsy bitsy spider crawled up the water spout.
Down came the rain and washed the spider out.
Out came the sun and dried up all the rain.
The itsy bitsy spider went up the spout again.

Books for Finger Plays

Cheyney, Jeanne and Arnold Cheyney. 1990. *Finger Plays for Home and School* Scott, Foresman: Glenview, Illinois.

Graham, Terry L. 1984. *Finger Plays and Rhymes for Always and Sometimes.* Humanities Ltd.: Atlanta, Georgia.

Leighton, Audrey O. 1984. *Fingerplay, Friends.* Judson: Valley Forge, Pennsylvania.

SPECIAL TOUCHES

Ordering Movies and Videos

If you are fortunate enough to have excellent movies at your disposal in the district media center, be sure to use them. Before you become busy preparing for school you can thumb through the catalog and order movies for the first week of school. You can then have either movies or stories in the afternoon, when the children are tired. You develop your curriculum by ordering movies related to reading and social studies and using movies about values and morals. A science movie pertaining to the body can be shown before a science lesson later in the school year.

Preview a movie you have not shown before in the morning before school starts. List questions to ask the children after they view the movie.

Welcome-to-School Letter

Send a note to each child *before* school starts.

August 31, 1993

Dear

Good news for me! You will be in my class this year. I am looking forward to seeing you September 6th.

Sincerely,
Mrs. Mary Coons

Parents really appreciate this information.

Box 12.1

CALENDAR OF EVENTS

Sept. 2nd Open House for children and parents 11 to noon.

Sept. 6th First day of school. All children arrive before 8:30 a.m. and are dismissed at _____.

Sept. 7th–8th Child/Teacher interviews
15 minute appointments starting at 12:45 p.m.

Sept. 12th–15th Parent/Teacher Conferences
15 minute appointments starting at 12:45 p.m.

Sept 25th Parent helper orientation
Sign-up will be available mid-September

Sept. 29th Back-to-School night for parents

Oct. 3rd Classroom helpers start

Source: Sandra Lauer. Reprinted with permission.

Class Newsletter

Another thing parents appreciate getting and children love to contribute to are class newsletters. The example below is easy to fill out quickly and keeps parents up-to-date.

Box 12.2

WEEK OF_____

KINDER-QUICKIE

Multi-Disciplinary Unit_____

Math Focus_____

Language Focus_____

Class Project_____

Special Person_____

Birthdays_____

Optional Home Activity_____

Needs_____

Other_____

Source: Sandra Lauer. Reprinted with permission.

Curriculum Highlights

You can give parents an outline of the year's curriculum during a conference or at Back-to-School night. Be sure to avoid jargon and explain your goals. The example below, for kindergarten, is reprinted with the permission of Sandra Lauer.

Language Arts

- ◆ A literature-based approach, including poetry
- ◆ Both oral and written language
- ◆ Alphabet letter and sound recognition is taught through a letter-of-the-week format

Math

- ◆ A hands-on approach using manipulatives with key experiences in sorting, classifying, patterning, and measuring
- ◆ Rote counting: 1–10; 1–50; 1–100
- ◆ Skip counting by 5's and 10's
- ◆ Numeral functions
- ◆ Geometric shapes

Social Studies

- ◆ Ourself, our family, and our community
- ◆ Multicultural awareness with activities at home and school

Science

- ◆ Self awareness, including health and nutrition
- ◆ Plants, animals, insects
- ◆ The four seasons
- ◆ The five senses
- ◆ Geology and natural resources
- ◆ Ecosystems

Art

- ◆ A wide variety of mediums is used throughout the curriculum on a daily basis. The children are encouraged to develop perceptual and fine motor skills while maintaining their own creative expression and growth.

Music

- ◆ A variety of songs, rhythms, and games are incorporated into each day. The district music specialist visits weekly.

Physical Education

- ◆ Activities that promote developmentally appropriate physical skills

◆ A variety of equipment is used: bean bags, hoops, balls, jump ropes, scarves

Teacher's Blue Box

We all welcome a pat on the back on those days when a lesson flops or a parent is upset with us. I have saved all of the lovely notes I have received from parents thanking me for some part I have played in helping their child. I still have them, and I find that ten minutes spent reading some of these makes me feel better. This was especially true when I was first starting to teach. A note from a master teacher, supervisor, or principal will do wonders in helping to build self-esteem.

Student of the Week

From the information on the children's interests, families, and activities, that you have gathered in your reading conference files, you can make a "Student-of-the-Week" chart. Give each child a turn by drawing her name from a box. Display a chart all about that child on the Student-of-the-Week bulletin board (see Figure 12.1). Third graders can fill out the chart themselves, and the younger children can be asked the questions with the teacher filling in the blanks. On Friday, that student is questioned by the class about her interests and opinions. The child may decline to answer certain questions if she wishes by saying, "I pass." No silly questions are accepted.

SPECIAL EVENTS

Fundraisers for Class Projects

When the children want something special that would help them as a class, you can organize a fundraiser to raise money. Have the children suggest ideas for the fundraiser, and involve them in its organization. When my children wanted a rocking chair like mine to sit in, we organized a cupcake sale. We soon had enough money to buy a rocker.

Guest Speakers

Guest speakers can be a wonderful source of expert information about subjects being studied. Parents who are artists explain painting, veterinarians discuss animal care, and dental hygienists talk about how to care for teeth. Community employees such as a firefighter, police officer, mail carrier, museum director, and librarian can be invited to visit the classroom. These visits are especially meaningful before a trip by the class to their place of work.

Figure 12.1

STUDENT OF THE WEEK

Name:_____Birthday:_____Birth year:_____

Address: _____

Brothers & sisters: _____

Pets:_____

Favorite: Sports:_____ Foods:_____

Movies:_____ T.V. show:_____

Music:_____ Food to cook:_____

I'm especially good at: _____

My best school subject: _____

I would like to improve my: _____

I would like to know more about: _____

When I grow up : _____

My best time: _____

_____

My worst time: _____

_____

I would like to change: _____

_____

I would like to wish for: _____

_____

My favorite thing I do with my family:_____

My favorite thing to do with my friends:_____

A gardener at the nearby park came to invite one of my classes to visit his garden. We were all enthralled with this relaxed man. When he asked the children if they had any questions, one child with a quizzical look on his face asked, "Do you have your pajamas on under your jeans?" The gardener laughingly admitted it, saying he woke up late and only had time to put his clothes on over his pajamas. The children loved him and his honesty and thought he was very funny.

Field Trips

Field trips are exciting days for the children. They are going to experience something first-hand. There are so many places to visit to broaden their knowledge.

The responsibility of having twenty-four or more children in five different cars can be frightening; make sure the parents have had their cars inspected for safety by the police department and that each is fully insured. You can relieve your burden when each parent is responsible throughout the trip for the children who ride with them. But remember that you are still responsible for the behavior of all your children.

To avoid problems, I had my children help develop the following rules for the class to follow on field trips (see Figure 12.2). Before each trip these rules were read to the children and given to each parent along with the names of the children who would be with them. The names of the drivers and the list of the children in each of the driver's cars were written on the blackboard the night before. Review these rules before each trip, and give this list of rules to each parent before the trip.

Figure 12.2

Dear

1. The children are to stay with the parent they are riding with while walking to the car, upon arriving at the destination, and during the trip. It is easier for each child to watch the parent than it is for one parent to watch five children.
2. Everyone is to fasten his or her seat belts.
3. The parent will choose a place for the children to meet if you become separated from the group. Everyone should be certain to know where it is.
4. If there are any problems such as improper language or disobedience, the parent will report this incident to the teacher. The person who misbehaves is telling us that he does not want to go on field trips.
5. Use quiet voices in the car. If there is too much noise in the car, the parent will stop the car by the side of the road and wait until everyone's voices are softer.
6. Understand and practice safety.
7. Your cooperation and helpfulness means more field trips for everyone.

Thank you for driving.

A field trip's success depends on good planning. A prior visit to the field trip site will give you ideas as to what to expect. Your notes and observations can provide ideas for a map of the places to visit with a star by places to observe. A treasure hunt of things to find out about on the trip with a check-off sheet as to what they found is a good motivator for children.

A tour guided by several docents with small groups of six children is an ideal situation. Well-trained, knowledgeable docents are invaluable.

The children can write about their field trip experiences during creative writing and discuss what they saw and heard in a class meeting. From these observations the teacher can revise, expand on, or eliminate future trips to that site.

Walking Trips

Rules of orderly conduct also apply when the children go with the teacher on a walking trip to a nearby fire station, post office, bakery, park, or lake. Review these rules with the class:

1. Stay on the sidewalk and be careful of the homeowners' grass and plants.
2. Talk in a soft voice; sometimes we may sing our favorite song along the way.
3. Stay behind the teacher in an orderly fashion while walking to the destination.
4. When you arrive at the destination, the teacher will tell you the boundaries so that she can always see you.

Walking to the local park to have lunch, playtime, and a story was a way for me to be with the children and observe them in a relaxed situation. Year-end walks for a day of picnicking and fishing at a nearby lake the next to last day of school was a tradition for my classes.

Open House

Open House is a favorite time and is the children's night to shine. I had them prepare for Open House by having them color a huge envelope in the Writing Area with their names clearly written on the top.

In the Writing Area they prepared all of their creative writing papers by coloring pictures to go with what they had written and put their papers together to make a book.

Before they colored a picture about their writings, many of them read all of their papers and become proud of their noticeable progress. Start this preparation at least two weeks before Open House, so the children will not be rushed and can take time to read their papers. They will also see mistakes in punctuation and spelling errors, which they are now able to correct.

Next give them their journals. Time is needed to read these. Send a letter home to the parents at the beginning of January, explaining that starting February 1, no papers will be coming home until Open House. As the children go through the rest of their papers, some will arrange them by dates, others by categories. It is fun to hear them remark, "I remember when I was adding this simple stuff."

Two days before Open House, discuss with the children the correct way to introduce their family to their friends and other parents. They should think about what they want to show their parents. Explain to them that they are the hosts and their parents are guests. Compile a list of their suggestions. A booklet, put together by the children for their Open House program, and typed by the aide, might look like Figure 12.3.

Figure 12.3

1. **Introduce your guest**
2. **Show them your** creative writing book folder with papers
3. **Show them your:**
   All About Me
   The Me I Know
   Here I Am
   Math book
   Reading paper
   Following directions
   Crossword Puzzles
   Sight Word Search
   Handwriting paper
   Punctuation paper
   Capitalization paper
   A.B.C. paper
   Spelling book
   Dictionary
   Reading book
4. **Show them your:**
   Mailbox
   Journals
   Science book
   Cubby
5. **Show them our:**
   Calendar
   Class rules
   Meeting rules
   Helpers' Chart
   Pictures
   Library

MORE ABOUT CLASSROOM MANAGEMENT

Pupil Self-Evaluation

During a one-to-one conference with a child, you can discuss with him his goals and help him make a self-evaluation. This helps the child focus on what he wants to achieve. Another good time to do pupil self-evaluation is before report cards are due. Review the report card with each child and discuss how he thinks each category should be marked and why. See Figure 12.4 for an example of a pupil self-evaluation form.

Changing the Children to Different Groups

Changing color groups every six weeks is important. The children are then able to get to know other children they would usually not be closely associated with, thus building more friendships and class unity. After six weeks of school, take time during the first hour of school (when no one is absent) to take children one at a time from the Reading Area to the reading conference desk where it is private. Explain that this is a very private conversation and you will not tell what is said. Ask the children not to tell what they have said either. (Some of the following has been excerpted with permission from "Conducting a Sociometric Study," by Mary Reiss Collins, Ph.D.)

Be diplomatic. You could ask:

"Which three children in our class would you like to have as a close friend?" or, "Which three children would you like to sit near?" or, "Which three children in our class would you most like to play with during recess?"

Or you could be direct and ask which three children they would like to have in their color group. "Who are your first, second, and third choices?"

If you can, complete this task before recess. Otherwise the students may go out and plot, "I will choose you if you choose me."

Have enough 3" × 5" cards for each child. Put the chooser's name at the top with the three chosen names below.

Barry

1. Dale
2. Dominic
3. Noel

Figure 12.4   Student Self-evaluation Form

Date_____

Reading
    _____ At my own speed
    _____ Below my speed
    _____ I am trying to learn in reading   Yes_____ No_____
    This is how: *Ask what words I don't know so I will learn them.*

Math
    _____ At my own speed
    _____ Below my speed
    _____ I am trying to learn more in math   Yes_____ No_____
    This is how: *Try to do more in one day.*

Writing
    _____ At my own speed
    _____ Below my speed
    _____ I am trying to improve handwriting   Yes_____ No_____
    This is how: _____

Things I learned this week: *If I don't get started into work right away I won't have enough time to finish.*

My favorite activities were: *Math*
This is the way I was in the classroom with others and myself:

    _____ I feel good about myself
    _____ I care to learn
    _____ I start activities by myself
    _____ I usually keep at things I have begun
    _____ I feel good about the way I use my time in class
    _____ I gave warm fuzzies and was nice to people

After the sociometric study, organize the results that day. Give the child who is not chosen at all or by a very few the first choice to be in a group with his friend. Try not to put two people together who do not get along or have a tendency to upset or disrupt a group. (See Figure 12.5 for how to tally the results.) Mabel, Noel, and Barry would be placed in a group with their first choices, which are Dale and Peggy. If Noel and Barry do not work well together then one will go with their second choice. Then go to Candace and Dominic's first choice. When you have three groups that might work well together, put the new groups on the blackboard for the next day. Explain to the child that with a class of twenty-seven children it is difficult to give each person her first choice. Make a note of the children who received a second or third and are due for first choice next time.

Figure 12.5

Chooser	Barry 1	Dale 2	Dominic 3	Noel 4	Jarvis 5	Ralph 6	Dirk 7	Percy 8	Peggy 9	Candace 10	Anne 11	Mabel 12
1 Barry		1	2	3								
2 Dale					3	3	1					
3 Dominic		2					3	1				
4 Noel		1					2	3				
5 Jarvis	1	2	3		1							
6 Ralph		3				3	2	3				
7 Dirk					1		2					
8 Percy		1										
9 Peggy		2			3						3	
10 Candace					2				3	1	1	2
11 Anne								3	1		2	
12 Mabel									1	3	2	

				Orange	Yellow	Green
Dale	7	Candace	2	Barry	Noel	Mabel
Dirk	6	Dominic	2	Dale	Ralph	Peggy
Jarvis	4	Barry	1	Candace	Dirk	Dominic
Anne	4	Noel	1	Anne	Jarvis	Percy
Ralph	3	Mabel	1			
Peggy	3					
Percy	3					

Results from the study tell who you need to help, build up, draw out, and give duties to (such as passing out paper, collecting scissors, and so on) that will put them in a leadership role.

The results can be quite revealing:

- What appears that you had expected?
- What appears that you had not expected?
- Why are certain children the most chosen?
- Why are certain children not chosen?
- What seems to account for the mutual choices?
- Can you think of an arrangement that would help each child?

Helping a Substitute Teacher Be Successful in Your Classroom

This list was prepared by one of my principals and has proven to be very useful.

1. Leave a plan on your chalkboard for the day so that your class knows that the sub is doing what you want the children to do.

2. Leave detailed plans on your desk.

3. Organize your desktop with all the books and materials to be used in the order they will be used.

4. Plan the first period of the day as one that requires little direct supervision of the children. This will make it possible for the substitute to have time to get organized and will let the children know that this is a serious, get-down-to-work type of day.

5. If you are absent on a day when you have extra duties, leave a description of what those are and when and where they are to be carried out...or make a trade with a faculty friend for that day.

6. A description of any special arrangements for children being outside the classroom, who, when, where, prevents misunderstandings.

7. Brief descriptions of children with exceptional learning or behavior patterns helps both the children and the substitute.

8. There are always children who finish early or who can't do the work who need some extra special assignment that is not busy-

work. Leave things you know these children can do and leave for everyone more to be done than can possibly be accomplished that day.

9. A sentence or two outlining the disciplinary measures that your children are used to will help.

10. Indicate the kind of supervision to be provided to the children when going to lunch, during lunch, going to the library.

11. Leave an outline of any special paper grading or checking arrangements you would like followed.

12. Don't be hesitant in suggesting things the sub should try to have prepared for you on the following day.

13. Leave a request of the special things you would like the sub to report on at the end of the day. You might want her to complete some form with specific details of what was accomplished.

14. Have a folder prepared with at least three days of lesson plans not attached to what you are doing in class. That way, when you are sick, you won't feel compelled to come in to keep things going.

15. Do expect your substitute to be a skilled professional. He expects to work hard and be responsible. He would like to do more than just control your children while you're gone. It is your class even when you are absent, so do whatever you can to help the sub help your children.

What to Do with Completed Papers

Completed papers should be taken from the finished-paper basket and corrected each day. If there are several mistakes on a child's paper, file the paper in the color group that corresponds to the one the child is in. Then, on Friday, schedule one area for journals and correcting papers . When the children come to the area, their color-group folder is taken out. If they have no papers to correct, they are to work in their journals. If there are papers to be corrected or to complete, the child is given a lesson or help from the teacher in the area until he understands the corrections that need to be made.

The papers that do not have to be corrected are filed in an open posting tub in alphabetical order. On Friday, the week's papers for each child are stapled together and put in her cubby to take home. File all of the children's completed papers to take home except the journals and creative writing papers. Put these alphabetically in a box and save them until April for Open House.

File papers for a parent conference in alphabetical order in a folder for each child. Just before the conference, you can gather that child's folder from the finished-paper file, his folder from the reading conference file, and his journals, math book, and reading book to refer to during the conference.

Evolving from Groups into Independent Learning

During a reading conference, a second grader asked me if she could share a double desk with a friend. I said that I would think about it. Six other children asked the same question. It became obvious to me that these children were asking to work on their own and were ready for independent study.

As I reviewed the class, I decided that perhaps all but six children were ready to be independent and that this was the appropriate time to change the program. I held a conference again with the first child. I told her I would help her move a double desk from the Math Area for her and a friend. I moved on to the next child who had made a similar request. Upon noticing that the remainder of the class was becoming interested in the move, I announced to the children what we were doing, and that I would take one person at a time for a desk assignment. Only those who were continuing with their seat work and were helping by being quiet could be moved. Not everyone needed to move to a desk if they did not wish. The half circle table could accommodate six to eight children who did not want to move. The aide would stay at this desk to help them. Within half an hour the room was transformed from areas to individual double desks in rows. To my relief, the dependent children who needed extra help decided to stay in a group of six with our aide.

For the remainder of the year the children worked with check-off requirement sheets directing them as to what their assignment was each day. The check-off sheets were similar to the ones explained in Appendix B.

Conclusion

*One of the greatest failures of our contemporary
training of teachers is that they become mere
technicians....They do not learn the beliefs and motives
and values for the sake of which the classroom exists.*

— Alexander Meiklejohn,
American educator (1872)

hether you are facing your first class or your
twentieth, the beginning of the school year is
an anxious time for teachers. You want to do the
best job you can. What will make you a better
teacher? Too often teachers teach as they were
taught, using the same methods over and over,
without questioning why these methods are
used or if there are other more effective methods. But teaching should be dynamic; we cannot rest on tradition. We must apply what
research has taught us about learning and effective teaching. Teachers of the primary grades
must make the best use of the limited time they
have with children to teach them not only the

259

appropriate academic subjects but also social and emotional skills. In this book I have shared with you the fruits of my many years in the classroom. Here is a summary of my best advice to a beginning teacher.

1. Be prepared. Take the time to properly prepare each lesson. Plan every minute and more. Have all the materials you will need ready at your fingertips. You will lose the children's attention if you are always scrambling to find the materials for the next activity.

2. Slow down. Be sure that the children understand the rules of the class before you rush into academic subjects, and that they understand the first step of a lesson before you move on to the next step. Remember that rapid speech and movement make the children excitable. If you move slowly and smoothly through the day you will set a calmer tone for yourself and for your class.

3. Set down rules. One of your first priorities at the beginning of the school year should be establishing the class rules. Let the children know what behavior you expect from them. Ask the children for suggestions, and discuss why each rule is important. When a rule is broken, be consistent in your reactions; follow through. Explain to the rule-breaker what he has done wrong, listen to his ideas about his behavior, and be sure to notice good behavior in the future.

4. Use positive reinforcement. Look for behavior to praise. You will do more to promote orderly, happy children by noticing good behavior than by punishing bad behavior. If a child is having a problem with motivation or actions, meet with that child privately and agree on a system where she will be noticed for acting in the desired way.

5. Be sensitive to the individual. This means taking the time to find out about the individual's personality, learning modality, and level of development. A child will become frustrated if she is feeling pressured to learn too quickly or too slowly. Understand that each child has different needs, and work to understand and meet these needs.

6. **Educate yourself.** Remember that teaching is a learning process, and fresh ideas will keep you from getting in a rut. Keep up on the latest theories on teaching and child development by taking classes and reading the literature. Visit other classrooms looking for new ideas and techniques, and adapt the ones you like to your own teaching style. With constant ongoing training you will always be growing as a teacher.

7. **Observe and listen.** Write down and then discuss with an aide or student teacher your daily observations of each child. This can help you learn each child's needs. Listening to each child's ideas gives you a feeling of closeness. The child gains a sense of respect that is needed to develop self-esteem.

To My Class

I wrote this letter before I left my class in California in 1984. I never gave it to them, but have kept it to remind myself how I felt about all of my classes.

Dear Class,

I am writing this letter to let you know why I think all of you are so special. You came together in September as a mixture of kindergartners, first, and second graders. In this blend of ages and grades, I have seen an atmosphere of helpfulness, caring, and cooperation. You have accepted each person for what they are.

By your hard work and helpfulness to others, it was obvious you were in this classroom to learn and teach. You all have accomplished both.

Love,
Mary Coons

Thoughts to New Teachers

You are lucky. You have the privilege of shaping the minds of our youth through your guidance and leadership. You will need a strong commitment to your profession and to children. You will need energy, for the work is hard. But all this will be worth it when you see the looks of loving gratitude on the faces of your children, and you know that you have had a positive impact on their lives.

Always train yourself by enrolling in courses, looking for new ideas and techniques from classroom visits, or talking to fellow teachers. Try not to go back to your classroom and use these techniques and ideas exactly the way the course or person was using them. Develop the ideas to fit your style, by adding a technique or not using the areas that you are not comfortable with. With constant training and searching, you will grow as a teacher.

You have ahead of you years of growth, participating in exciting changes in your profession, and shaping the minds of our youth. Setting an example through your guidance and leadership is a privilege of your profession.

You will need a strong commitment to what you are doing. You will experience mistakes and failures, in order to learn. You bring new ideas and enthusiasm to the classroom, opening many doors of learning and providing insights into children and teaching.

▼▼▼▼▼▼▼▼▼▼▼▼▼▼▼▼▼▼▼▼▼▼▼▼▼

Appendix A: Sample Class Schedules

Second Day Schedule for a Few Kindergarteners, First, and Second Grades

The first day's schedule (discussed in Chapter 3) was very brief. The next day can have five minutes added to each area.

8:55	Meet the children outdoors at the designated area promptly
9:00–9:15	Take attendance, recite Pledge of Allegiance, discuss helpers, discuss and form room rules chart, and explain schedule
9:15–9:30	Area I: Reading
9:30–9:45	Area II: Listen to a record
9:45–10:00	Area III: Writing in Journals

Rotate the groups as described in Chapter 3

10:00–10:20	Class and teacher make rules for the classroom
10:20–10:25	Snack time
10:25–10:40	Recess
10:40–10:45	Meet children outside to bring them in to the Meeting/Rug Area
10:45–10:55	Read a familiar story
10:55–11:00	Explain schedule
11:00–11:20	Area I: Puzzles (Individual)
11:20–11:40	Area II: Art (Color pictures in journal)
11:40–11:55	Area III: Dot-to-Dot math

Rotate the groups three times

11:55–12:00	Prepare for lunch
12:00–12:40	Lunch (stay 10 minutes with the children), kindergartners go home
12:40–12:45	Meet children outside promptly
12:45–1:00	Story
1:00–1:20	Game–Steal the Bacon
1:20–1:40	Movie
1:40–1:55	Discussion–what did you do today in the classroom?
1:55 –2:00	Dismissal

Second Week Schedule for a Few Kindergarteners, First, and Second Grades

8:55–9:15	Attendance, Pledge of Allegiance, sing *Star Spangled Banner*, class discussion, explain schedule
9:15–9:35	Area I: Reading, give individual reading tests
9:35–9:55	Area II: Listening
9:55–10:20	Area III: Writing in journals

} **Rotate the groups as described in Chapter 3**

10:20–10:25	Snack
10:25–10:40	Recess
10:45–11:00	Feedback to the children about their work habits and behavior during the first hour. ("You people are showing everyone you know what to do when you get to work. You learned the class rules fast.") Explain schedule
11:00–11:20	Area I: Math tests for entry level placement
11:20–11:40	Area II: Paper about colors
11:40–11:55	Area III: Art

} **Rotate the groups as described in Chapter 3**

11:55–12:00	Clean up, come to the Meeting Area, teacher checks each area for neatness and cleanliness (If an area is not clean the group who was at that area last goes back to clean up.)
12:00–12:45	Lunch, walk to the designated lunch area with the children, staying long enough to be certain all is functioning well (Kindergartners go home.)
12:45–1:00	Story
1:00–1:25	Handwriting (the entire class observes and writes each letter formation as the teacher demonstrates the proper strokes)
1:30–1:50	Games
1:50–2:00	Dismissal after discussion of the school day, what they did and learned (Give positive feedback on their behavior and learning attitude. Introduce something for tomorrow or tell them to look at the schedule on the board tomorrow for a surprise.)

Third Week Schedule for a Few Kindergarteners, First, and Second Grades

8:55–9:15	Attendance, Pledge of Allegiance, discussion, explain schedule
9:15–9:30	Area I: Reading, give individual reading tests
9:30–9:45	Area II: Listening
9:45–10:00	Area III: Creative Writing: (If I Could Be...)
10:00–10:10	At the rug, discuss what they did, how they worked to deserve an early snack time
10:10–10:20	Snack
10:20–10:40	Early recess
10:40–10:45	Meet to come into the room
10:45–11:00	Discuss rules and behavior going to and from the library and while in the library
11:00–11:20	Area I: Math paper
11:20–11:40	Area II: Pattern blocks
11:40–11:55	Area III: Clock lesson and library visit (Have clock faces stamped on paper ready for each child. The first group will need a clock reading 11:15 a.m., the second 11:35 a.m., the third 11:55 a.m. They are to take the clock faces as their group leaves and compare the face with the clock in the library in order to return to the classroom on time.) **Rotate three times.**
12:00	Dismiss for lunch, kindergartners go home
12:00–12:45	Lunch
12:45–1:00	Story
1:00–1:20	Manuscript writing practice
1:20–1:50	Game
1:50–2:00	Discussion–what did you do and learn today?
2:00	Dismissal

> **Rotate the groups as described in Chapter 3** (applies to 9:15–10:00 blocks)

October Schedule for a Few Kindergarteners, First, and Second Grades

8:25–8:40	Monday: Yard duty
8:55–9:15	Pledge of Allegiance, new duties, attendance, explain language arts
9:15–9:35	Area I: Reading, reading conferences
9:35–9:55	Area II: Creative writing (What I Will See on Halloween)
9:55–10:20	Area III: Listening (Georgie's Halloween record and books)
10:25–10:40	Recess
10:45–11:00	Half of the class—music with music teacher, the other half—math skills
11:00–11:15	Area I: Math books
11:20–11:40	Area II: Art (Draw what you will see on Halloween night.)
11:40–12:00	Area III: Discovery blocks
12:00–12:45	Lunch, kindergartners go home
12:45–1:10	Story
1:15–1:35	Game: Kickball
1:35–1:55	Movie: "Georgie the Ghost"
1:55–2:00	Discussion—what did you learn in school today?
2:00–2:10	Recess for the children who remain for reading skills
2:10–3:10	Reading skills group

Area I through Area III (9:15–10:20): } Rotate three times

Area I through Area II (11:00–11:40): } Rotate three times

November Schedule for a Few Kindergartners, First, and Second Grades

8:25–8:40	Tuesday: Yard duty
8:55	Meet the children promptly
9:00–9:15	Sing the *Star Spangled Banner*, Pledge of Allegiance, attendance, explain areas
9:15–9:35	Area I: Reading
9:40–10:00	Area II: Creative writing
10:05–10:25	Area III: Dukane

} **Rotate three times**

10:25–10:40	Recess
10:45–11:00	Go to the library for a story read by the librarian
11:00–11:15	Area I: Math papers
11:20–11:40	Area II: Geo boards
11:40–12:00	Area III: Science

} **Rotate three times**

12:00–12:45	Lunch
12:45–1:00	Discussion, everyone reads
1:00–1:25	Social studies
1:30–1:50	Game: Steal the Bacon
1:50–2:00	Discussion–what did you learn today?
2:00–2:10	Recess for skills group
2:10–3:10	Reading skills group: three letter blends/long vowels

January Schedule for a Few Kindergartners, First, and Second Grades

8:55–9:15	Attendance, news, explain the program	
9:15–9:35	Area I: Read	} **Rotate**
9:35–9:55	Area II: Journals	**three**
10:00–10:20	Area III: Crossword Puzzles	**times**
10:20–10:40	Recess	
10:45–10:55	Addel reads to the class	
11:00–11:30	Upside down day	
11:30–12:00	Clean the room	
12:00–12:45	Lunch	
12:45–1:00	Ecology day (the monitor goes out to clean our designated area)	
1:00–1:25	Assembly in the auditorium	
1:30–1:50	Games	
1:55–2:00	Dismissal	
2:00–2:10	Recess for skills group	
2:10–3:10	Reading skills: controlled vowels	

March Schedule for a Few Kindergarteners, First, and Second Grades

8:55–9:15	Attendance, Pledge of Allegiance, sing *America*, news, explain the schedule
9:15–9:35	Area I: Read
9:35–9:55	Area II: Spelling test for some, Sight Word Search for others
10:00–10:20	Area III: Creative Writing (Things you hear in the night.)

} Rotate three times

10:25–10:40	Recess
10:45–11:00	Paul reads to the class
11:00–11:20	Area I: Library
11:20–11:40	Area II: Art
11:40–12:00	Area III: Math skills group

} Rotate three times

12:00–12:45	Lunch, kindergartners go home
12:45–1:00	Story
1:00–1:20	Science
1:20–1:40	Game
1:40–2:00	Art with resource teacher
2:00–2:10	Recess for skills group
2:10–3:10	Reading skills: long vowels

May Schedule for a Few Kindergarteners, First, and Second Grades

8:55–9:15	Attendance, Pledge of Allegiance, news, explain schedule for tests
9:20–10:20	Test second graders (The remainder go the library or playground with an aide. Put on board all second graders' names who are to stay IN on blue paper. Red will be for those who go OUT.)
10:25–10:40	Answer questions, recess
10:45–10:55	Test first graders (Put their names on red paper. Place on the board under IN. Blue will be for those who go out with aide or helper.)
12:00–12:45	Lunch (Kindergartners now stay at school until the end of the year. They are requested to stay to be ready for a longer day next year.)
12:45–1:15	Music
1:15–1:35	Kickball
1:40–2:00	Movie
2:00–2:10	Recess for skills group
2:10–3:10	Skills test for the remaining children

Typical Third Grade Schedule

8:55–9:10	Attendance, agenda items for children and teacher in the Meeting Area
9:10–9:15	Dismiss the monitor to get requirement sheets and give them to the children when they are settled at their desks
9:15–9:35	Silent reading at their desks while teacher conducts individual reading conferences, aide answers questions and gives help
9:35–10:25	Language Arts period (Required tasks are worked on in any order and student may choose a task when the required tasks are completed.
	Spelling Study for test (with desk partner)
	*Dictionary Skills (paper)
	*Sight Word Search (paper)
10:25–10:40	Recess
10:45–11:00	Introduction to health lesson, health discussion
11:00–12:00	*Health paper
	*Math book
	*Math paper
	Five papers are due by 11:45 in the finished-paper basket
12:00–12:45	Lunch
12:45–12:55	A student reads followed by discussion
12:55–1:15	Social studies discussion
1:15–1:30	Social studies movie
1:30–1:50	Game: prison ball
1:50–2:00	Discussion about the following day and math homework. Dismissal for everyone but a skills group.
2:00–2:20	Recess for skills group
2:10–3:10	Skills: syllables

▼▼▼▼▼▼▼▼▼▼▼▼▼▼▼▼▼▼▼▼▼

Appendix B: Third Grade Ideas

Program for the Third Grade

These ideas for third grade are included because you need to plan for an assignment other than the grades you have experience in. It happened to me one year. I was elated and amazed because I would have children in my class whom I had taught before. I had taught most of the upcoming third grade children since kindergarten and first grade. If you ever have this opportunity, *take it!* You will never experience more rewards or more closeness to the children.

I was also excited because I had never taught third grade before and felt a real challenge, a chance to teach something different. Third grade was just what I had hoped for. I could now continue my ideas for an independent program.

First, I studied the Course of Study for the third grade. I took home all of the required books, all of the ditto material that accompanied the books, and materials that a friend had given to me. I put everything into subject areas. I was delighted to find that most of the subjects overlapped. I could integrate the curriculum. Social studies, health, geography, science all intermingled!

Preparing the Classroom

Each person had his own desk. I put a dictionary, ruler, pencils, crayons, and the required texts for Health, Social Studies, and English in each desk.

I did not include reading or math books until after I gave the entry-level tests in these subjects.

Each child sat with a partner. I had a few single desks for those who could not function with someone else. The half-circle table was used for the children who needed extra help. (See Figure B.1 for a sample third grade classroom layout.) They could leave their desks and go to the table to receive help from the aide. By spring very few children used this table.

Partner Work: Talking Their Way into Learning

Ten reasons why students should do school work with a partner:

1. To talk is to think.

2. Talking clarifies misunderstandings. Partners are teachers to each other.

Figure B.1

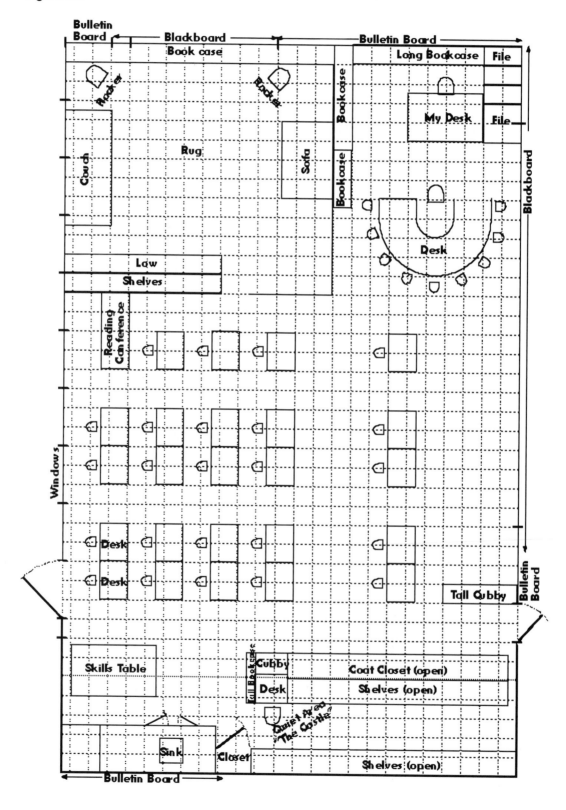

3. Talking reinforces learning and is a major aid to the memory.

4. Talking with a partner produces more knowledge than if the individual works alone.

5. Talking releases energy and reduces the build-up of tension that leads to discipline problems.

6. Talking is a social need. Interaction with peers is interesting and pleasant. The tediousness, difficulty, and boredom of school work is lessened.

7. Partner work releases the teacher from front-of-room teaching, freeing her to attend to partner groups. Her relationship with the partner group is immediate, personal, and comprehensible as opposed to front-of-room teaching which is distant and formal.

8. Talking focuses the attention and greatly increases the time a student can stay on task. In silent seat work, children can usually only concentrate for a minimal time. Because the mind is highly susceptible to distractions, it needs to be anchored down. Talking aloud can act as an anchor.

9. Through talking about schoolwork, the student begins to know how he learns and how he may better learn.

10. Partner work produces more success; success produces self confidence. Partner work fosters self discipline, cooperation, reliability, and social responsibility.

New responsibilities that go with partner learning include:

◆ keeping voices in a low conversational tone

◆ attending to the task; partner talk must be school talk

◆ managing time so task is completed

◆ participating equally with the partner; a 50-50 basis

◆ conducting on-going self, partner, and teacher evaluations

Welcoming Third Graders

Third graders require a different kind of attention than first and second graders. I sent a letter to each student before school opened, letting them know how happy and lucky I was to have them in my classroom again. To help them feel more grown up, I gave them a list of things they needed for third grade, such as a folder to carry homework in and a pencil sharpener that caught the shavings (to cut down on trips to the classroom sharpener). I also listed optional items, such as personal pencils, a pencil box, and binder. The parents told me that their children looked forward to making their small purchases and felt grown up having a folder for homework. The children felt special receiving a letter from their teacher.

Check-off Requirement Sheets

Each day I wrote check-off requirement sheets which were given to the majority of the students who were now independent. I put these at each desk so that every day they knew what they were to do. Putting individual assignments in writing takes the teacher out of the nagging role. The students knew they must complete their requirements each day. They could choose whichever subject they wanted to do first, before recess, except reading. Everyone read silently at the same time from 9:15 to 9:35—this gave me time to hold individual reading conferences. During the reading conferences, I could hear them read, assign new books, and ask questions. After they completed a book, I gave them an entry-level test to take at their desks. My aide acted as a floater during the conferences and answered questions if they raised their hand or put a card on the corner of their desks.

The students handed in their papers with the requirement sheets stapled to the front. Notice in Figure B.2 that there are stars in front of certain requirements. This meant that, for example, if there were three stars, they needed to have three papers total with their requirement paper stapled on top in the finished-paper basket by 11:45 a.m.

If no one needed help, the aide and I checked the papers in the finished-paper basket, and, if a paper had many errors, it meant we had missed helping this person as we roamed around the room. The paper was then taken to the child's desk to be explained. We spent the last twelve minutes before lunch checking and helping. These papers were sent home each week. Those students who finished early could complete a project, read a book, or do something for extra credit. We provided extra papers for them to complete in a special area. The children received special mention for doing extra work by a note home and on their report card. To encourage the students to finish quickly, those who finished first went to lunch first. I would take the stapled papers from the bottom of the basket and dismiss that person for lunch, and so on, until I came to the top papers, which had been turned in last. Either my aide or I was near the basket checking the finished

Figure B.2

MONDAY

Name:_____

Date: September 5, 1993

    1.   Read your book for 25 minutes.
  *2.   Write in your reading log.
  *3.   Do creative writing.
  *4.   Practice following directions.

    –Recess–

  *1.   Do a math page.
  *2.   Practice cursive writing.
  *3.   Draw a picture.

After you have finished your requirements you may choose an activity.

    1.   Find a book from last year.
    2.   Ditto on table in the back.

WEDNESDAY

Name: _____

Date: _____

  *1.   Read your book.
  *2   Write in your reading log.
  *2.   Take your spelling test.
  *3.   Do your English paper.
  *4.   Practice alphabetizing.

–Recess–

  *5.   Do graphing.
  *2.   Work in your math book.
  *3.   Practice mapping.

Extra work for extra credit.

papers for corrections, thus discouraging someone from slipping his paper into the bottom.

Reading Logs

I found that most children were reading so much that we needed a way to keep track of what they had read. I had them keep reading logs where they wrote down the last page they had read after our reading period. They brought this reading log up to me during their reading conference.

Gearing Requirements to Individuals

Early in the year I noticed three or four children who did not finish their work by noontime. One student had a learning disability. I went to that student's desk and crossed off some of the required papers. Knowing he could not do all of the work, I required fewer papers from him to ease his frustration. I explained to him that because he was out of the room for a certain time each day with the special teacher, he did not have time to do so much work.

One child could not concentrate. I made up a special paper for him. Each time I found him doing his work, he received a mark. Marks were given if he didn't talk or play from the last time I was by his desk. If he finished his work, he received five marks. If he earned twenty-five marks in a day, I sent the paper home, and he received praise from his family and a special treat. With this motivation, he easily earned twenty-five points the first day.

I held the small, homogeneous reading skills groups in the afternoon from 2:10 to 3:10 p.m. The remainder of the children went home. I taught the math skill groups from 11 to 11:30 a.m., once a week. For those participating in this skill group, one requirement on their checksheet was crossed out and math skills written in its place.

As the year progressed, I was amazed at how the third graders observed so intently and learned so quickly. I was constantly preparing for the next step, because they were always ready to move on. I seemed to spend less time reviewing and repeating. They were on their own!

Check Sheet for Homework

Each morning the children put their homework papers in the finished-paper basket. The aide gathered the papers and checked their name on a class list if the homework was in. I reminded those who did not have papers in by reading their names from the class list. At first there was usually a scurry to get the forgotten papers until they got into the habit of remembering where to put them.

I sent the note shown in Figure B.3 home if no paper was unearthed.

If math was to be assigned as my homework, my aide and I went to each desk with our class list and check the top of the next page for them to tear out for homework. The number of the page was written on a class list.

Figure B.3

Dear _____,

    An important part of your child's education is completing assignments on time. Therefore, we expect the assigned papers completed and returned on the due date.

    Your child has papers: _____ overdue, and they should be completed and returned.

    Please help your child find these papers and return them completed by tomorrow.

Thank you,
Mary Coons

Recreational Reading as Homework

    I developed a recreational reading program to supplement the third grade reading textbooks. I sent the letter shown in Figure B.4 home to introduce the parents to the program. The check sheet (see Figure B.5) went home each week and was filled out by the child.

Book Report Ideas

    A child could be turned off to reading if a written book report is assigned. Try the following ideas to make book reporting more enjoyable.

Group Oral Presentations
- Give a dramatic presentation of part of a book with others who have read the same book.
- Use the story for the basis of a continuous story told by several people.
- Give a puppet show based on the book.

Figure B.4

Dear Parent,

The interest you parents have in your child's education is wonderful. It is obvious that your child's education is important to you.

I believe reading should be something to enjoy. Books can be enjoyed for their pictures, entertainment, and information. The more a child reads, the more a child can learn to read. Your child will have an assigned recreational book to read each week at home. Please note the attached slip.

Please do not force your child to read aloud to you. These books are for extra practice in reading silently, aloud only if they wish. Hopefully each member of the family will be reading his or her own book at the same time. If your child does not know 3 or 4 words per page, that is all right. If your child knew all of the words on each page, there would be no new words to learn, so do not be alarmed if they ask you to pronounce a word. Please tell it to them immediately so they can go on to enjoy the story. I will teach the phonics skills of learning new words during the reading skill groups.

If your child realizes that the book she or he is reading is not interesting, that is O.K. I have found books like that too. Have your child return the book to school, and we will jointly—your child and I—find another book. Or if they have a book at home they like to read, have them bring the book to school for me to check.

I hope you can all find time to spend 15 minutes to an hour reading for pleasure while your child is reading his or her book.

Perhaps you can also help your child fill out the assignment form each night. These forms are *due each Monday*.

I am looking forward to a continued positive approach to this important aspect of your child's education, reading.

Thank you all for your time and interest in your children and their education. What a wonderful investment you are all making.

Sincerely,
Mary Coons

Figure B.5

RECREATIONAL READING FORM

(To be filled out by the student.)

Name:_____

The book I am reading: _____

I have read my book 5 days this week for 15 minutes each day.

Please check the 5 days.

_____Sunday

_____Monday

_____Tuesday

_____Wednesday

_____Thursday

_____Friday

_____Saturday

Date Due:_____

Individual Oral Presentations
- ◆ Give a short dramatization of part of the book.
- ◆ Act out one character or situation in pantomime.
- ◆ Give a good sales talk or commercial for the book.
- ◆ Retell the funniest, most exciting, or saddest part of the story.

Art Activities
- ◆ Create a diorama or miniature stage setting for the story.
- ◆ Make paper or fabric cutouts for a flannelboard story.
- ◆ Make models in clay, or papier-mâché of the book characters.
- ◆ Create a series of original illustrations for the book.
- ◆ Make a "broomstick roller" movie in a cardboard box.
- ◆ Make puppets of the story's main character or several characters.

- Do a large comic strip drawing of the story.
- Make a poster or advertisement to promote the book.

Written Activities

- Add a chapter to the end of the book, or create a new adventure or mystery.
- Write a rebus of the story.

▼▼▼▼▼▼▼▼▼▼▼▼▼▼▼▼▼▼▼▼▼▼▼

Select Bibliography

I list only the books that have been of use in the making of this book. This bibliography is by no means a complete record of all the sources I have consulted. It indicates the substance and range of reading upon which I have formed my ideas, and I intend it to serve as a convenience for those who wish to pursue the study of teaching.

Ashton-Warner, Sylvia. *Spearpoint: Teacher in America.* New York: Random House, 1964. Useful when teaching journal writing.

Austin, Mary C. and Morrison Coleman. *The First R. The Harvard Report on Reading in Elementary Schools.* New York: Macmillan, 1963.

Bassett, Evelyn and Gena McMillan. *Sponge Activities Using Time Productively.* Ventura, California: Pleasant Valley Superintendent of Schools.

Beggs, David W. III and Edward G. Buffie. *Nongraded Schools in Action.* Bloomington, Indiana: Indiana University Press, 1967.

Benjamin, Robert. *Making Schools Work.* New York: Continuum, 1981.

Betts, Emmett Albert. *Foundation of Reading Instruction.* New York: American Book Co., 1946.

Biggs, Edith E. and James R. MacLean. *Freedom to Learn, An Active Learning Approach to Mathematics.* Ontario, Canada: Addison-Wesley, 1969.

Bloom, Benjamin S. *Taxonomy of Educational Objectives, Cognitive Domain.* New York: MacKay Co., 1967.

Bloomfield, Leonard and Clarence L. Barnhart. *Let's Read, A Linguistic Approach.* Detroit: Wayne State University Press, 1961.

Bond, Guy L. and Eva Wagner. *Teaching the Child to Read.* New York: Macmillan, 1966.

Bruner, Jerome S. *The Process of Education.* New York: Vintage Books, 1960.

Coombs, Arthur. *Perceiving, Behaving, Becoming.* Washington, D.C.: Association for Supervision and Curriculum Development, 1962.

Coopersmith, Stanley. *Antecedents of Self-Esteem.* New York: W. H. Freeman, 1967.

283

Copeland, Richard W. *How Children Learn Mathematics, Teaching Implications of Piaget's Research*. New York: Macmillan, 1970.

Durkin, Dolores. *Teaching Young Children to Read*. Boston: Allyn and Bacon, 1980.

Durrell, Donald D. and Helen Blair Sullivan. *Building Word Power*. New York: Harcourt Brace and World, 1941.

Featherstone, Joseph. *Schools Where Children Learn*. New York: Liveright, 1971.

Flesch, Rudolf. *Why Johnny Still Can't Read: A New Look at the Scandal of Our Schools*. New York: Harper and Row, 1981.

Freed, Alvyn M. *T.A. for Tots (and Other Princes)*. Sacramento, California: Jalmar Press, 1973.

French, Ruth A. *Multi-Sensory Reading, The Child's Way of Learning*. Sacramento, California: Frank Adam Products, 1975.

Gans, Roma. *Facts and Fiction About Phonics*. New York: Bobbs-Merrill, 1964.

Gibbs, Jeanne. *Tribes: A Process for Social Development and Cooperative Learning*. Santa Rosa, California: Center Source Publications, 1987.

Ginott, Haim G.. *Between Parent and Child*. New York: MacMillan, 1965.

Ginsburg, Herbert P. and Sylvia Opper. *Piaget's Theory of Intellectual Development, An Introduction*. Englewood Cliffs, New Jersey: Prentice-Hall, 1969.

Glasser, William. *Reality Therapy: A New Approach to Psychiatry*. New York: Harper Collins, 1975.

Glasser, William. *The Quality School*. New York: Harper Collins, 1990.

Goodlad, John I. *A Place Called School*. New York: McGraw-Hill, 1984.

Goodman, Yetta M. and Carolyn L. Burke. *Reading Miscue Inventory*. New York: Macmillan, 1971.

Gordan, Thomas. *T.E.T. Teacher Effectiveness Training*. New York: Peter H. Wyden, 1974.

Guszak, Frank J. *Diagnostic Reading Instruction in the Elementary School*. New York: Harper Collins, 1978.

Hart, Louise. *The Winning Family*. Oakland, California: Life Skills Press, 1987.

Heilman, Arthur W. *Phonics in Proper Perspective*. Columbus: Macmillan, 1968.

Holt, John. *How Children Fail.* New York: Dell, 1988.

Jersild, Arthur T. *When Teachers Face Themselves.* Columbia: Teachers' College Press, 1955.

Johnson, D.W. and R.T. Johnson, R.T. *Learning Together and Alone.* Englewood Cliffs, New Jersey: Prentice Hall, 1989.

Jones, Fredric H. *Positive Classroom Instruction.* New York: McGraw-Hill, 1987.

Kohl, Herbert R. *The Open Classroom.* New York: Random House, 1969.

Kohl, Herbert R. *Thirty-six Children.* New York: Signet Books, 1988.

Kovalik, Susan. *Teachers Make the Difference: With Integrated Thematic Instruction.* Village of Oak Creek, Arizona: Susan Kovalik and Associates, 1986.

Lakein, Alan. *How to Get Control of Your Time and Your Life.* New York: The New American Library, 1973.

Lee, Doris M. *Diagnostic Teaching.* Dept. of Elem-Kindergarten, Nursery Ed., National Ed. Assoc., 1966.

Leonard, George. *Education and Ecstasy.* New York: Dell, 1987.

Mary Caroline, Sister. *Breaking the Sound Barrier, A Phonics Handbook.* New York: MacMillan, 1960. I used this book for spelling and phonics lessons.

Moffett, James and Betty Jane Wagner. *Student-Centered Language Arts and Reading, K-12, A Handbook for Teachers.* Boston: Houghton Mifflin, 1976.

Olson, Ken. *The Art of Hanging Loose in an Uptight World.* Greenwich, Connecticut: Fawcett Crest, 1974.

Park, Joe. *Bertrand Russell on Education.* Athens, Ohio: Ohio State University Press, 1963.

Patterson, Gerald R. and Elizabeth M. Gullion. *Living with Children, New Methods for Parents and Teachers.* Champaign, Illinois: Research Press, 1974.

Peale, Norman Vincent. *The Power of Positive Thinking.* New York: Prentice Hall , 1987.

Postman, Neil and Charles Weingartner. *The School Book.* New York: Delacorte Press, 1973.

Postman, Neil and Charles Weingartner. *Teaching as a Subversive Activity.* New York: Dell, 1989.

Rogers, Carl R. *Freedom to Learn for the Eighties.* Columbus: Charles E. Merrill, 1983.

Sharp, Evelyn. *Thinking Is Child's Play.* New York: Discovery Books by Avon, 1969.

Silverman, Charles. *Crisis in the Classroom.* New York: Random House, 1970.

Simon, Sidney B., Leland Howe, and Howard Kirschenbaum. *Values Clarification.* New York: Hart Publishing, 1972. A good resource to use during circle discussions.

Smith, James A. and Lloyd M. Dunn. *Peabody Language Development Kit.* Circle Pines, Minnesota: American Guidance Service, 1967. This kit contains many useful activities for when you have five minutes of unplanned time.

Spache, Evelyn B. *Reading Activities for Child Involvement.* Boston: Allyn and Bacon, 1972.

Trelease, Jim. *The New Read-Aloud Handbook.* New York: Penguin Books, 1985.

Trelease, Jim. *Hey! Listen to This.* New York: Penguin Books, 1992.

Veatch, Jeannette. *Reading in the Elementary School.* New York: The Ronald Press, 1966. This book may be older, but her ideas are farsighted. A good reference for all you want to know about reading.

Westerman, Gayle. *O.A.T. Operation Assessment Tool Reading and Spelling Program.* San Anselmo, California: The Child Center, 1975. A progressive guide through reading and spelling.

Wood, Paul and Bernard Schwartz. *How to Get Your Children to Do What You Want Them to Do.* Englewood Cliffs, New Jersey: Prentice Hall, 1977. Although the title of this book implies manipulation, it is not about that at all. It is helpful for ways to relate to children.

Index